Intelligent Vehicular Networks and Communications

Fundamentals, Architectures and Solutions

Intelligent Vehicular Networks and Communications
Fundamentals, Architectures and Solutions

Anand Paul

Naveen Chilamkurti

Alfred Daniel

Seungmin Rho

ELSEVIER

AMSTERDAM • BOSTON • HEIDELBERG • LONDON • NEW YORK • OXFORD • PARIS
SAN DIEGO • SAN FRANCISCO • SINGAPORE • SYDNEY • TOKYO

Elsevier
Radarweg 29, PO Box 211, 1000 AE Amsterdam, Netherlands
The Boulevard, Langford Lane, Kidlington, Oxford OX5 1GB, United Kingdom
50 Hampshire Street, 5th Floor, Cambridge, MA 02139, United States

Library of Congress Cataloging-in-Publication Data
A catalog record for this book is available from the Library of Congress

British Library Cataloguing-in-Publication Data
A catalogue record for this book is available from the British Library

ISBN: 978-0-12-809266-8

For information on all Elsevier publications
visit our website at https://www.elsevier.com/

Working together
to grow libraries in
developing countries

www.elsevier.com • www.bookaid.org

Publisher: Todd Green
Acquisition Editor: Brian Romer
Editorial Project Manager: Amy Invernizzi
Production Project Manager: Priya Kumaraguruparan
Designer: Mark Rogers

Typeset by Thomson Digital

Contents

Preface

The evolution of vehicular networks has advanced significantly with the introduction of intelligent transportation systems (ITS) dating back to the 1990s, and it keeps evolving with technological innovations. The solutions involved in this multifaceted problem area range from planning to safety implementations, and it is one of the long-term goals of smart city transportation planning and development. Recently, as vehicular communications have been identified as a key technology for enhancing road safety and transport efficiency, governments have started to allocate fixed portions of their communication spectrum to intelligent transport systems.

The diversity of services and communications has introduced new challenges in the design of both network architecture and protocols. Thus, a significant research effort has been put in the definition of complete network architectures, new standard protocol stacks, new routing solutions, and redesigning existing media access control (MAC) [1].

Vehicular communications are mainly classified into vehicle-to-vehicle (V2V) and vehicle-to-infrastructure (V2I) communications. V2V communications are between vehicles and V2I is vehicle to roadside unit (RSU) communication. An intelligent vehicular network is a network of vehicles that interact with one another and with infrastructure to transmit and receive data. As vehicular networks are expected to become somewhat ubiquitous by 2016, security elements of these types of networks would also come into the picture. It is clear that false or unauthorized data communication or attacks leading to denial of service within such a vehicular area network (VAN) could cause devastating results, compromising the driver's judgment and/or safety [2].

The rapid development and availability of mobile computing systems and environments have created a highly heterogeneous vehicular network. As a consequence, the provision of seamless connectivity across different wireless networking technologies is very complex, especially in terms of quality of service, routing, and security. Thus, it is expected that the next generation of ITS will reflect a more holistic approach to network solutions [3].

Localization in vehicular networks is critical, especially when used in safety applications. These applications require more reliable and highly accurate localization values to be effective. Generally a satellite-based positioning system such as GPS is used in each vehicle, but these systems are not accurate and are not always available. Reliable and more accurate ubiquitous localization techniques are to be used by vehicles in critical safety and emergency applications and will likely be provided by a combination of different techniques and data fusion [3].

Vehicular communications have been allocated the 5.9-GHz spectrum bandwidth for dedicated short-range communication (DSRC). Still, having a large number of vehicular wireless nodes communicating in a limited space may quickly exhaust the available spectrum. Due to stringent QoS requirements on the DSRC spectrum, it is not possible for all applications to depend only on the licenced DSRC spectrum. To solve the problem of possible spectrum resource starvation in vehicular networks, cognitive radio (CR) has been considered as a potential solution to exploit licenced but unused frequency bands [4]. However, spectrum sensing in vehicular environments is a challenging task due to mobility, shadowing, and other factors.

Big Data endows the novel technique of probability to collect, manage, and analyze vast quantities of data, which indeed offers a smart and intelligent transportation system. This technique enables vehicular networks to store large quantities of real-time data for further analysis [5]. But there are various challenges for empowering Big Data in the vehicular network, such as the need for centralized access to image and video traffic data storage at various locations. In addition, the sole purpose of Big Data is to optimize utilization of massive data storage of vehicle monitoring data for as long as possible to supply information for intelligent transport of vehicles.

For this enormous choice and collection of data, adaptive models have to be built to help transportation companies decide on the best routes to optimize the time of delivery, safety, cost, and fuel consumption. Using Big Data, this collected data can be analyzed, and by quantifying traffic behavior in bad weather, transport companies can make decisions on alternative routes, which allows them to optimize various factors for better fuel efficiency [6]. The need is to develop predictive models and use the data for realistic benefits to the company. Big Data analytics for vehicular ad-hoc networks (VANETs) can be used to improve road safety, optimize routes for drivers, and improve fuel efficiency.

This book is intended for researchers and students who are in the field of vehicular communications, providing detailed insights into fundamentals, architectures, and solutions for ITS. This book includes nine chapters, each further broken down into numbered sections.

Chapter 1 deals with the background of vehicular communications—its evolution models and methods, the standardization of vehicular communication, and technologies in transportation communications. The first section outlines a concern for road safety that has increased across the globe over the past few years due to the reporting of large numbers of traffic accidents. It also points out that road traffic efficiency and marketing policy are areas that could harness the benefits of intelligent transport systems. The next section discusses the evolution of transport systems, starting as a result of massive highway construction in the 1950s, coupled with the advancement of IT in the 1980s. In brief, transportation models generally can be classified into microscopic, mesoscopic, macroscopic, and metascopic models. The third section deals with the advancement in wireless technologies which has brought about various standards in vehicular communications such as ISO, ETSI, IEEE, and so on. The final section highlights the technologies in vehicular communications, categorizing them into existing and possible vehicular communication technologies.

Chapter 2 introduces ITS, which emerged as a result of the growth and advancement in IT for sensors/actuators, artificial vision, control systems, data storage management, and so on. The first part discusses the aims of IT in terms of fostering safety, efficiency, and economy for owners/drivers. The second section details the application and implementation of a comparative study on various ITS projects around the globe. Finally, this chapter discusses the computational technologies and sensing methodologies in ITS—which is the integral part of Chapter 3, Vehicular Network Model.

Chapter 3 targets a brief presentation of the design goals and challenges in a vehicular network model. The first section deals with cluster models in the ITS network: active, beacon, and other clustering models. The second section explains vehicle platooning, a technique where the highway traffic is organized into groups of close-following vehicles referred to as a platoon or convoy. Section 3 discusses the vehicular cloud in ITS: a detailed study and analysis of the vehicular cloud, where vehicles can share computation, storage, and bandwidth resources amongst themselves. Various other items, such as privacy issues related to vehicular networks from the ITS perspective, are also discussed. Section 4 investigates the integration between wireless sensor networks and vehicular networks. Section 5 deals with the Internet of vehicles (IoV), which is actually an integration of three networks: an inter-vehicle network, an intra-vehicle network, and a vehicular mobile Internet. This chapter concludes with a discussion of the working model of vehicular networks, outlining some of the research challenges that still need to be addressed to enable the ubiquitous deployment and widespread adoption of scalable, reliable, robust, and secure ITS architectures, protocols, technologies, and services.

Chapter 4 concentrates on analysis and evaluation of proposed system models, providing deep insight into vehicular communications measures such scalability, latency, and reliability of the particular network. This chapter discusses the feasibility of using alternative technologies for the vehicular network model. The chapter begins with a detailed description of data dissemination models, and continues with a discussion of the mobility management and architectures in vehicular network. The chapter includes a thoroughly investigated case study on mobility management of an IPv6-based vehicular network. The chapter also looked at different type of routing mechanisms and protocols used in vehicular networks.

Chapter 6 explores the essence of cooperative cognitive vehicular networks, and deals with spectral efficiency, spectral scarcity, and high mobility in the same. Additionally, various techniques and strategies of spectral sensing in CR of vehicular communication have been explored, along with case studies. The architectural viewpoint of the cognitive vehicular network is also illustrated. Finally, the chapter ends up with a discussion on various research issues and challenges.

Chapter 7 discusses the practical and experimental peripheries of vehicular communications. Section 1 deals with context awareness in vehicular networks while section 2 focuses on cloud application in transport networks, in design and architectural views. A trust-based information dissemination framework for vehicular networks is investigated in section 3. Knowledge-based intelligent Transportation Systems are the subjects of Section 4. The last two sections discuss hybrid sensor and vehicular networks and intravehicular communications, respectively. Overall, this chapter explores the working principles of controller area network (CAN) protocol and the working function of the onboard unit (OBU), both of which are integral to establishing communication between vehicle or infrastructure nodes. The working principles of roadside unit (RSU) and other infrastructure nodes are also examined.

Chapter 8 explores the possibility of applying Big Data analytics principles in vehicular networks. The chapter discusses technologies of big data for vehicular networks, data validation, Vehicular Carriers for Big Data. In this chapter, we discuss the role of descriptive analytics and predictive analysis, to exploit the historical data and to predict future trends and occurrence in vehicular networks. Various tools that are applicable for Big Data analysis in vehicular networks are discussed. Further, issues and challenges related to real time Big Data analysis in a vehicular network are illustrated. In conclusion, this chapter determines how market policies translate into facilities for both scientific understanding and improving the forecasting, planning, policy-making, and evaluation of vehicular networks.

Chapter 9 discusses the next generation and future trends of ITS, particularly the standardization. It focuses on autonomous vehicles and their effect on ITS. Further, this chapter discusses various research issues and challenges related to ITS and possible solutions where applicable to real world scenarios.

REFERENCES
[1] Fonseca A. Instituto Superior Tecnico. Portugal antonio.fonseca@ist.utl.pt: Available from: http://www.ist.utl.pt
[2] Faezipour M, Nourani M, Saeed A, Addepalli S. Progress and challenges in intelligent vehicle area networks. Commun ACM 2012;55(2):90–100.

[3] da Cunha FD, Boukerche A, Villas L, Viana AC, Loureiro AF. Data communication in VANETs: a survey, challenges and applications. [Research Report] RR-8498, INRIA Saclay; 2014.

[4] Qian X, Hao L. On the performance of spectrum sensing in cognitive vehicular networks. IEEE PIMRC Aug. 30, 2015–Sept. 2, 2015, p. 1002–6.

[5] Daniel A, Paul A, Ahmad A. Near real-time big data analysis on vehicular networks. IEEE International Conference on Soft Computing and Network Security (ICSNS), Feb. 2015, p. 1–7.

[6] Bedi P, Jindal V. Use of Big Data technology in vehicular ad-hoc networks. ICACCI, 2014 International Conference on Advances in Computing, Communications and Informatics, New Delhi; 2014. pp. 1677–83.

INTRODUCTION: INTELLIGENT VEHICULAR COMMUNICATIONS

1.1 BACKGROUND OF TRANSPORTATION NETWORKS

The World Health Organization (WHO) statistics depict that annually road accidents cause approximately 1.2 million deaths worldwide, one fourth of all deaths caused by injury. In addition about 50 million people are injured in traffic accidents annually. This scenario calls for immediate steps to revamp the present vehicular safety services. The main motivation behind the vehicular communication systems is to promote safety and also eliminate the excessive costs of traffic collisions. Although the main advantage of vehicular networks is safety, there are several other benefits such as avoiding congestion, finding the most optimal path by processing real-time data, vehicle behavior analysis, examining road capacity, pedestrian flow rate analysis, and so forth. The US regulator officials are planning for the technology to become mandatory by 2017 for intelligent transportation system (ITS). Allowing cooperation among vehicular network entities, which require a persistent, stable, and reliable underlying communications service. Currently, the US Federal Communications Commission (FCC) has allocated 75 MHz and the European Telecommunications Standards Institute (ETSI) allocated 30 MHz of spectrum in 5.9 GHz band for the operation of ITS services.

The vehicular network research deals with a multifaceted real-world system, the transportation system. The research implications deal with theoretical values and practical methods that can be implemented and applied in different aspects, including planning, design, construction, operations, safety, and so forth. One unique characteristic of a vehicular network is that it advances intensively with scientific innovations. In order to change the elementary characteristics of the vehicular networks the technological achievement provides an innovative path for observing, monitoring, and managing transportation systems. One of the earliest and most representative transportation models is the fundamental diagram of relationships among speed, flow, and density by Greenshields in the year 1935. From that time, vehicular networks investigation has advanced significantly with respect to practically all features of the transportation system, particularly with the growth of ITS technologies since the 1990s.

Road safety has been a significant concern in the world over the past few decades because millions of people die or are injured in car accidents every year. Current statistics show that road traffic accidents in the Member States of the European Union annually claim about 39,000 lives and leave more than 1.7 million people injured, representing an estimated cost of 160 billion euros. In 1900 there were 240 km of surface road in the United States, and this total had increased to 6,400,000 by the year 2000, with effectively 100% of the US population having almost instant access to paved roadways. The growth (and decline) of transportation networks perceptibly disturbs the communal and financial happenings that a region can support, yet the dynamics of how such growth occurs is one of the least understood areas in transportation. This lack of understanding in recent times can be seen in the long-range planning and development of urban and rural transportation projects. If one looks at the difficulty and governance involved in transportation infrastructure organizations and management, one might conclude that it is impossible to perfect the transportation network. Nevertheless, the current advancement in transportation network results in abundant primary and secondary valuations by various functionalities such as property holders, companies, manufacturers, townships, cities, states, provinces, and countries and so forth. It's necessary to understand how markets and policies convert into amenities on the ground and how it is crucial for scientific permissive filtering prediction, scheduling, policymaking, and valuation. In general, a transportation network is a multilayered system that reflects self-organization and illustrates the subtleties related to conveyance systems, focusing on traffic projection or assessment. However, the dynamics of vehicular network development require various enhancements.

Automated highway systems and ITS were introduced to quicken the growth and use of incorporated safety systems that use information and communication technologies (ICT) as an intelligent solution to address issues of road safety and to decrease the number of accidents. With the advances in mobile wireless devices, which are becoming an indispensable part of our lives, and increasing interest in ubiquitous connectivity methodologies, Internet access from a vehicular point of view is in huge demand. The propagation of cooperating system methodology for ITS, the focus on ICT, and the growing number of communication infrastructure–enabled vehicles has opened up new business models and key market segments for investors in the ITS market.

Vehicular communication networks (VCNs) are the foundation for the much-anticipated ITS. By enabling vehicles to communicate with each other via intervehicle communication (IVC) networks as well as with roadside base stations via roadside-to-vehicle communication (RVC), vehicular networks could promote safer and more well-organized infrastructures for transportation. The prospects in the areas of applications in a vehicular network are growing rapidly, with several vehicle companies and private organizations vigorously pursuing research and development in vehicular networks. The combination of onboard sensor structures and the dissemination of onboard localization methods (global positioning system or GPS) make vehicular network appropriate for active safety applications, including collision and warning systems, driver assistance, intelligent traffic management systems, and so forth. Furthermore, IVC opens up possibilities for online vehicle entertainment such as streaming video and gaming file sharing, and thus facilitates the incorporation of Internet services and applications. Fig. 1.1 illustrates the functionalities of vehicular communication scenarios: IVC, RVC, and VCNs.

Vehicular network organization assessments made at one point of time can influence future developments. Although vehicular networks are characteristically depicted as being static in representations, an enhanced understanding of the growth pattern of infrastructures will provide valuable guidance to shape the next-generation network.

Vehicular ad hoc networks (VANET) should, upon implementation, collect and distribute safety information to massively reduce the number of accidents by warning drivers about the danger before they actually face it. Such networks comprise of sensors and onboard units (OBU) installed in the car as well as roadside units (RSU). The data collected from the sensors on the vehicles can be displayed to the driver, sent to the RSU or even broadcasted to other vehicles depending on its nature and importance. The RSU distributes this data, along with data from road sensors, weather centers, traffic control centers, and so forth, to the vehicles and also provides commercial services such as parking space booking, Internet access, and gas payment. The network makes extensive use of wireless communications to achieve its goals but although wireless communications reached a level of maturity, a lot more is required to implement such a complex system. Most available wireless systems rely on a base station for synchronization and other services; however, using this approach means covering all roads

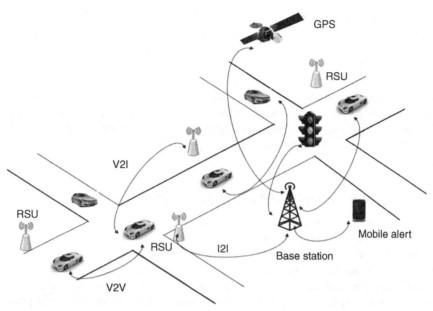

FIGURE 1.1 Vehicular Communications Scenario

with expensive infrastructure. Ad hoc networks have been studied for some time but VANET will form the biggest ad hoc network ever implemented, and issues of stability, reliability, and scalability are of concern. VANET therefore is not an architectural network and not an ad hoc network but a combination of both; this unique form combined with high-speed nodes complicates the design of the network. When we entered VANET research with the Fleet-Net project in mid-2001, ad-hoc research was largely dominated by efforts to standardize mobile ad hoc network (MANET) protocols in the same-named IETF working group. Consequently, these protocols were tailored to transporting IP unicast datagrams, enabling the variety of IP applications to be run transparently over these networks. Thus, early MANET research focused on the network layer, since (1) wireless network hardware including layers 1 and 2 could already be bought off-the-shelf, and (2) everything above IP was already there. So the ultimate challenge seemed to lie in the problem of how to reach nodes not directly within radio range by employing neighbors as forwarders.

MANET research itself tried to treat the networks as generally as possible, following the idea that worst-case engineered protocols also fit special-case scenarios. For example, the widely used random-waypoint mobility model proposes node movement by means of randomized sequences of linear movement, combined with randomized periods of standing still. Being able to parameterize the random distributions, this created a powerful tool to create scenarios with various degrees of mobility. However, these scenarios do not exist in reality, so the basic assumption was that a protocol able to cope with worst-case (because unpredictable) node movements of a random movement model would also be able to cope with the more correlated movements occurring in reality. At this point, there seemed to be an obvious chance to do some original research. If we regarded street-bound vehicles as a MANET, we could at least study well-known methods or create modifications or even novel proposals for these scenarios. And, as a matter of fact, we partially succeeded by exploring and extending position-based routing methods for vehicular scenarios. Actually, we were so successful that when observing the route-finding capability of position-based methods on highways, the theoretically achievable number of hops seemed to be almost unlimited. However, informal probing of the IETF MANET people quickly showed that getting a protocol proposal on the standards track would require a tremendous effort and would encounter significant opposition, since they were fiercely trying to reduce the number of candidate protocols. Nevertheless, since the Fleet Net agenda called for a proof-of-concept demonstration platform, we felt it appropriate to implement position-based routing in Linux with the ultimate goal of performing some real-world measurements on the road.

1.2 EVOLUTION OF TRANSPORTATION MODELS

A transportation network can be categorized in numerous different ways. Nevertheless, we are more interested in tracking the evolution of transportation modes in response to the trends in technology advance, methodology concepts, and practical requirements over a long time horizon. From this perspective, transportation models can be classified into different generations. By summarizing what has been achieved in the past generations, we can offer some projections of what may be expected in future generations (e.g., the next 30 years) of transportation models, considering some promising ITS technologies that are being, or expected to be, implemented. If one looks back into the history of the transportation research, three major waves can be identified.

The first wave began in the 1950s with the construction and massive use of freeway systems worldwide, such as the US interstate system, which was based on earlier experience with the German autobahn and American turnpikes. These projects provided new perspectives in transportation engineering. Researchers and engineers were motivated to study the detailed characteristics of the new transportation systems and explore methods of operating and managing the expanding systems. Due to the difficulty and complexity of collecting data at that time, models during this period were primarily empirical and static. Models and theories are developed based on either ideal assumptions, or very limited experimental and survey data. However, they still serve as basic guidelines that help plan, construct, and operate the early transportation systems. Transportation models developed during this time period (1950s–1980s) are here referred to as first-generation models.

The second wave was triggered by the rapid development of information technologies after 1980, as well as the legislation progress regarding transportation systems, such as ISTEA, which is the emergence of the ITS technologies. During this time period, the most critical issue that emerged was the balance between the limited supply that can be added to the existing infrastructure and the ever-growing travel demands. Different approaches have been taken, including exploring the additional capacity of the existing infrastructure and using planning strategies to balance the transportation supply and demand by promoting alternative transportation modes. Tackling such issues relies on more detailed and dynamic information regarding travelers' demands and road conditions. Information technologies, along with the developments in vehicle sensing technologies, allow engineers and researchers to collect, analyze, model, and predict transportation phenomena more rapidly, more efficiently, and more accurately than ever before. During this period, dynamic, statistical, and disaggregated transportation models with rigorous formulations and efficient numerical methods originating from physics, economics, computer science, and other scientific fields, suitable for network or system performance evaluation, were widely developed. We refer to models that have these features and that emerged during the 1980s–2000s as second-generation models. Most early ITS models lie within this generation, even though the scope of ITS has been greatly extended by more advanced technologies and models. The third and current wave has been primarily driven by rapidly growing wireless communication technologies in the new century. Reliable connectivity between all elements (human, vehicle, and infrastructure) in transportation systems can now be achieved. Such connectivity facilitates not only the real-time data collection of transportation systems but also the active coordination of vehicles in real-time. Models in this period have the characteristics of real-time capability, active control, and integration among different data sources and different applications.

However, these models still assume that the natural characteristics of flow in the transportation system, such as human driving, local perception, and so on, will remain largely unchanged. With the future development of communication technologies along with smart vehicle technologies in the automobile industry, fully automated and controlled transportation systems may become possible. This advancement may start the next wave in transportation model development, since traffic flow can be changed fundamentally to automated, proactive, well-informed, and fully controlled flow, which may be triggered by several new technologies that are under development, such as cloud computing, Internet of Things, and distributed computing. Fourth-generation models in this wave may be highly integrated, highly reliable, distributed, and system optimized, based on the above new characteristics of traffic flow. There are several key differences between the third- and fourth-generation models. First of all, the third-generation models deal with the increased automation in driving and traveling with the development of the connected vehicle technologies, while the fourth-generation models study the potential of fully automated traveling in the future. The difficulty in the third-generation models is to describe the impact of the increased connectivity and control within mixed noninformed, informed, and connected driving and traveling, while the difficulty in the fourth-generation model is to explore system-wide and customized solutions to stochastic travel demand by data mining over the massive amount of data. The latter one may sound trivial but is, in fact, a very complicated system optimization problem in the evolution of transportation models.

1.2.1 EVOLUTION OF METHODOLOGY IN TRANSPORTATION RESEARCH

Transportation models generally can be classified into microscopic, mesoscopic, macroscopic, and metascopic models. Microscopic models study individual elements of transportation systems, such as individual vehicle dynamics and individual traveler behaviors. Mesoscopic models analyze transportation elements in small groups, within which elements are considered homogeneous. A typical example is vehicle platoon dynamics and household-level travel behavior. Macroscopic models deal with aggregated characteristics of transportation elements, such as aggregated traffic flow dynamics and zonal-level travel demand analysis.

Major research objects in transportation engineering include traffic flow, travel behavior, transportation networks, traffic control and management, freight systems, and other transportation modes. The study of traffic flow includes its micro-, meso-, and macroscopic characteristics, human factors, autonomous vehicles, and so on. Common approaches include empirical studies, and statistical and computer science modeling motivated by new data collection technologies. Theories and models developed for similar physical objects, such as fluid and particles, are sometimes introduced and improved to fit traffic flow characteristics. The research topics of travel behavior include demand analysis, route choice, day-to-day dynamics, and activity choices. Research methods usually involve survey-based methods and travel choice models that originated from economics and logistics. Traffic control and management involves the design and management of traffic control devices, traveler information provision, and more recently vehicular communication system. Optimization and control methods are usually involved. Transportation network consists of traffic flow, traveler behavior, and traffic control. Its design and performance evaluation usually rely on integrated models of both planning and operations.

The study of freight systems involves the performance, optimization, and management of commodity flow. Other research objects also include several alternative modes such as public transportation, bicycles, and pedestrians, which are important components in transportation systems and can either be studied along with behavior model or operational models or together with passenger vehicles as alternative studies. These basic research objects remain relatively static throughout the history of transportation research; however, models to describe and analyze those objects have evolved from generation to generation. Meanwhile, technologies play important roles in studying these research objects. More detailed data sets can reveal new characters of those objects and lead to new methodologies and models. For example, from traditional license-plate matching to inductive loop detectors and to probe vehicle technologies, the methodology of estimating and managing traffic flow dynamics on both freeways and arterials has evolved from empirical relationship analysis to complicated traffic state estimation and advanced traffic control models. Furthermore, similar to the other engineering fields, the evolution of transportation models usually involves four major types of contributions: (1) the discovery and introduction of new principles and relationships, (2) the integration of models, (3) the relaxation of ideal assumptions, and (4) performance improvement. The first two types of contributions usually come during the transition period between major generations; the second two types of contributions occur regularly during all periods. The term *model* is not used in the contribution because this type of contribution refers only to truly fundamental and original models. Typical examples include the fundamental diagrams of traffic flow, kinematic models, and gravity models. One should not underestimate the contribution of the latter four types of contributions, since usually the first type of contribution results in raw and ideal models and formulations that sometimes take years to evolve into practically accurate and efficient models that can be applied in the real world, which is quite important for a practical field such as transportation. A famous example is the development of the cell transmission model that made solving the traffic dynamics inferred from LWR model truly efficient and scalable for traffic operations, even though it is a category-D contribution. Table 1.1 summarizes the major existing and expected contributions and their corresponding types in different generations and different types of models.

1.2.2 VEHICULAR NETWORKS AND ITS

Research of vehicular networks toward the development of an ITS can be readily segmented into following application areas, such as advising or warning the driver (collision warning), moderately controlling the vehicle either for steady-state driver assistance or as an emergency intervention to avoid a collision (collision avoidance), and fully controlling the vehicle (vehicle automation). From an ITS perspective, collision-warning systems include functions such as a forward-collision warning, blind-spot warning, lane-departure warning, lane-change or -merge warning, intersection collision warning, pedestrian detection and warning, backup warning, rear-impact warning, and rollover warning for heavy vehicles. A special category of collision warning is driver monitoring, to detect and warn the driver of drowsiness or other impairments that prevent the driver from safely operating the vehicle. If

Table 1.1 Evolution of Transportation Networks

Attributes	First Generations	Second Generations	Third Generations	Fourth Generations
Period	1950s–1980s	1980s–2000s	2000s–near future decades	2000s–distant future decades
Technological background	Massive construction of transportation infrastructures	Early ITS technologies	Wireless communication technologies	Cloud computing, Internet of Things, supercomputers
Objectives	Operate early transportation systems	• Create potential supply from existing infrastructure • Balance supply and demand	Accommodate both human and automated driving Active supply and demand management	• Real-time control and management of transportation systems • Proactive control and management
Key characteristics	• Empirical models • Static models	• Descriptive models • Dynamic model • Statistical models • Partial macroscopic control • Independent models • Behavioral models • Actuated control	• Rich data environment • Partial macroscopic/microscopic control • Interaction with vehicular network • Transition between human and automated traveling	• Massive data environment • Automated environment • Fully integrated models • Feedback-control models • System optimal
Data and control environment	• Very limited data • Static data • Empirical data • Basic control	• Sampled and archived data • Automated traffic management • Indirect and unidirectional communication • Macroscopic dynamic control • Localized perception • Low market penetration	• Detailed real-time and archived data • Direct and bidirectional communication • High market penetration	• High-resolution real time and archived data • User-specific control • Full or near-full market penetration
Issues	• Lack of dynamic data • Lack of dynamic theories • Suitable for design and planning, but not reliable for operations • Planning models lack a clear relationship to traffic flow theory • No representation of interaction at intersections	• Limited coverage (spatial/temporal or both) • Limited accuracy • Limited resolution	• Heavy data processing • Complex data fusion and integration • Strong interactions (V2V, V2I, and I2I) • User interface • Need to accommodate the transition from autonomous vehicle to fully controlled vehicles • Privacy and system security	• Data mining on massive data • Integration with existing information and control systems • System reliability and robustness • User-oriented services • Stochastic demand management • Privacy and system security

the driver does not adequately respond to warnings, collision-avoidance systems might take control of the steering, brakes, or throttle to maneuver the vehicle back to a safe state. Driver-assistance systems include functions such as adaptive cruise control, lane keeping, precision docking (which will be discussed later), and precise maneuvering. Vehicle-automation systems include low speed automation, autonomous driving, and close-headway platooning (which provides increased roadway throughput), and electronic vehicle guidance in segregated areas such as busways and freight terminals. These systems can be autonomous, with all instrumentation and intelligence of the vehicle, or cooperative, where assistance comes from the roadway, other vehicles, or both. Roadway assistance typically takes the form of passive reference markers in the infrastructure. Vehicle–vehicle cooperation lets vehicles operate in close proximity for increased efficiency, usually by transmitting key vehicle parameters and intentions to following vehicles. The general philosophy is that autonomous systems will work on all roadways in all situations at a useful performance level and take advantage of cooperative elements, as available, to augment and enhance system performance.

In ITS, each vehicle takes on the role of sender, receiver, and router to broadcast information to the vehicular network or transportation agency, which then uses the information to ensure safe and free flow of traffic. For communication to occur between vehicles and RSU, vehicles must be equipped with some sort of radio interface or OBU that enables short-range wireless ad hoc networks to be formed. Vehicles must also be fitted with hardware that permits detailed position information such as a GPS or a differential global positioning system (DGPS) receiver. Fixed RSUs, which are connected to the backbone network, must be in place to facilitate communication. The number and distribution of RSU are dependent on the communication protocol to be used. For example, some protocols require RSU to be distributed evenly throughout the whole road network, some require RSU only at intersections, while others require RSU only at region borders. Although it is safe to assume that the infrastructure exists to some extent and vehicles have access to it intermittently, it is unrealistic to require that vehicles always have wireless access to RSU. Fig. 1.1 depicts the possible communication configurations in ITS. These include intervehicle, vehicle-to-roadside, and routing-based communications. Intervehicle, vehicle-to-roadside, and routing-based communications rely on very accurate and up-to-date information about the surrounding environment, which in turn requires the use of accurate positioning systems and smart communication protocols for exchanging information. In a network environment in which the communication medium is shared, highly unreliable, and with limited bandwidth, smart communication protocols must guarantee fast and reliable delivery of information to all vehicles in the vicinity. It is worth mentioning that intravehicle communication uses technologies such as IEEE 802.15.1 (bluetooth), IEEE 802.15.3 (ultra-wide band), and IEEE 802.15.4 (Zigbee) that can be used to support wireless communication inside a vehicle, but this is outside the scope of this chapter and will not be discussed further.

1.3 VEHICULAR NETWORK STANDARDIZATION

To achieve safety in vehicular network management and to coordinate the diverse standards in the vehicular network, the recent developments in the Wireless Communication Technology and ITS have been combined. The US Department of Transportation (USDOT) and ETSI extending the worldwide harmonized standards for cooperative-ITS (C-ITS), these practices continue to emerge. In addition to that, Japan took this initiative along with ETSI and USDOT. Furthermore, countries such as Australia and South Korea want to follow this. With significant advances in alternative fuels and connected vehicles reworking automobile transportation, it is time to unify the association for nursing an intelligent future in transportation worldwide and engulf cross-disciplinary approach to shorten the considerable time required to promote transportation standards.

1.3.1 EUROPEAN ITS STANDARDS INITIATIVES

1.3.1.1 European Committee for Standardization (CEN)

ITS can contribute to a cleaner, safer, and more efficient transport system. They use ICT in order to control traffic flow, collect road tolls (electronic fee collection, EFC), provide timely traffic and safety information, notify emergency personnel about accidents (eCall), and give priority to emergency vehicles.

The European Commission has laid down the legal framework in order to accelerate the deployment of ITS across Europe (Directive 2010/40/EU) and has requested the European standardization organizations to develop and adopt European standards in support of this framework (EC M/453), in order to ensure interoperability across countries. European standards and technical specifications in the domain of ITS are being developed by the CEN Technical Committee "Intelligent Transport Systems" (CEN/TC 278). These standards cover a variety of aspects including: cooperative systems, travel and traffic information, route guidance and navigation, public transport, emergency vehicles, and EFC. CEN and CENELEC (European Committee for Electrotechnical Standardization) cooperate closely with ETSI and ISO in order to ensure a coherent approach to standardization on this topic. In 2015, CEN is expected to adopt European standards regarding the eCall system, which allows emergency services to be notified automatically in the event of a traffic accident (EN 15722 and EN 16072). It will also publish a technical specification relating to EFC, that is, secure monitoring for autonomous toll systems (CEN/TS 16702-2). In addition, a major programming exercise will be undertaken in relation to ITS involving a wide range of relevant partners such as UITP, EUROCITIES, and so forth. Furthermore, major initiatives are carried out in relation to C-ITS with UITP, EUROCITIES, and so forth. Table 1.2 illustrates the work group CEN/TC 278 and its applications.

Table 1.2 CEN/TC278 Work Groups and its Applications

Work Group	ITS Application
1. WG13	Architecture
2. WG12	Automatic vehicle identification (AVI) Automatic equipment identification (AEI)
3. WG1	EFC
4. WG8	Road data
5. WG4	Traffic travel information (TTI)
6. WG3	Public transport
7. WG16	C-ITS

Table 1.3 ISO/TC 204 Work Group and its Applications

Work Group	ITS Application
WG1	Architecture
WG3	Database technology
WG4	AVI AEI
WG5	Fee and toll collection
WG7	General fleet management and commercial/freight operations
WG9	Integrated transport information, management and control
WG10	Traveler information systems
WG14	Vehicle/roadway warning and control systems
WG16	ITS communications (CALM)
WG18	C-ITS

1.3.1.2 International Standard Organization (ISO)

In 1993, ISO created the ISO/TC 204 that covers ITS activities. The ISO/TC 204 activities are performed in 16 operating teams. The protocol suite that's standardized by ISO is denoted as continuous air interface long- and medium-range (CALM). CALM considers infrared (IR) communications, additionally as radio systems and includes communication technologies, such as GSM, UMTS, DSRC, and so forth. ISO/TC 204 WG 16 and ETSI TC ITS are closely cooperating with each other in effective transportation models. CEN in collaboration with ISO/TC 204 ITS organized ISO/TS 19321 in line with the Vienna agreement (a technical cooperation between ISO and CEN). As per C-ITS, informing the driver about the traffic situation and road regulation forms a vital component of road operations. See Table 1.3 for the work group ISO/TC 204 and ITS applications.

By using messages such as cooperative awareness messages (CAM), decentralized environment notification messages (DENM), or basic safety messages (BSM) we can notify the road user about the traffic situation in the C-ITS, an initiative undertaken by ISO/TS 19321. Furthermore, ISO/TS 19321:2015 stipulates the in-vehicle information (IVI) data organizations that are required for various ITS services (e.g., refer to ISO/TS 17425 and ISO/TS 17426) for exchanging information between ITS stations as depicted in Table 1.2. ISO/TS 19321:2015 latest edition is referenced by ETSI/TS 102 894-2 V1.1.12, ITS; users and application requirements.

1.3.1.3 ETSI

ETSI is a standard for ICT, which includes fixed, mobile, radio, converged, broadcast, and Internet technologies and is legitimately acknowledged by the European Union as a European Standards Organization. ITS can significantly contribute to a cleaner, safer, and more efficient transport system. In 2010 the European Parliament and Council adopted the ITS Directive to accelerate the deployment of these innovative transport technologies across Europe. This directive is an important instrument for the coordinated implementation of ITS in Europe. It aims to establish interoperability and seamless ITS services while leaving Member States the freedom to decide which systems to invest in. Under this directive the European Commission has to adopt specifications to address the compatibility, interoperability, and continuity of ITS solutions across the European Union.

ETSI has published the first release of standards for the initial deployment of C-ITS, which will enable vehicles made by different manufacturers to communicate with each other and with road infrastructure systems. ETSI ITS Committee (TC ITS) is a prominent initiative to achieve global standards for C-ITS that will empower vehicles made by different companies to communicate with each other and with the road infrastructure arrangements. In order to be productive, ETSI along with the European Committee for Standardization (CEN), and in response to the European Commission (EC) Mandate M/453, has published the first set of standards to enable the initial deployment of C-ITS in 2014, called Release 1. Also, the committee has begun the work on the requirements for Release 2. In Release 2 numerous novel features and functionalities will be included with the specifications to safeguard susceptible road users such as cyclists and motorcycle riders, for cooperative adaptive cruise control (C-ACC) and for platooning. ETSI has also started work on mitigation procedures to avoid interference between European CEN Dedicated Short-Range Communication equipment and ITS. Other efforts comprise local dynamic maps, cross-layer decentralized congestion control (DCC) for the management of C-ITS, and intersection collision risk warning (ICRW).

ETSI has published two new European Standards for ITS: the specification of Cooperative Awareness Basic Service (EN 302 637-2) and the specification of decentralized Environmental Notification (DEN) Basic Service (EN 302 637-3). They outline the message sets required for running C-ITS safety essential applications. The Cooperative Awareness Service allows the exchange of data between road users and roadside infrastructure, providing the positions, dynamics, and attributes that are required. In an ITS environment the road users can be cars, trucks, motorcycles, bicycles, or perhaps pedestrians, whereas margin infrastructure instrumentality includes road signs and traffic lights. Creating awareness is the basic necessity for road safety and traffic influence applications. The application mentioned earlier is often achieved by the regular exchange of data from the vehicle-to-vehicle (V2V) network, and between vehicles to infrastructure (V2I and I2V) network supported by various communication technologies. Henceforth, EN 302 637-2 specifies the syntax and semantics of the CAM and provides elaborated specifications for message handling in ITS.

The DEN (EN 302 637-3) supports road hazard warning in ITS environment. The DENM contains information associated with a road hazard or contains uncharacteristic traffic condition information. Usually in ITS application, a message is sent to ITS stations that are located at a particular region to direct V2V or V2I communications, in order to alert commuters of a dangerous incident. From the road user's point of view the message is processed, and the application enable assessment of the possibilities. Published as Technical Specifications in Release 1 of ETSI ITS, the standards are already taken into consideration. The feedback from testing ability workshops organized by ETSI for the trade as well as the feedback from ITS implementation emphasize the need of the above-mentioned standards. These two European Standards pave the way to new applications that will offer safer and more efficient driving conditions for the vehicular paradigm.

Standards for C-ITS are established by the experienced technical committees of CEN and ETSI. These technical committees bring together experts from that automotive industry, including car manufacturers as well as infrastructure system suppliers. In order to move forward, progressive work has been undertaken by the technical committee to develop the next package of standards. Some of the research projects funded by the European Union such as eCoMove, Drive C2X, and COMeSafety are major contributors to the standards committees. On the other hand infrastructure manufactures and the automotive industry are organizing their requirements through functional groups such as the ERTICO–ITS Europe, Amsterdam Group, and the Car 2 Car Communication Association, for further enhancement of standardization. In addition to that international cooperation with ISO, IEEE, and the SAE pave way for global harmonization of ITS deployment.

1.3.2 INTERNATIONAL TELECOMMUNICATION UNION (ITU)

ITU is a part of the United Nations organization in the field of telecommunications technologies. There are a few initiatives for the establishment of a joint task force on ITS communications between ITU and ISO. The joint task force is responsible for ITS applications, telecommunication manufactures, and other existing work on networking, in order to attain a global ITS standards. The intent of this joint task force is to collaborate with globally renowned forum for the establishment of a globally harmonized set of Intelligent ITS Standards. This harmonization should provide the utmost quality in the most efficient way possible to empower the rapid placement of fully interoperable ITS communication-related products in the global marketplace. Hence a convergent, harmonized, and incorporated approach provides ITU with an emerging ITS communication standard.

1.3.2.1 United States' Initiatives for ITS Standards

Table 1.4 provides links to standard development organizations (SDO) and some of these are specific ITS Standards efforts and their applications. In the United States, the DOT's ITS Joint Program Office (JPO) involved with ITS standards development includes the ISO and the National Institute of Standards and Technology (NIST).

1.3.2.2 IEEE

IEEE plays a vital role in C-ITS standards. Some of the working groups that are responsible for deriving standards in ITS are IEEE 802, IEEE 802.11p, IEEE 1609 (WAVE), and IEEE SCC42 Transportation. The IEEE 802 LAN/MAN Standards Committee develops and maintains networking standards and recommended practices on a global basis. The IEEE 1609 Family of Standards for Wireless Access

Table 1.4 SDO and its Applications	
SDO	**ITS Applications**
AASHTO, ITE, NEMA	Traffic management center to other centers Traffic management center to field devices
AASHTO, ITE	Traffic management center to other centers
ANSI	Commercial vehicle operations (CVO)-related system interfaces
ASTM	Archived data management center interfaces
ASTM, IEEE, SAE	Vehicle to vehicle; field to vehicle
IEEE	Emergency management center to other centers
APTA	Transit center to other centers and transit vehicles
SAE	Traveler information (information service provider interfaces) Location referencing

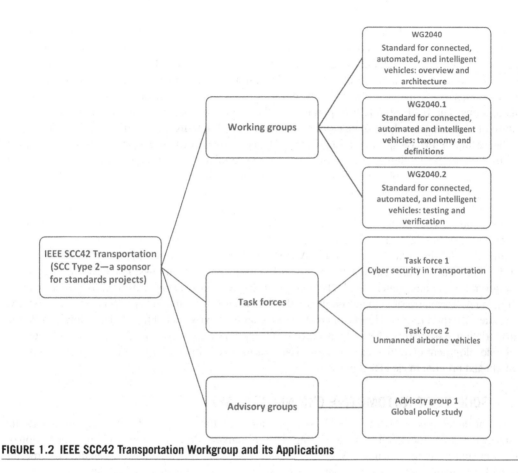

FIGURE 1.2 IEEE SCC42 Transportation Workgroup and its Applications

in Vehicular Environments (WAVE) defines an architecture, services, and interfaces that mutually facilitate secure V2V and V2I communications. In addition to that, IEEE 1616 is for motor vehicle event data recorders and IEEE 1512 is a multiple standard for traffic safety and emergency communications. In addition to that, we have IEEE 802.20/802.21/802.22 series of communication standards for connecting vehicles.

IEEE SCC42 Transportation is a new initiative toward global effort to promote transportation standards as mentioned in Fig. 1.2. IEEE invites the engagement of trade, government, and academia, globally in order to ensure that the IEEE SCC42 transportation's work is helped by a broad variety of views and demands. IEEE SCC42 transportation is developing guides, endorsed practices, standards, and customary definitions of terms in order to facilitate this.

1.3.2.3 SDO

The IEEE SCC42 transportation is functioning proactively with varied communities and corporations in transportation. Standardization of these functionality efforts leads toward coordination of IEEE standardization activities for transportation technologies, notably in the areas of connected vehicles, autonomous vehicles, and inter- and intravehicle communications. These techniques embrace (but are not restricted) to mobile applications, device networks, and communications that alter human-to-vehicle information flow, a vehicle-to-vehicle information exchange, a vehicle-to-infrastructure flow, a vehicle-to-platform flow, and vehicle to everything information and data flow. Wherever a need for standardization exists, the SCC will develop guides, advised practices, standards, and customary definitions of terms. The IEEE SCC42 transportation will assemble connected disciplines to help guarantee a future of transportation that can be extra related, automated, intelligent, electrical, and electronic.

The Institution of Transportation Engineers (ITE) is a global instructional and scientific association of transportation professionals. ITE supports the purpose of technology and scientific principles for the analysis, planning, implementation, operation, policy development, and management of vehicular networks. National Electrical Manufacturers Association (NEMA) is a trade association for electrical productions. NEMA member firms manufacture products employed in the Traffic Management Center. The National Transportation Communications for ITS Protocol (NTCIP) is a joint standardization project of AASHTO, ITE, and NEMA.

American National Standards Institute (ANSI) is the official US representative to the International ISO, US National Committee, and International Electrotechnical Commission (IEC). The American Society for Testing and Materials (ASTM) establishes international standards to enhance the quality, safety, and performance of vehicles on the roads. Particularly from the industry point of view, ASTM contributes in expert testing of parts and materials for automotive manufacturers. The American Public Transportation Association (APTA) has played an important role in creating active working structure for the development of vehicular standards. Their various activities have been carried out in order to maintain and procure these ITS standards.

1.3.3 SOCIETY OF AUTOMOTIVE ENGINEERS (SAE)

The recent development of SAE J2678 2015 provides recommendations for Navigation and Route Guidance Function Accessibility while driving. This initiative endorses practice and implementation of navigation and route management. SAE J2365 2015 states recommendations for calculating time for in-vehicle navigation and route guidance. This standard suggested practices on both original equipment manufacturer (OEM) and aftermarket route-guidance and navigation system functions for passenger vehicles by providing a method on time required to compute the navigation-related mission. SAE J2400 deals with the human factor in Forward Collision Warning (FCW) Systems, emphasizing user-interface requirements. This SAE standard provides an FCW operator interface, as well as necessities and test approaches for systems capable of warning drivers of rear-end collisions.

1.3.3.1 Japan's Initiatives

In Japan the bands 58,355,840 and 58,455,850 MHz were allocated for uplink and 57,905,795 and 58,005,805 MHz for downlink for the Association of Radio Industries and Businesses standard ARIB STDT55. The system relies on road architecture, as with DSRC, and provides ETC service. The standard uses ASK modulation for a data rate of 1 Mbps with 8-slot TDMA/FDD to provide service for a maximum of eight cars within a range of 30 m. Currently a new standard (ARIB STDT75) is being developed [3]. These systems can be regarded as the first generation of vehicular communications. The different standards and frequencies hindered the implementation of ITS systems since each country has its own specifications and operating systems. Moreover the low data rates and short distances were only suitable for a limited number of applications.

1.3.3.2 ARIB

ARIB is a leader in research and development studies, and is also responsible for setting standards and providing services for radio spectrum coordination and cooperation with international counterparts. ARIB STDT109 is also referred as Radio Equipment of 700 MHz BAND Intelligent Transport Systems. The main purpose of this standard is to provide drivers on the roads with vastly reliable safety information from traffic management systems through I2V communications, as well as to interchange safety-related information among nearby vehicles. ARIB STDT109 operates at the 700 MHz radio frequency band, and it comprises base stations, RSU stations, and mobile vehicles that exchange this valuable information among themselves. ARIB STDT110 is for the DSRC application interface. DSRC applications and its interface are already specified in ARIB STDT75, which denotes DSRC System and ARIB STDT88 specifications. DSRC application sublayer has two standards for the communication between a mobile station and base station in a DSRC system. ARIB STDT110 standard specifications state six basic application interfaces for I2V communication within a DSRC system. The first application discusses the onboard equipment (OBE) instruction response application. The second application focuses on OBE memory access application. In the third application, an IC card access application is discussed. The fourth application focuses on push-type information delivery in DSRC systems. OBE ID communication is the fifth application. The sixth concentrates on OBE basic indication application in DSRC systems.

ARIB STDT55 and ARIB STDT75 standards are the main platforms for the Japanese ITS [4]. The minimum requirement for the communication between OBUs and RSU is the focus of ARIB STDT55. Furthermore it validates the lowest level of provisions required to establish a primary connection. It supports both point-to-point and point-to-multipoint topologies. ARIB STDT75 Communication Standard is developed to work with DSRC 5.8 GHz band. The ARIB STDT55 Standard provides a limited connection between the RSU, base station (BS), and the vehicles. The applications include electronic toll collection and provide miscellaneous information related to parking assistances, logistics, and so forth. To take advantage of these promising opportunities, Japan has made huge investments with various cooperative initiatives such as national projects in Europe and North America to promote the cooperative realization of ITS. Furthermore, the Internet Engineering Task Force (IETF), which is an organized activity of the Internet society (ISOC) and Mobility Extension for IPv6 (MEXT) has been in effect in order to provide effective standards for safer means of transportation respectively.

1.4 VEHICULAR COMMUNICATION TECHNOLOGIES

By means of the development and extension of wireless communication technologies, substantial research efforts have been made in the area of vehicular network. The objective is to increase driver safety and comfort by relaying required information from vehicle to vehicle. Future vehicles are expected to anticipate and avoid possible collisions, navigate the quickest route to their destination making use of up-to-the-minute traffic reports, identify the nearest available parking slot, and minimize their carbon emissions. One of the most important challenges to convert all these dreams into reality is that these future applications have diverse communication requirements and will be used in different countries following different traffic rules and even different legal frequency bands. Therefore, understanding the communication requirements of target applications is key to selecting an appropriate communication channel. To achieve this, we need to define a set of communication parameters on the basis of which we can judge the suitability of a communication medium within a particular environment.

The vehicular standards are dedicated short-range communication (DSRC) and IEEE 802.11p; other than that, researchers are working on short-range communication protocols such as Zigbee, Wi-Fi, and so forth. Several technologies are involved in vehicular ad hoc networks, especially as enablers of ITS. These are GSM, UMTS, WiMAX limited Wi-Fi, and a new and specific technology for these kind of applications, namely WAVE, also known as IEEE 802.11/p [11]. This implicitly suggests that a car should have on board different radio interfaces (and/or network card). WAVE is a member of the IEEE 802.11 family. This suggests that this solution (currently at the stage of draft) is borrowed from IEEE 802.11 and adapted for the vehicular context. The vehicular communication scenario can be classified according to a range of communication between vehicles or between infrastructures as depicted in Fig. 1.3. The following are the classifications of vehicular communication scenarios:

- existing vehicular communication
- possible vehicular communication

In ITS the communication technologies can classify as traditional or existing mode of communication and then the possible or favorite mode of communication technologies as depicted in Fig. 1.3, which is discussed in the next section.

1.4.1 EXISTING VEHICULAR COMMUNICATION

1.4.1.1 DSRC

Dedicated short-range communications (DSRC) has close association with the discussed WAVE systems. The FCC in the United States, allocated 75 MHz of spectrum in the 5.95 GHz band for intelligent transportation. The purpose of DSRC is to provide high data transfers and low communication latency in a small communication area on vehicular networks. Hence, this type of communication covers a wide range of applications such as V2V safety messages, traffic information updates, toll-fee collection, and several other applications. DSRC-based systems are used in the majority of places all around the globe, particularly by EU Member States; however, these systems are currently not compatible. Therefore, the role of standardization is important in order to ensure interoperability, specifically in applications such as toll collection, for which the European Union imposes a need for interoperability of systems. Harmonization of different standards will ensure the provision and promotion of additional services using DSRC systems in ITS. CEN TC 278 produced the following standards for DSRC, EN 12253, EN 12795, EN 12834 [ISO 15628], and EN 13372 for ITS. On the other hand, SAE has SAE J2735 for DSRC message set dictionary used for intelligent transportation.

1.4.1.2 WAVE

WAVE system intended to provide continuous, interoperable services for ITS. The focus of WAVE is about the communication between vehicles and vehicle to infrastructure. This service is acknowledged by the United States' national ITS architecture and other research and industrial sectors. In order to specify the technologies associated with WAVE, the term DSRC is frequently used. The FCC has allocated bandwidth for DSRC system mobile services in ITS, and SAE J2735 has specified 5.9 GHz DSRC for the purpose of applications intended for the utilization of WAVE. With respect to vehicular networks, the WAVE systems currently visualize the design to meet the communication requirements. The IEEE WAVE standards documents, includes IEEE Std 1609.-2013, IEEE Std 1609-2010, IEEE

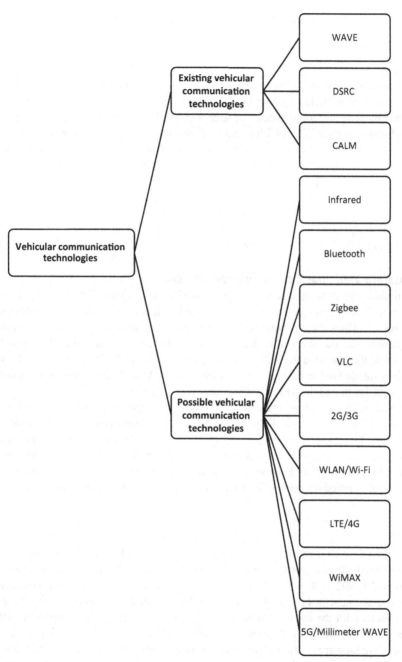

FIGURE 1.3 Vehicular Communication Technologies

Std 1609.-2010, IEEE P1609, IEEE Std 1609.11-2010, IEEE Std 1609.1, and IEEE Std 802.1-2012, respectively.

1.4.1.3 CALM

CALM standards are communication-centric and according to the requirement this application varies. The application of CALM includes communication protocols, allowing dynamic selection according to the need of the applications, competencies of access technologies, existing condition of the communication channels, and so forth. The ITS international SDO and other ITS communication international standards derived a set of CALM international standards for basic ITS vehicular networks around the globe. The ISO TC204 WG16 has developed the International Standards ISO 24102 for ITS Station Management and ISO 29281 for Non-IP Networking, which are a basic set of CALM communication standards. Furthermore, ISO 29281 contains the basic specifications of the ITS FAST networking and transport protocol that are part of CALM standardization. In addition to that, ISO 15628 access technologies and its applications are currently used for electronic toll services. ISO 24102 contains the specification of ITS FAST Service Advertisement.

1.4.1.4 Possible Vehicular Communication Systems

IR is most suitable for short-range communication in ITS. IR is appropriate for some specific ITS applications such as lane-specific communication due to its highly directional nature and increased data transfer rate, up to 1 Mbps. In addition, IR doesn't require licenses and agreements with providers and there are no restrictions on bandwidth allocation. IR is the possible candidate for line-of-sight communication. It can thus be used for V2I communication between RSU and vehicles. This technology is successfully implemented in several ITS projects such as Vehicle Information and Communication System (VICS) in Japan and the Truck Tolling Scheme in Germany.

Bluetooth technology is a possible candidate for short-range communication, and operates in an unlicensed band at 2.4 GHz over small distances of 10 m. The fundamental characteristics of bluetooth technology include low power, low cost, low complexity, and robustness. This technology is intended to provide wireless connection between different portable or fixed electronic devices in the vehicle basically suited for communication, such as onboard communication devices. In addition it can be used for technology that is wired but with an interface that is free to move, such as Internet over mobile and other existing networks.

1.4.1.5 Zigbee

In vehicular communication particular attention is given to IEEE 802.15.4 Zigbee communication since it is well suited for an adaptive network. IEEE 1609 standard, which is a fundamental standard, can also assist IEEE 802.15.4, which helps in improving network services, multichannel operations, and resource management in ITS. Zigbee is especially intended to support sensing, monitoring, and control applications with the lowest power consumption, respectively. In comparison with the traditional GPS navigation system, the IEEE 802.15.4-based driver assistance system is cost-effective and along with the navigation application, it provides warning capabilities to vehicles. Additionally, Zigbee can accommodate various network topologies such as star, peer-to-peer, mesh, and so forth. Also, there are various other features of Zigbee, such as support for low-energy devices requiring time-critical, medium data rate, non-line-of-sight operation, and reliable communication for ITS.

1.4.2 VISIBLE LIGHT COMMUNICATION (VLC)

VLC uses lighting sources as transmitters and utilizes photodiodes as receivers for establishing communication. Various research organizations are working on VLC applications like such as Visible Light Communications Consortium and the IEEE task group, 802.15.7 and so forth. With reference to vehicular network, the merits are that VLC data rate is up to 500 Mbps and VLC is energy efficient due to the use of LEDs. In ITS environment, VLC can be used for processing minor application scenarios such as sensor data and so forth. The sensors are used to provide efficient environmental monitoring. There are also a few drawbacks to VLC, such as how it supports line-of-sight (LOS) communications, which can be used only at a short range.

1.4.3 CELLULAR SYSTEMS (2G/3G)

The cellular networks such as 2G/3G are suitable for vehicular communication technology context because of their virtually ubiquitous nature. In cellular networks, a base station or access point is widely deployed in almost all cities and cover an enormous geographical region. In comparison with other networks such as IEEE 802.11b/g, wireless local area networks (WLANs), cellular networks have low data rates. On the other hand, emerging cellular network technologies such as long-term evolution (LTE) is offering high data rates for ITS.

1.4.4 WLAN/WI-FI

WLAN or wireless fidelity (Wi-Fi) can provide efficient wireless access to empower intelligent transportation between vehicles and the infrastructure. IEEE 802.11 standards can be used to provide wireless connectivity between ITS environment. Furthermore, IEEE 802.11a provides a data rate of 54 Mbps and, with a communication range of at least a 140 m range, it can be effectively used in a vehicular networking scenario. In addition to that, we have IEEE 802.11g, which has the same characteristics of IEEE 802.11a, like similar data rates, but works at 2.4 GHz.

1.4.5 4G/LTE

In 4G networks, worldwide interoperability for microwave access (WiMAX) and LTE are the two important developing wireless technologies that aim to provide a broadband Internet speed of 100 Mbps. Recently, the focus of various academicians and researchers has been on the performance evaluation and improvement of 4G/LTE/WiMAX vehicular networks. These kinds of high-speed broadband connections have become the need of the hour for intelligent transportations. For high-bandwidth demand and QoS requirements in vehicular networks, LTE provides the current feasible alternative solution. The application of LTE includes cloud access, video streaming for entertainment perspective, VoIP, web browsing, vehicular social networking, and so forth. The basic need for vehicular communication that is providing road safety and traffic competence is still under investigation. With the major setback in message latency in a centralized LTE system design, the safety-related application in VANET is a matter of concern in LTE-based vehicular networks. ISO is currently working on alternative or complementary role for IEEE 802.11p, hence LTE or 4G would support the role in C-ITS.

1.4.6 WIMAX

WiMAX is based on the IEEE 802.16 standard. The ultimate goal of WiMAX technology is to provide seamless wireless access over extensive distance via multiple means, from point-to-point to mobile-centric access. The mobile-centric WiMAX is defined as IEEE 802.16e, which supports predominant mobility as per consumer requirements. This technology offers portable and high-speed connectivity, and WiMAX can be used with cellular setups as a layover to increase the capacity of a particular network. Hence, WiMAX can be effectively utilized for V2I or I2I communications, and it also provides long-range communications, which can be used for various applications.

1.4.7 5G/MILLIMETER-WAVE (MMWAVE) TECHNOLOGY

The 5G/MMWAVE is a next-generation technology that operates between 60 and 64 GHz, a band that can support direct V2V communication. There are various other features involved in this technology because it is less affected by weather and also supports non-line-of-sight communication for long-distance communication. In addition to that, MMWAVE supports smaller antenna sizes that can easily be integrated in a vehicle in an ITS environment. Hence, this technology is best suited for high data rates. Therefore, the above-mentioned communication technologies would be beneficial in different aspects or different modes of communication in the ITS environment.

1.5 CONCLUDING STATEMENT

Vehicular technologies commonly apply to car safety systems that have self-contained autonomous electromechanical sensors generating warnings that can be transmitted within a specified target area of interest, for example, within 100 m of the transceiver. In ground applications, intelligent vehicle technologies are utilized for safety and commercial communications between vehicles or between a vehicle and a sensor along the road. Various innovative paths for observing, monitoring, and managing transportation systems are discussed in this chapter, along with the available technologies to implement them.

INTELLIGENT TRANSPORTATION SYSTEMS

2

2.1 INTELLIGENT TRANSPORTATION SYSTEMS

Intelligent transport systems (ITS) is a general term for the unified application of communications, control, and information processing technologies to vehicular networks. The subsequent benefits save lives, time, money, energy, and the environment. The acronym ITS is flexible and capable of being understood in a broad or a narrow way. In Europe ITS is called *transport telematics,* a group of technologies that support ITS. Fundamental attributes of ITS cover all approaches of transport and imitate all features of the transportation system: the vehicle, the infrastructure, and the driver or user, collaborating together dynamically. The universal purpose of ITS is to develop decision making in real time by vehicular network controllers and other users, thereby filtering the operation of the entire transport network. The explanation covers a wide array of methods and tactics that may be achieved through stand-alone technological applications or as enhancements to other transportation schemes. Information is at the core of ITS, whether it is static or real-time traffic information. Presently, ITS tools are based on the collection, processing, integration, and supply of information around transportation networks.

Data generated by ITS may offer real-time information about current conditions of roads, or information for journey planning, enabling highway authorities and agencies, and individual travelers to make better informed, safer, more harmonized, and more "intelligent" decisions on using the networks. ITS adds information and communications technology to transport infrastructures and vehicles in an effort to improve their safety, reliability, efficiency, and quality. ITS comprises advanced technologies that aim to provide innovative services relating to different modes of transport and traffic management. It enables various users to be better informed and make safer, more coordinated, and "smarter" use of transport networks. Compared with the traditional transportation system, the most significant characteristic of ITS is the combination of artificial intelligence and a transportation system. ITS encompasses a broad range of wireless and wire line communications-based information and information processing, control algorithm, electronics, and other technologies. When integrated into the transportation system's infrastructure, and in vehicles themselves, these technologies relieve congestion, improve safety, and enhance productivity.

The development of ITS in different countries can be divided into two stages. The typical characteristic of the first stage is primarily transportation information acquisition and processing intelligence. Transportation telematics probably originated in the early 1970s in Japan, where several technological programs were conducted to deal with the large number of traffic deaths and injuries as well as the structurally ineffective traffic process. In Europe, the first formalized transportation telematics program, PROMETHEUS (Program for European Traffic with Highest Efficiency and Unprecedented Safety) was initiated by European automotive companies in 1986, while in 1988 the DRIVE program (Dedicated Road Infrastructure and Vehicle Environment) was set up by the European authorities. The

United States followed in 1990 by forming Mobility 2000 in 1989 and in 1990 by establishing the Intelligent Vehicle Highway Systems (IVHS) program which was renamed ITS in 1994.

National ITS architectures for several countries were designed and planned at this stage, including the research area and transportation service. ITS services are also designed to optimize transport times and fuel consumption, thus providing greener and safer transportation. However, the deployment of intelligent transport systems and the provision of corresponding services are not only limited to the road transport sector, but also include railway, aviation, and maritime domains, among others. ETSI, well known for producing standards for fixed telecommunications, mobile, radio, broadcast, and Internet technologies, supports the ITS domain with comprehensive standardization activities. Release 1 of a set of basic ITS standards has now been published. The full list of standards in ITS Release 1 is available in ETSI Technical Report TR 101 607. This first set of standards will lead to the harmonized development of ITS-related products and their deployment on the market, responding to market demands.

Technological innovation is essential for sustainable, efficient, and competitive mobility in Europe. ITS in particular can address the challenges that Europe faces in the transport sector. Deployment of ITS in Europe needs to be accelerated in a coordinated way and European standards—for example, for the exchange of data—should be set. This is the thrust of the European Commission's action plan for the deployment of ITS in Europe— the "ITS action plan" for short—and the accompanying proposal for a directive laying down the framework for the deployment of ITS, both adopted on Dec. 16, 2008. The plan aims to make road transport and interfaces with other transport modes more environmentally friendly, more efficient, and more safe and secure. ITS can make a significant contribution to the EU's efforts to pursue its broader goals for transport via a variety of applications for the different modes. And ITS can make it easier to link the modes, for example, by means of multimodal trip planners.

The EU wants to encourage "co-modality" in freight logistics chains, which means the efficient use of different modes on their own and in combination, and aims to cut congestion and reduce the number of accidents on Europe's roads. The goals also include reducing energy consumption and improving energy efficiency, cutting greenhouse gas emissions and reducing dependence on fossil fuels. ITS applications in road transport include electronic tolling, dynamic traffic management with variable speed limits, parking guidance and reservations, navigation devices, and driver assistance systems like electronic stability control and lane departure warning systems.

ETSI's Technical Committee for Intelligent Transport Systems (TC-ITS) creates and maintains standards and specifications for the use of information and communications technologies in transport systems. Most of the Technical Committee's ongoing standardization activities focus on wireless communications for vehicle-to-vehicle and vehicle-to-roadside communications. The goal is to address the safety of life through the reduction of road fatalities and injuries (in Europe, over 40,000 road fatalities per year and more than 1.25 million injuries), to address traffic efficiency with a reduction in transport time and the related economic consequences, and to decrease polluting emissions such as CO_2. This is a global issue and ETSI is cooperating with standardization bodies worldwide in order to achieve global interoperability and harmonized deployment of ITS. As a consequence, the work of TC-ITS is supported by a large variety of companies who actively contribute to standardization work. These include carmakers along with automotive industry suppliers. Equally, there are silicon vendors, network operators, and research bodies as well as test houses.

Intensive links are maintained at the European Commission, whose ITS-related initiatives aim to stimulate the deployment of ITS. In parallel, industry organizations such as the Car-to-Car Communication Consortium (C2CCC) provide important input to the standardization work. Due to the international nature of this work ETSI cooperates closely with other international standardization organizations such as ISO, CEN, IEEE, SAE International, ARIB, and IETF in order to achieve internationally deployed and harmonized standards on ITS, which are essential to worldwide interoperability.

2.1.1 CURRENT STANDARDIZATION ACTIVITIES OF ITS

Standardization currently focuses on cooperative systems, electronic fee collection, and interoperability of these technologies. Since ITS has a global dimension, great attention is given to the creation of commonly agreed-on standards for the network architecture, protocols, and transmission formats. Having such a set of commonly approved standards helps lead to a global harmonization of ITS services and applications. A key issue when working on such standards ensures interoperability. Here, ETSI's Centre for Testing and Interoperability (CTI) provides expertise in all aspects of interoperability. Since the Release 1 set of standards has been completed, ITS-related standardization continues in 2014 with the maintenance of Release 1 and the development of Release 2, which supports additional ITS-related use cases, functionality, and features. The following list shows some potential topics for which ETSI TC-ITS will develop standards and technical specifications for autonomous driving, integrated transport supporting smart cities, roadside platform architecture, integration of existing infrastructures, digital maps, in-vehicle platform architecture, urban mobility management, and freight and fleets services.

   ITS is the integration of information and communication technologies in the transportation system, which would improve safety, efficiency, and sustainability. Companies and government are working in tandem to address the current transportation challenges in the present fiscally constrained environment. High investments are being made in ITS to develop cost-effective measures that can lessen the traffic strain, congestion, and carbon emissions, while modernizing the present traffic operations, optimizing system performance, and improving access to transportation alternatives. The navigation and communication technologies that are typically used in ITS are global positioning system (GPS), dedicated short-range communication (DSRC), and CALM (carrier access for land mobiles). The vehicle detection system, traffic information, and variable message signs are the essential elements in an ITS, all of which improve the efficiency and reliability of the transportation infrastructure. This chapter discusses various systems that are being used in ITS, namely the Advanced Traffic Management System (ATMS), Advanced Traveler Information System (ATIS), ITS-Enabled Transportation Pricing System, Advanced Public Transportation System (APTS), and Commercial Vehicle Operation (CVO). These systems are used for various applications like asset monitoring, parking management, collision avoidance systems, traffic monitoring, and traffic enforcement cameras among others. The ITS market is also segmented based on the geographical regions covering certain key countries such as the United States, Canada, China, Japan, Australia, India, and Japan, taking into consideration the influence of ITS in these countries. The report also focuses on the driving factors for the market such as government support and environmental benefits, the safety parameters and, traffic congestion solutions that resulted in the reduction of accidents, and many more factors. The restraints and the opportunities for the ITS market are also highlighted, covering the current market scenario. The major trends in the ITS market are forecasted from 2013 to 2020, based on the market growth factors. The major players in the ITS market are Thales group (France), Nuance Communications Inc. (United States), Garmin International Inc. (United States), Kapsch Trafficomm AG (Austria), and TomTom N.V. (The Netherlands), among others.

Standardization for road transport focuses on wireless communications for cooperative ITS, with a priority on safety. ITS offers numerous benefits including increased travel safety, minimized environmental impact (in terms of CO_2 emissions and fuel consumption), and improved traffic management. ITS has applications in road safety, traffic control, fleet and freight management, and location-based services, supporting emergency services and providing driver assistance and hazard warning. Our ITS committee (TC-ITS) is leading the drive to achieve global standards for cooperative ITS, unlocking the enormous potential of vehicle-to-vehicle and vehicle-to-roadside communication. The completed Release 1 will enable the initial deployment of cooperative ITS and includes key standards for Cooperative Awareness Messages (CAM), Decentralized Environmental Notification Messages (DENM), Geo networking protocols, common data dictionaries, harmonized channel usage in the 5.9 GHz frequency range, and identity management and protection. Road hazard signaling for longitudinal and intersection collision warnings, as well as electric vehicle charging spot notification, is also addressed. A European standard (EN) on cross-layer decentralized congestion control (DCC) is being developed, coordinating with similar activities in the United States. Most of this Release 1 work has been done in response to the EC Mandate M/453 on Cooperative ITS.

To achieve harmonization of ITS services and applications, ETSI promises to produce commonly agreed-on standards for the network architecture, protocol, and transmission formats. ETSI's CTI provides expertise on interoperability matters. Release 2 is being developed and will provide additional ITS-related use cases, functionalities, and features to enable a large installed base of cooperative ITS and support additional available networks as required by the various stakeholders. This release will address service continuity in multiaccess environments, crash avoidance, intersection collision avoidance, traffic management, and enhanced point-of-interest notification services, geo-casting, geo-messaging, enhanced decentralized congestion control (DCC) for ITS-G5, and the inclusion of social networks.

2.2 ITS APPLICATIONS AND ENABLING TECHNOLOGIES

In recent years the term ITS has emerged, which refers to the methods of transforming transportation systems through the use of ICT and its related infrastructure. ITS can be defined as the application of advanced sensor, computer, electronics, and communication technologies and management strategies in an integrated manner to improve the safety and efficiency of the surface transportation system. ITS has the potential to solve the most common challenges related to recent transportation systems such as heavy traffic congestion in large cities, poor traffic management, unreliable services, and so forth. Moreover, it is shown that ITS has the possibility to act as a key factor for economic growth in many countries. However, the diversity of data sources and multiple distributed traffic departments make ITS development complex. Further, ITS should support a wide range of core services ranging from traveler information to ICT infrastructure. Even though the possibilities of ITS have been recognized, they have not yet been employed as real-world solutions in public transport systems. Therefore, in order to deploy ITS for public transport systems, the architecture needs efficient sharing of real-time traffic and road conditions among operated vehicles and transport authorities. This will increase road safety and improve traffic flow by operating traffic signals intelligently and assisting drivers to avoid potentially dangerous road conditions by sending prior traffic advisories such as road repairs, blocked lanes, and so forth.

2.2.1 APPLICATION FRAMEWORK OF ITS-AMERICA

According to the conceptual framework of future ITS development planned by the US Department of Transportation and ITS-America, the relationship between ITS services was defined to ensure the compatibility and the interchangeability. Seven functions and thirty users' services provided to drivers in an ITS environment are defined as follows:

1. **Travel and transportation management**
   a. Driving information during travel
   b. Route guidance
   c. Travel service information
   d. Traffic control
   e. Incident management
   f. Emission monitoring and improvement
   g. Railroad level crossing
2. **Travel demand management**
   a. Demand management and operation
   b. Pretrip information
   c. Carpool matching and prebooking
3. **Public transportation operation**
   a. Public transportation management
   b. Public transportation information during travel
   c. Personalized public transportation
   d. The security of public transportation
4. **Electronic payment**
   a. Electronic payment service
5. **CVO**
   a. The electronic customs clearance of commercial vehicle
   b. Automatic security roadside inspection
   c. Security monitoring in car
   d. Commercial vehicle management program
   e. The incident response of dangerous goods
   f. Cargo flexibility
6. **Emergency management**
   a. Emergency notification and personal security
   b. Emergency vehicle management
7. **Advanced vehicle control and safety system**
   a. Back-up collision prevention
   b. Side collision prevention
   c. Intersection collision prevention
   d. The vision improvement of traffic accident prevention
   e. Security preparation
   f. Collision prevention before accident
   g. Automatic highway system

Unlike traditional traffic engineering, ITS is considered to be a smart technology that integrates information, communication, control, computer technology, and other modern technologies to deploy a real-time, flexible, reliable, and efficient transportation management system. The concept of ITS was proposed by the United States in the 20th century, but nowadays it is known all over the world, especially in Japan, Singapore, Korea, and some of the European countries at a significant level. In order to solve the problems related to transportation and to advance the research related to people-centric ITS for public and private sectors, European Road Transport Telemetric Implementation Coordination Organization (ERTICO) was formed in 1985. ITS can offer five key benefits over traditional traffic infrastructure:

1. reduce congestion and hence increase operational performance,
2. increase safety for travelers and vehicles,
3. enhance mobility and flexibility for travelers,
4. ensure compliance with environmental regulations,
5. raise employment opportunity, and therefore support economic growth.

There are different technologies that need to be integrated in order to design a concrete architecture for ITS. Furthermore, a general infrastructure for ITS includes three key steps: (1) data collection, (2) data processing, and (3) information delivery. Each step involves a set of diverse technologies, devices, platforms, and entities that require seamless interaction in order to deliver reliable services to end users.

Crash prevention and safety in ITS is proposed to increase the level of safety and efficiency of the overall transportation system. In developing as well as in developed countries, the rate of accidents on the roads during the past few years has constantly declined because of the implementation of ITS on the roads. There are signs on the roadsthat provide information about roadway conditions, weather conditions, and other useful messages for drivers, which are required. On the other hand, road weather management in ITS also provides road weather management facilities to the drivers. Numerous systems are mounted on the roads for weather information, which is used to monitor different conditions. Sensors in the cars provide data such as air and pavement temperatures, wind speed and direction, visibility, humidity, and precipitation. Another system for weather management is the Wind Warning System and messages concerning the level of snow on roads, which alerts the drivers about hazardous conditions at bridge crossings and along coastal highways. These systems monitor warning signs and provide necessary travel advisories.

Optimized timing of real-time traffic signals is an integral part of the urban traffic control system. Providing effective traffic signal control for a large, complex traffic network is an extremely challenging problem. The developed intelligent system makes real-time decisions about whether to extend the green time for a set of signals. The increase in urbanization and traffic congestion creates an urgent need to operate the transportation systems with maximum efficiency. One of the most cost-effective measures for dealing with these problems is traffic signal control. Traffic signal control is a system for synchronizing the timing of any number of traffic signals in an area, with the aim of reducing stops and overall vehicle delay or maximizing throughput of the traffic. It provides functions such as controlling traffic by adjusting and coordinating traffic signals at intersections, surveillance by monitoring traffic conditions with vehicle detectors and cameras, and maintenance of equipment by monitoring for equipment failures.

Enhancing mobility and convenience in an ITS advances transportation mobility, convenience, and productivity by incorporating advanced communications technologies into transportation infrastructure and into vehicles. ITS incorporates a broad range of wireless and traditional communications-based information and electronic technologies.

2.2.2 APPLICATIONS AND USE CASES

Vehicular networking applications can be classified as active road safety applications, traffic efficiency and management applications, and infotainment applications. Active road safety applications are those that are primarily employed to decrease the probability of traffic accidents and the loss of life of the occupants of vehicles. A significant percentage of accidents that occur every year in all parts of the world are associated with intersection, head-on, rear-end, and lateral vehicle collisions. Active road safety applications primarily provide information and assistance to drivers to avoid such collisions with other vehicles. This can be accomplished by sharing information between vehicles and roadside units that is then used to predict collisions. Such information can represent the vehicle position, intersection position, speed, and distance heading. Moreover, information exchange between the vehicles and the roadside units is used to locate hazardous locations on roads, such as slippery sections or potholes. Some examples of active road safety applications are given subsequently, as derived from the use cases described.

An intersection collision warning is used during the risk of lateral collisions for vehicles that are approaching road intersections and is detected by vehicles or roadside units. This information is indicated to the approaching vehicles in order to lessen the risk of lateral collisions. Lane change assistance is used to determine the risk of lateral collisions for vehicles that are accomplishing a lane change with a blind spot for trucks. Overtaking vehicle warning aims to prevent collision between vehicles in an overtake situation, where one vehicle, say vehicle 1, is attempting to overtake a vehicle, say vehicle 3, while another vehicle, vehicle 2, is already doing an overtaking maneuver on vehicle 3. Collision between vehicle 1 and vehicle 2 is prevented when vehicle 2 informs vehicle 1 to stop its overtaking procedure.

Head-on-collision warning that determines the risk of a head-on collision sends early warnings to vehicles that are traveling in opposite directions. This use case is also denoted as "do not pass warning." A rear-end-collision warning is provided to avoid the risk of rear-end collisions, for example, due to a traffic slow down or road curvature (e.g., curves, hills). The driver of a vehicle is informed of a possible risk of rear-end collision in front. The risk of forward collision accident is detected through the cooperation between vehicles called "cooperative forward collision warning." Such types of accidents are then avoided by using either cooperation between vehicles or through driver assistance. Emergency vehicle warning activates emergency vehicles, for example, ambulance, police car, informs other vehicles in its neighborhood to free an emergency corridor. This information can be rebroadcast in the neighborhood by other vehicles and roadside units.

Pre-crash sensing/warning considers that a crash is unavoidable and will take place. Vehicles and the available roadside units periodically share information to predict collisions. The exchanged information includes detailed position data and vehicle size and it can be used to enable an optimized usage of vehicle equipment to decrease the effect of a crash. Such equipment can be actuators, air bags, motorized seat-belt pretensioners, and extensible bumpers. In cooperative merging assistance vehicles involved in a junction merging maneuver negotiate, and cooperate with each other and with roadside units to accomplish this maneuver and avoid collisions. Emergency electronic brake lights allow a vehicle that has to suddenly brake to inform other vehicles, by using the cooperation of other vehicles and/or roadside units, about this situation. In a wrong-way-driving warning, a vehicle detecting that it is driving the wrong way signals the situation to other vehicles and roadside units. Stationary vehicle warning provides information regarding a vehicle that is immobilized due to an accident, breakdown, or any other reason, informing other vehicles and roadside units about this situation.

In traffic condition warning any vehicle that detects some rapid traffic evolution informs other vehicles and roadside units about this situation. Signal violation warning in one or more roadside units detects a traffic signal violation. This violation information is broadcast by the roadside units to all vehicles in the neighborhood. In collision risk warning a roadside unit detects a risk of collision between two or more vehicles that do not have the capability to communicate. This information is broadcast by the roadside unit toward all vehicles in the neighborhood of this event. Hazardous location notification provides any vehicle or any roadside unit signals to other vehicles about hazardous locations, such as an obstacle on the road, a construction worker or slippery road conditions. The control loss warning is an additional use case which is defined to enable the driver of a vehicle to generate and broadcast a control-loss event to surrounding vehicles. Upon receiving this information the surrounding vehicles determine the relevance of the event and provide a warning to the drivers, if appropriate.

2.3 EMERGING ITS APPLICATIONS
2.3.1 ITS ACTION PLAN AND DIRECTIVE

The 2008 ITS Action Plan 3 and 2010 ITS Directive 4 established a clear framework for the technological development and deployment of road transport ITS. The focus of the review was on the deployment and the effects (benefits) of ITS; the development of ITS is not directly within the scope of this work. On Dec. 16, 2008, the European Commission adopted the ITS Action Plan [COM (2008) 886] for road transport and interfaces with other modes. The Action Plan aims to accelerate and coordinate the deployment of ITS in road transport. One of the key priority areas involves the optimal use of road, traffic, and travel data. The scope of this study falls within that priority area.

The ITS Action Plan provided the basis for the ITS directive, which defines a series of basic elements to be considered when elaborating on "the necessary requirements to make EU-wide real-time traffic information (RTTI) services accurate and available across borders to ITS users." In Dec. 2012 the EC commissioned a study regarding "the provision of EU-wide real-time traffic information services." This final report provides an overview of the results of the study and presents its findings, conclusions, and recommendations. Technological innovations have fundamentally changed the RTTI services landscape. New technologies have created new ways of collecting more and more road and traffic data, at decreasing costs. Big data analytics have enabled the cost-efficient processing and enrichment of available data. And technological developments have introduced new services platforms such as smartphones and personal navigation devices. The desk research showed that this trend is likely to continue in the coming decade as new technologies will enter the market that also can cause a paradigm shift in the way road and traffic data is collected, processed, and distributed to end users. The technology that connects vehicles to the Internet (the connected car), to each other, and to roadside equipment (cooperative technology), for example, is expected to lead to a significant increase in available RTTI data at a much lower cost.

Technological developments also lead to different road and traffic data needs. As more and more driving tasks are automated, the need for human comprehensible traffic information (e.g., incident and traffic jam reports) will decrease and the demand for machine-readable road and traffic data will increase. Because machines can process much more data much faster than humans, the demand will shift to high-volume, accurate road and traffic data that is much more accurate and updated much more frequently. Automated vehicles will in particular require RTTI that will allow them to look past the range of their sensors and their cooperative range, providing them with a forward awareness of potential traffic build-up (forecasts) and potentially dangerous traffic situations downstream (accidents, dangerous driving conditions, etc.).

The new data and services platforms can potentially provide road authorities with powerful means to manage traffic on their roads more efficiently and more effectively. Roles in the RTTI value chain will likely change in the coming years. Private traffic information service providers are well positioned to develop the new traffic information services, as they have the technology to process the volumes of new traffic data and develop profitable business models. Public authorities will, however, retain a key role in assuring societal interests in the RTTI value chain. How the new technology, the RTTI markets, and the roles in the value chain will develop is difficult to predict. What does seem clear is that changes will occur and that both public and private organizations will have a role to play. Establishing a forum where public and private stakeholders in road data and traffic information find a platform to regularly discuss technical, organizational, and legal issues, would allow for the gradual incorporation of new technologies, development of new cooperation models, coordinated development of new data coding, location coding, quality standards, and so forth. The impact assessment showed that significant benefits to road safety and congestion reduction can be achieved against limited investments by mandating the deployment of public traffic management information and road data updates on the Core and Comprehensive Trans-European Road Network (TERN).

In addition to the quantified impact there are also important additional impacts that should be taken into consideration. Respondents to the online survey, for example, believed that RTTI can have high impacts on both road safety and road user satisfaction. Responses to the online survey showed broad support for actions by the EC to ensure and foster the provision of EU-wide RTTI. Traffic management information is in general poorly developed and not available to service providers. In addition there is reluctance from Traffic Managers to share such information with ITS service providers, as they are concerned the information might be used to recommend routes that are in the interest of the individual driver but not in the public interest. Service and satnav providers, however, indicate they would like to receive this information to better guide their customers away from traffic congestion and other incidents. Various trials have proven that it is possible to develop a cooperation model that serves both needs. Key to the solution is that road authorities classify their traffic management information (informative, recommended, mandatory) and that service and satnav providers present the information as such to their customers. A Memorandum of Understanding between road authorities and service and satnav providers could resolve this issues, wherein road operators commit to publishing traffic management information, and service providers commit to timely publishing of traffic management information, leaving the choice of whether to abide to the information, recommendations, or instructions from the road authorities to the end user. Data privacy and service liability will become key issues for increasing amounts of data originating from vehicles and communities. The EC should encourage harmonization of access conditions for data originating from the car, drivers, and passengers, by requesting the industry to draft guidelines and submit them to the joint European data protection authorities. Table 2.1 illustrates ITS directives and action plans.

2.3.1.1 ITS taxonomy
Directorate General for Mobility and Transport (DG MOVE) of the European Commission engaged AECOM to carry out a study on key performance indicators (KPIs) for ITS. The Final Report outlines the process that AECOM has utilized to establish current levels of KPI use, consult with industry

Table 2.1 ITS Action Plan and ITS Directives

ITS Directives	ITS Action Plan	
Priority Area A: optimal use of road, traffic, and travel data	Priority Area B: real-time traffic information services	Action 1.1: EU-Wide real-time traffic and travel information services
		Action 1.2: road data traffic circulation plans, traffic regulations, recommended routes
		Action 1.3: public data for digital maps and their timely updating
	Priority Area C: free safety-related traffic information	Action 1.4: free minimum universal traffic information services

experts, and establish a set of recommended KPIs for implementation within and across the EU. The objectives of the study as a whole were: to undertake a state of the art review of KPIs relating to ITS, with particular focus on the type, method of calculation, terminology used, and approaches, and how these vary between member states; and to define/recommend a set of common KPIs for road transport, with supporting guidance on their application, presentation, and reporting.

As defined in the study's terms of reference, the work is to provide the Commission with a recommended set of KPIs that can be adopted across the European Union. It is recognized that significant investment has been made in ITS, although the approaches developed for monitoring have remained fragmented, with little pan-European consolidation. As such, this study has built upon this existing evidence base, incorporating a review and assessment of the scope, rigor, and relevance of indicators already adopted. Table 2.2 illustrates the number of levels that are identified to classify ITS services with increasing levels of detail, from level 0, representing the ITS directive priority areas, through to level 4. For the purposes of defining where each KPI sits within this taxonomy, we have recorded the Level 2 system within the state of the art database. This allowed for both an aggregation to Level 1 and 0 within the analysis, and the consideration of Level 3 and 4 systems. Mapping the defined KPIs against Level 2 of the taxonomy allowed an assessment of ITS coverage to be undertaken. A central challenge in defining common KPIs was ensuring sufficient and proportionate coverage across the ITS deployment areas.

2.3.2 COOPERATIVE INTELLIGENT TRANSPORTATION SYSTEMS

Modern vehicles equipped with driver assistance systems can sense by sensors and see by cameras, and in the future modern vehicles will speak through communication systems. The new technology of cooperative ITS and related services enables communication between vehicles and traffic infrastructure. It is based on the principle that cooperative parties like ITS stations, that is, in vehicles and in roadside units, exchange information among each other in terms of standardized message sets. The receiving ITS station analyses the incoming data and makes use of them, resulting in a self-organizing principle on a local level. Services and applications being subjected to competition between companies cover up-to-date traffic information and improve road safety by avoiding accidents and reducing injury severity, increasing efficiency by supporting a consistent traffic flow, foresighting driving needs and enhancing driving comfort. By involving public transport, bicyclists, and pedestrians, intermodal and environmental capabilities, autonomous driving and further functions will be addressed in a second step when

Table 2.2 ITS Taxonomy

Level 0	Level 1	Level 2	Level 3	Level 4
ITS road safety and security applications	Emergency services	Transport-related emergency notification and personal security	eCall	
		Emergency vehicle management		
		Hazard materials and incident notifications		
	Road-transport-related personal and freight transport safety	Public travel security		
		Safety enhancements for vulnerable road users		
		Safety enhancements for disabled road users		
		Safety provisions for pedestrians using junctions and links		
		Commercial vehicles secure parking		
		Road-safety-related traffic information		
	Disaster response management and coordination services	Disaster data management		
		Disaster response management		
		Coordination with emergency agencies		
	Driver assistance and vehicle control	Safety readiness	Driver impairment	Alcohol interlock
			Intelligent vehicle safety systems or safety systems	Adaptive headlights
				Local danger warnings
				Collision avoidance
				Lane keeping
			Vision enhancement	Blind-spot monitoring
			Speed control (including ISA—intelligent speed adaption))	
Linking the vehicle with the transport infrastructure	Intelligent vehicle services	Automated vehicle operation	Platooning	
		Cooperative systems	Vehicle to vehicle (V2V)	
			Vehicle to infrastructure(V2I)	
			Vehicle to X (V2X)	
			Value-added services	

C-ITS has reached a sufficient market penetration. Based on European Mandate M/453, the minimum set of standards for C-ITS is developed and essentially finalized in 2013. The cooperative ITS scenario and its possible applications are discussed in Fig. 2.1.

The vehicle manufacturers announced they will start Day One deployment of C-ITS in Europe based on ITS-G5 technology beginning in 2015. Some front-runners of road operators and road authorities aim at strengthening this voluntary deployment process by investing in cooperative roadside units on the infrastructure side.

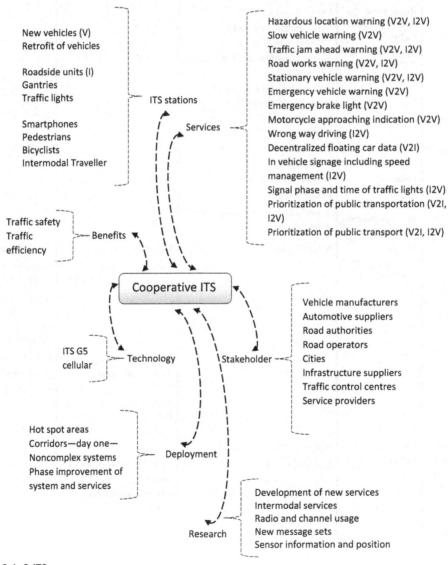

FIGURE 2.1 C-ITS

C-ITS applications are complex and may not all be implemented at the same time. Instead, a phase model will be applied. For cities in the first phase, applications related to traffic lights are of primary interest. The technology enables the transparent prioritization of public transport (bus, tram) and of emergency vehicles at intersections. Signal phase and timing information support "green driving" of all vehicles and safe and comfortable crossing of intersections, even by blind and visually impaired pedestrians. Collecting probe vehicle data from all C-ITS users provide a detailed up-to-date picture of the traffic situation and improves traffic control and intermodal traffic management. Energy and emission savings result from facilitating a consistent traffic flow, reducing the number of accidents as well as traffic congestion caused by drivers searching for suitable parking areas. Furthermore local information on P&R and public transport offers could contribute to a modal shift toward environmentally friendly transport modes.

2.3.3 IMPORTANT SPECIFICS OF C-ITS

The cooperative system and dedicated functions have been tested and demonstrated in many European cities. Cities that are involved in the most important field operational tests are discussed. In Frankfurt, Germany, a national large-scale field operational test by the simTD project has been carried out. The simTD project (2008–13) in its first phase defined the overall cooperative architecture and the system design, the implementation, integration, and test of individual subsystems, as well as the experimental design. Then the cooperative infrastructure on motorways, rural roads, urban roads, related traffic control, and management centers and vehicle fleets of more than 100 test vehicles were implemented. The third project phase focuses on the large-scale field operational trial under real conditions. In Paris, France, a national field operational test by the SCORE@F project (2010–13) focuses on cooperative V2V and V2I services increasing the safety and comfort for passenger cars and long-distance lorry drivers. The test field comprises special test tracks, motorways including tunnels and urban roads, in the southwest of Paris. Project results were fed in standardization at the European Standardization Organizations ETSI and CEN.

Tampere, Finland; Gothenburg, Sweden; Helmond, the Netherlands; Frankfurt, Germany; Yvelines, France; Brennero, Italy; and Vigo, Spain, are some of the European fields where operational test by the DRIVE C2X project is carried out. The European DRIVE C2X project (2010–13) lay the foundation for rolling out cooperative systems in Europe, leading to safer, more economical, and more ecological driving. It focuses on communication among vehicles (C2C) as well as between vehicles and roadside and backend infrastructure system (C2I). Thereby, it also enables commercial services based on C2X communication data to private and commercial customers. Besides testing and demonstration, it brought together all stakeholders involved, prepared an implementation roadmap, contributed significantly to the European ITS standardization, and provided the necessary certainty for decision making toward the market introduction by investigating socioeconomic and business-economic aspects of cooperative driving.

In Braunschweig, Germany, an Application Platform Intelligent Mobility (AIM) framework has been developed. The project AIM, which is an independent, cooperative ITS infrastructure covering the city, was started in 2010 on urban roads and urban motorways. By the end of 2012, it comprised 30 roadside units for ITS-G5, six roadside units for W-LAN for the inclusion of pedestrians and cyclists in cooperative scenarios, and GSM/UMTS5 connection for infrastructure/vehicles. By the end of 2015, at least 60 roadside units will be in operation for the next 15 years. The service-oriented architecture

(SOA) and 23 basic services were designed to meet project-specific demands covering mobility research, different transportation modes, and intermodality. In Vienna, Austria, a Cooperative Mobility Demonstration during the ITS World Congress 2012 was demonstrated. The Testfeld Telematik project (2011–13) was established for telematics testing in cooperative services aiming at the mutual exchange of real-time information between vehicles and infrastructure to increase safety, efficiency, and environmentally friendly mobility. It was of particular importance that the passenger transfer to public transport was made attractive and simple, which was achieved by comprehensive co-modal traffic information for all means of transportation. About 3,000 drivers tested cooperative services for 12 months on the main test route, which has a length of about 45 km and is located in the area of the motorway intersection A2/A23-A4-S1. In Madrid, Spain, a cooperative road information pilot project called mVia used various applications like Adaptive Traffic Control for 15% of city intersections. The mVia project implemented travel time calculation and dynamic VMS with use of on-board equipment and data capture (including ODB connection) on a 40 km northbound freeway corridor. Servers already processed the geo-referenced information and served data for driver's notifications. Additionally Madrid has implemented adaptive traffic light regulation, aiming at providing smooth adaptation of traffic plans to changes in traffic conditions. By now, nearly 350 intersections of the 2.200 have been working in adaptive mode for the past 10 years, implementing near closed-loop regulation.

2.3.4 RESEARCH ON ITS

At the same time as industry players are taking advantage of evolving information and communications technology to develop telematics and infotainment systems for commercial benefit, governments are working with standards bodies and industry stakeholders to develop ITS that use telematics to allow for automatic communications among vehicles, infrastructure, and pedestrians to improve traffic safety and efficiency. Vehicle-to-vehicle or Connected Vehicle systems are a key component of ITS, focusing on surface transportation. First-generation V2V systems involve the transmission of a basic safety message between vehicles so as to warn drivers of imminent collisions. Second-generation systems are expected to use vehicle sensors to trigger automatic safety-related actions.

In addition to the promise of improved road safety, V2V, and more broadly, ITS, is touted as easing traffic congestion and lowering overall carbon emissions. By directing drivers to less congested routes, helping to eliminate unnecessary stops, and providing drivers with real-time information on traffic, weather, and alternative transportation options, such systems are expected to reduce commute times, cut traffic emissions, and help people make greener and more efficient transportation choices. ITS can also be used by the state to identify and track vehicles for purposes of law enforcement. For example, Brazil is moving ahead with a mandatory electronic tag-based vehicle identification program aimed at ensuring that drivers pay vehicle registration fees and taxes, road tolls, and parking fees. The system will also be used for police identification of vehicles involved in crimes or stolen or unregistered for automatic monitoring of vehicles will be in place across the country by 2017. Following the lead of the United States, Canada launched a national ITS strategic plan in 1999 and in 2010 released version 2.0 of the National ITS Architecture for Canada.

The basis for stakeholders to work together on standardization of ITS technologies and ensure interoperability of technologies used at Canada-US border crossings is under contemplation. There are now over 200 ITS-related projects underway across Canada, including two Connected Vehicle test beds at the Universities of British Columbia and Alberta. Similar Connected Vehicle research and development initiatives are underway elsewhere. In addition to funding ITS projects such as these test beds, Transport Canada is working with the Ministries of Transportation in Ontario and Quebec to develop a "Smart Corridor" for more efficient multi-modal commercial movement of goods. The City of Toronto, Canada's largest city, recently adopted a Congestion Management Strategy that involves ITS projects and the potential for Big Data analytics. Meanwhile, the US Department of Transportation (DOT) and National Highway Transportation Safety Administration (NHTSA) announced in Feb. 2014 that it will begin taking steps to enable V2V technology in light vehicles with a view primarily toward improving traffic safety. In Aug. 2014, the NHTSA issued an advance notice of proposed rulemaking in which it invited comment from the public and stakeholders on various issues, including privacy and security of V2V systems, as it works to deliver a Notice of Proposed Rulemaking by 2016. It is expected that the United States will soon mandate the provision of V2V telematics technology in new vehicles. Canada is collaborating in the development of V2V systems standards for use in North America and is expected to follow suit once the NHTSA determines that a V2V system is ready for implementation. These inter-vehicle communications are variously referred to as *V2V systems* and *connected vehicles*, among other technology-specific terms.

While Canada has not yet required vehicle manufacturers to build emergency calling capability into cars, there is a good chance that it eventually will do so, following the lead of the European Union (EU) and Russia. The European Union has established standards for a pan-European in-vehicle emergency service known as eCall that will detect collisions and automatically call public emergency services, providing GPS-based location of the vehicle, time of the accident, direction of driving, number of occupants, and vehicle identification number. Manual emergency calling must also be facilitated. All cars must be equipped with eCall compliant technology by Oct. 1, 2017. Russia has moved forward with a similar initiative, referred to as ERA-GLONASS, under which all new passenger vehicles as of Jan. 2015 must be equipped with a special device that can detect collisions and call emergency services automatically, relaying the location, speed, and other vehicle information. While the EU and Russian mandatory vehicle emergency call regimes are broadly similar in terms of the service provided, they differ markedly when it comes to the collection, retention, use, and disclosure of data collected by the system. The EU has designed its eCall system with privacy as a key principle: the system does not collect data unless triggered by an accident, only a minimal defined set of data is sent to emergency services, and the data is neither retained nor used for secondary purposes. In contrast, the Russian approach (as of Sep. 2014) was to collect, store, and make the data available for analysis and use by other state bodies (including state insurance agencies), local governments, vehicle owners, and others.

The Tenth Five-Year period (2001–05) first took the fields of ITS as content for national planning. In 2001, China had selected 10 cities as "model cities" for ITS field-testing and evaluation. Those cities included Beijing, Shanghai, Guangzhou, and so on. During this period, many important aspects and key issues in ITS research and development were addressed on a high scientific and engineering level: agent-based and vision based technologies; traffic modeling, control, and simulation; communication and location-based services; and driving safety and assistance, and so forth. For instance, the digital bus station systems have come into use in many cities, such as Beijing, Guangzhou, Chongqing, Shanghai, Hangzhou, Shenzhen, Nanjing, Shenyang, and so forth. Many information technologies of this system, such as computer control technology, wireless network communication technology and LED display control have been completely developed. During the Eleventh Five-Year period (2006–10), ITS had more opportunity to develop, especially in transport services for major international events.

Table 2.3 ISO/TC 204 Workgroup and Its Applications	
Work Group	**Application**
TC 204/WG8	Public transport/emergency
TC 204/WG15	Dedicated short-range communications for Transport Information and Control System applications

2.3.4.1 ITS Canada

ITS Canada defines an application of advance and emerging technologies such as computers, sensors, control, communications, and electronic devices in transportation environment with ultimate focus on safer roads. The ITS Canada is moving forward toward fully integrated transportation management system, with improving efficiency and general mobility in transportation. ITS Canada has a complex collaboration with Europe, the United States, and Japan. These counterparts invest billions of dollars in ITS solutions to solve transportation difficulties. ITS Canada provides valuable contributions in exporting the latest innovation in ITS technologies abroad. ITS Canada has two more working groups in ISO TC 204. The working group and its application are depicted in Table 2.3.

2.3.4.2 ITS South Africa

SABS (South African Bureau of Standards)/TC204) was previously known as Sub Committee 71 H (SC71H), which is the South African ITS standardized organization. The SABS/TC204, imitates the scope of ISO/TC204 standards. The scope of SABS/TC204 standardization includes the information, communication, and control systems in the field of urban and rural surface transportation, traffic management, emergency services, commercial services, and so forth.

SABS/TC204 which imitates the functionalities of ISO/TC 204 in the majority of its application, differs in a specific application that is ITS systems which are completely self-contained in the vehicle and do not interact with other vehicles or with the infrastructure; this includes the scope of ISO/TC 22/SC 3, respectively. There are five active working groups in operations as part of TC204, which is similar to the ISO/TC204 standards working group.

2.3.4.3 Global initiatives toward ITS

In order to initiate cooperative ITS, various processes are carried out all around the globe. In the European Union, ERTICO (European Road Transport Telematics Implementation Coordination Organization) focuses on this initiative. And in the United States, ITS America deals with the promotion of ITS and cooperative ITS development in that particular region. In Japan VERTIS (2) (Vehicle, Road, and Traffic Intelligence Society) took the initiative toward ITS deployment. The main objectives of VERTIS are to further enhance the research and development in the ITS-related arena and to establish communications with its counterparts in Europe and North America to create awareness globally.

2.3.4.4 ITS Korea

In 2001, Korea chose the establishment of ITS as one of the major plans of "Advanced Green City" and one of seventeen new growth engines of South Korea. In addition to that, through advanced IT technologies, the ITS makes great contributions to sharpening the Korea's ITS. By 2020 ITS deployment rate would increase from 14% to 30%. Furthermore, installation of RSU, sensor hardware which are essential for ITS, would effectively increase. An analysis portrays that ITS deployment and installation would result in an increase of average travel speed by 20% and a decrease of traffic congestion by 30%.

2.3.4.5 ITS Australia

ITS Australia is an independent not-for-profit organization representing ITS suppliers, academia and transport businesses and the commuters. ITS Australia has various collaborations with leading ITS organizations all around the globe. ITS Australia classifies the application of vehicular communication, data handling and transmission technologies for in-vehicle, V2V, V2I, and mode-to-mode systems to increase transport efficiency, to provide safety, and to improve the performance of Australia's transportation networks.

2.3.4.6 ITS Taiwan

Taiwan's geography is complicated, which demands a diverse range of professionals and experts to ensure the successful deployment of intelligent vehicular network model. Furthermore, Taiwan's future economic growth depends on solid transportation infrastructures and management systems. Hence, in order to make advances in this area of ITS, the Intelligent Transportation Society of Taiwan was established in 1998 to bring together Taiwan's professionals and experts from industry, government sectors, research institutes, and academies committed to the development of ITS. Furthermore, ITS Taiwan has fruitful collaboration with various ITS organizations around the world such as ITS America, ERTICO in Europe and ITS-Japan. In addition to that there are numerous countries which effectively participate in the development of ITS in their respective regions. The members of ITS Asia Pacific, a regional society member, include China, Hong Kong, Indonesia, Malaysia, India, Thailand, and New Zealand. Apart from that, countries like the United Kingdom and Singapore actively participate in the deployment of ITS installation.

2.4 ITS MARKET SEGMENTATION

ITS market can be segmented into four types, namely:

1. System based
2. Geography based
3. Component based
4. Application based

The ITS market segmentation and applications are illustrated in Fig. 2.2. The ITS market is also segmented based on the geographical regions covering certain key countries such as the United States, Canada, China, Japan, Australia, India, and Japan, taking into consideration the influence of ITS in these countries. The report also focuses on the driving factors for the market, such as government support and environmental benefits; safety parameters such as traffic congestion solutions, which may result in a reduced number of accidents; and many more. The restraints and opportunities for the ITS market are also highlighted, covering the current market scenario. The major trends in the ITS market are forecasted from 2013 to 2020 based on market growth factors. The major players in the ITS market are the Thales group (France), Nuance Communications, Inc. (United States), Garmin International, Inc. (United States), Kapsch Trafficomm AG (Austria), and TomTom N.V. (The Netherlands), among others. The ITS market has been broadly classified into four categories: ITS market by component, ITS market by systems, ITS-based application areas and ITS market.

The types of ITS component are interface boards (multifunctional board, communication board, and vehicle detection board), sensors (vehicle detection sensors, pedestrian sensors and speed sensors), surveillance cameras (thermal and AID cameras), software (visualization software, video detection

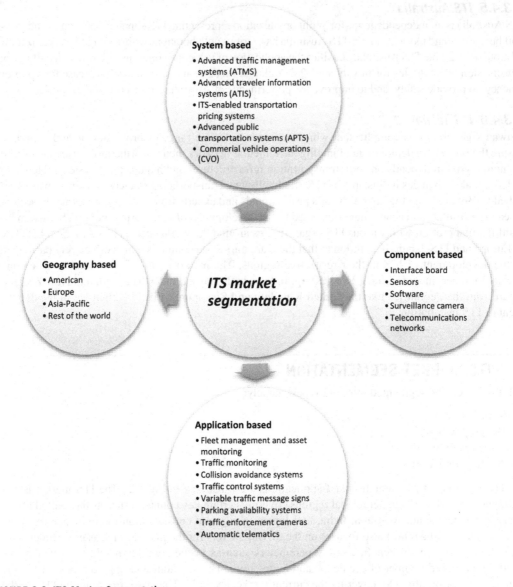

System based
- Advanced traffic management systems (ATMS)
- Advanced traveler information systems (ATIS)
- ITS-enabled transportation pricing systems
- Advanced public transportation systems (APTS)
- Commerial vehicle operations (CVO)

Geography based
- American
- Europe
- Asia-Pacific
- Rest of the world

ITS market segmentation

Component based
- Interface board
- Sensors
- Software
- Surveillance camera
- Telecommunications networks

Application based
- Fleet management and asset monitoring
- Traffic monitoring
- Collision avoidance systems
- Traffic control systems
- Variable traffic message signs
- Parking availability systems
- Traffic enforcement cameras
- Automatic telematics

FIGURE 2.2 ITS Market Segmentation

management software, transportation management software, and others), communication network (fiber optics, monitoring, detection systems), and others. Average selling prices (ASP) assist in calculating all kinds of suitable statistical and mathematical methods and considering external qualitative factors affecting prices. All the calculations interconnected between the tables are considered the finalized ASPs. Average selling price of all devices is kept standard for all geographical regions. The

ITS software market is calculated on the basis of resource value units pricing, and the resources that are used for the purpose of RVU calculation is the total number of transportation events accessed or managed by the software per month. The ITS market for applications includes fleet management and asset monitoring, traffic monitoring, collision avoidance system, traffic signal system, variable traffic message signs, parking availability system, traffic enforcement cameras, and automotive telematics.

2.5 CASE STUDY

2.5.1 IBM INTELLIGENT TRANSPORTATION

IBM Intelligent Transportation conforms to the National ITS Architecture, and follows the ITS common structure for the design of an ITS framework, as depicted in Fig. 2.3. The IBM Intelligent Transportation architectural design was developed around this framework. IBM Intelligent Transportation is tailored to meet the needs of the end user while maintaining the benefits of a common architecture. "Center" subsystems deal with the functions typically assigned to public or private administrative, management, or planning agencies. IBM Intelligent Transportation implements the center subsystems highlighted in Fig. 2.3, which include roadway information and reporting, traffic management, archived data management, and core services (such as administration, authentication, and authorization).

2.5.2 TRAFFIC MANAGEMENT

The traffic management subsystem consists of traffic surveillance and managing events or incidents.

2.5.3 TRAFFIC SURVEILLANCE

Traffic surveillance processes traffic data and provides basic traffic and incident management services through roadside and other subsystems. All preprocessed data about vehicles passing through the surface street and freeway network are collected by processes. The data are then sent to processes that distribute it to other facilities and load it into the current and long-term data stores. The data in these stores, plus weather and incident data, are used by processes to produce an analysis. (In future releases, a predictive model of future traffic conditions will be produced.) The results of this process, and the data stored by processes, are available for display by traffic operations personnel and the media. The processes that make up the Provide Traffic Surveillance facility within the Manage Traffic function include storing and managing the processed traffic data, displaying and outputing traffic data, and exchanging data with other traffic centers to analyze, correlate, and report traffic data.

2.5.4 MANAGE EVENTS/INCIDENTS

ITS provides the processes that make up the manage incidents facility within the manage traffic function. These processes manage the classification of incidents and implement responses when they actually occur. The facility will store, manage, and categorize traffic events static data.

It provides operator interfaces for events and it also provides traffic data analysis of traffic events and the major functionality is to review and manage events data. The event management processes divide events, or incidents, into three types: possible, predicted, and current data. For example, planned

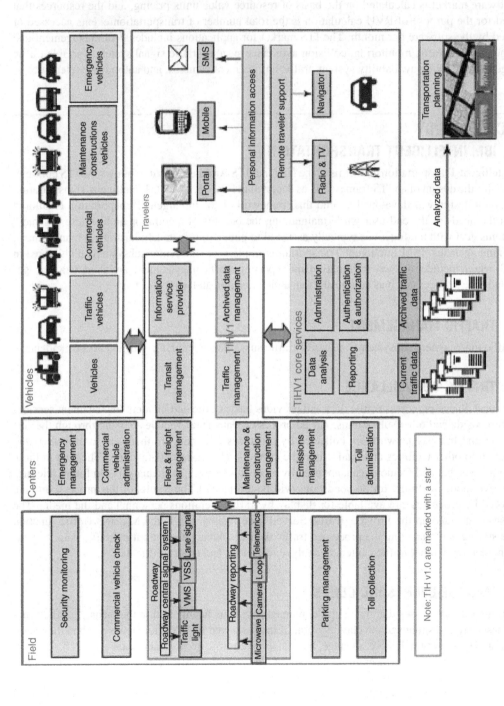

FIGURE 2.3 IBM Intelligent Transportation Systems

events could include special events, sports events, and maintenance and construction activities. Current incidents might include traffic accidents, natural disasters, and incidents caused by the effects of the weather.

2.5.5 ARCHIVED DATA MANAGEMENT

The archived data management subsystem collects, archives, manages, and distributes data generated from ITS sources for use in: transportation administration, policy evaluation, safety, planning, performance monitoring, program assessment, operations, and research applications. Key services of the archived data management subsystem include managing the archive data administrator interface, managing the roadside data collection, acquiring archive data, storing and managing archive traffic data, analyzing archives, and finally preparing report inputs.

2.5.6 APPLICATION IN FREIGHT MANAGEMENT

Facing a world that emphasizes reliance on foreign goods, the experts have suggested that ITS be used to streamline and optimize shipping, ensuring an uninterrupted flow of goods into and across the nations. In these scenarios, ITS could expand into the realm of detection and tracking. The increase in imported goods necessitates an improvement in goods scanning and tracking to enhance freight system security. Such technologies would need to rapidly and efficiently scan for radiological, biological, and chemical threats, intentional or otherwise. To improve the efficiency of "sniffer" technologies, these devices could be applied while the freight is in transit. When a threat is detected, it could be reported to security personnel at the port along with information on the cargo vessel's location, its expected arrival time, and vessel schematics, which identify where the threat is located. Such technologies could also alert emergency responders, ensuring the safety and efficiency of the freight system.

2.6 CONCLUSIONS

In this chapter we discussed ITS comprising advanced applications which form basic management systems such as vehicle navigation, traffic signal control systems, container management systems, number-plate recognition, parking guidance, and so forth. Some technologies and standards are used to support this advancing model, especially ITS for vehicular networks. We see how ITS can facilitate greater ease and safety by streamlining the vehicular data flow via detection and tracking, and this will continue to be the crux of our discussion in the next chapter.

VEHICULAR NETWORK (VN) MODEL

3

3.1 CLUSTER-BASED VEHICULAR NETWORKS

Over the past few years vehicular networks have received a lot of attention from academia, industry, standardization bodies, and the various transportation agencies and departments of many governments around the world. It is envisaged that in the next decade the intelligent transportation system (ITS) will become an essential part of our daily life. This book describes models and/or algorithms designed to investigate evolutionary solutions to overcome important issues such as congestion control, routing, clustering, interconnection with long-term evolution (LTE), and LTE-advanced cellular networks, traffic signal control, and analysis of performances through simulation tools and the generation of vehicular mobility traces for network simulations.

Automation has played a key role in the development of new technologies and in the maturation and improvement of existing ones. Automatic control launched its development with electronic devices since the mid-20th century, but many of the key mathematical tools for dynamic analysis and control synthesis were developed much earlier. It was necessary to join the mathematics with the electronics and other related areas such as simulation and modeling to raise this promising, now essential area of knowledge. The number of automatic processes applied to vehicles and transportation systems has increased dramatically in recent years due to the growing desire for environmental friendly and autonomous transportation. As technology advances, most complicated mathematical problems have to be solved in order to satisfy the increasing astringent expectations for safety, reliability, and performance of vehicular systems. Our intention with this special issue was to provide an opportunity for researchers to share their latest theoretical and technological achievements in control, modeling, and analysis of vehicular systems and to become a forum to contribute, from a mathematical point of view, to the solution of some of the challenges that the development of new trends of transportation has arisen.

As vehicular ad hoc networks (VANETs) have been used in various applications whose ultimate goal is to provide safety and comfort to the passengers sitting in the vehicles, hence there is a requirement of optimized solutions for clustering in VANETs. But due to a large number of nodes and lack of routers, a flat network scheme may cause serious scalability and hidden terminal problems.

A possible solution to the aforementioned problems is the use of an efficient clustering algorithm. As for efficient communication among the vehicles on the road, dedicated short-range communications (DSRCs) are used, so it would be a good idea to divide the vehicles into clusters so that vehicles within the same cluster may communicate using DSRC standards. These facts motivate us to categorize various clustering techniques in VANETs based upon predefined criteria.

However, there are a number of challenges that need well-designed solutions for clustering of vehicles. Some of the challenges are high mobility of the vehicles, sparse connectivity in some regions, and security. Due to a large number of parameters that have been considered in different clustering, it was difficult to consider some parameters as standard for the evaluation of reviewing protocols. To accommodate this diversity, all the parameters are analyzed and then synthesized into eight standard categories in this chapter.

The eight parameters have been broadly categorized into vehicle density and vehicle speed, which characterize the efficiency of clustering protocol; cluster stability; cluster dynamics; cluster convergence; and cluster connect time; transmission efficiency; and transmission overhead. This standardization will help us to provide a comparative analysis of all the reviewed clustering protocols. Some of the aforementioned parameters are illustrated as follows. Vehicle density, which is one of the most important parameters, defines the average number of vehicles in terms of vehicles per kilometer or vehicles per lane. For urban scenarios the high value of vehicle density is considered compared to highways. Vehicle speed is the range of speeds considered for simulation by a particular protocol in terms of m/s or km/h. A speed range that varies realistically indicates better adaptability. Transmission efficiency is described as the average number of messages or packets that are transmitted or received by a cluster member during a specified time duration. High transmission efficiency shows that a clustering scheme is more effective data dissemination. Transmission overhead is the average communication or control overhead required by a clustering scheme for cluster formation and maintenance in terms of number of packets. A clustering scheme that has lower transmission overhead is desired. Cluster stability is the average lifetime of a cluster. A high value of cluster stability indicates a better cluster-clustering protocol. The parameter cluster dynamics describes the average number of status changes per vehicle defined in terms of average number of cluster changes or cluster head changes in terms of total number of vehicles. A low value of cluster dynamics is more suitable. Cluster connects time refers to percentage time duration that a vehicle stays connected to a single cluster. A high value of cluster connects time indicates the higher suitability of a protocol. Cluster convergence refers to the duration required for all the nodes to join a cluster at the initiation of a clustering scheme. The suitability of a clustering scheme for VANETs is greater when it exhibits low clustering convergence.

3.1.1 TAXONOMY OF CLUSTERING IN VANETS

For efficient communication among the nodes in the network, stable clustering is required. In this direction, many researchers have used various techniques to form a stable cluster among the nodes. Some of these techniques consist of the use of the signal strength received, the position of the node from the cluster head, velocity of the nodes, direction, and destination of the node. Keeping in view the aforementioned issues, the detailed taxonomy of various clustering algorithms follows. Fig. 3.1 explains the classification of clustering methods.

3.1.2 TRADITIONAL CLUSTERING

The traditional clustering techniques used in VANETs are subdivided into active and passive clustering based upon the role of nodes in VANET.

3.1.2.1 Active Clustering

In case of active clustering protocols, there are continual updates of the clustering information and routing table for route discovery after a fixed interval of time. They generally initiate clustering process through flooding, which generates a sustained routing overhead. The various active clustering protocols are described as follows.

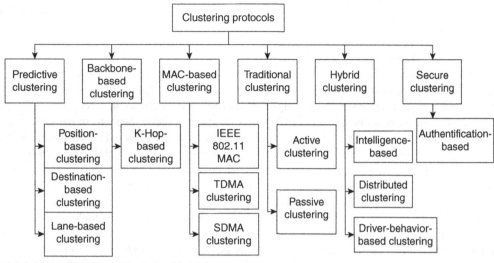

FIGURE 3.1 Classification of Clustering Model in VANET

3.1.2.1.1 Beacon-Based Clustering

In beacon-based clustering, clusters are formed based on some vehicular or network parameter detected by beacons of hello messages by the receiving vehicle. Little et al.proposed a beacon-based clustering model, which is an extension of the algorithm proposed. In this approach, the clusters are formed based on mobility metric and the signal power detected at the receiving vehicles on the same directed pathway. Received signal strength (RSS) value is used as criteria to assign weights to the nodes and based on these weights the CH is selected. Using this method, the proposed protocol helps in forming stable clusters. However, it does not consider the occurrence of losses in the wireless channel. In practical scenario effects of multipath fading are bound to affect the cluster formation method and thus the stability.

3.1.2.1.2 Mobility-Based Clustering

Mobility-based clustering is a distributed clustering algorithm that forms stable clusters based on force-directed algorithms. Every node applies to its neighbors a force according to their distance and their velocities. Vehicles that move in the same direction or toward each other apply positive forces while vehicles moving away apply negative forces. According to the current state of the node and the relation of its F to neighbors, every node takes decisions about the clustering formation, cluster maintenance, and role assignment. This work also proposed mobility metric based on forces applied between nodes according to their current and their future position and their relative mobility. A new stability-based clustering algorithm (SBCA), that aims to reduce the communication overhead that is caused by the cluster formation and maintenance, as well as to increase the lifetime of the cluster. SBCA makes use of mobility, number of neighbors, and leadership or CH duration in order to provide a more stable architecture. The nodes remain associated with a given cluster and not with any CH as is the case with most existing clustering approaches. When one CH is no longer in the cluster, another CH takes over; the cluster structure does not change but only the node playing the role of CH. This allows for stable cluster architecture, with low overhead and better performance. SBCA protocol significantly improves the cluster residence time, for each node, reducing the overhead and thus improving the performance/reliability also.

3.1.2.1.3 Density-Based Clustering

Density-based clustering (DBC) is an iterative algorithm named distributed construct underlying topology (D-CUT) in which each node discovers and maintains a geographically optimal clustering for the current network configuration. D-CUT algorithm partitions the network into geographically optimized clusters. The protocol is applied in two phases. In the first phase, beacons in the same cluster are aggregated by a CH in a synchronized manner. In the second phase, the CH disseminates a compressed aggregated beacon of its own cluster to its adjacent clusters. The vehicles produce a snapshot of the surrounding vehicle map, and update the clustering solution according to the changes in the network configuration. All neighboring vehicles share a matching partitioned vehicle map producing the same new partitioned map for each vehicle in the network. The algorithm updates the partitioning according to the most recent topological changes, thus maintaining the geographically optimized clusters. The proposed a multilevel cluster algorithm called the DBC based on several factors like connectivity level, link quality, relative node position prediction of a nodes position in futures, and node reputation.

This algorithm has three phases. In the first phase, anode estimates its connectivity level defined as the number of connections, which is used to discover the density of the local neighborhood of a node. Every node counts the number of received acknowledgments to find the number of active links. This information determines whether a node belongs to the dense or sparse parts of networks by comparing the connectivity level against a threshold value. The aim of the second phase is to select stable links from all the current links. This selection is made on some prediction about the future, but it also takes into account the past knowledge of speed and direction of the vehicle. This is the basis for estimating the link quality. In this evaluation a vehicle also uses signal-to-noise ratio of the link. In the last phase communication history is used to determine nodes reputation before it becomes a cluster member. The effects of multipath fading are also taken into account in this DBC algorithm.

3.1.2.1.4 Dynamic Clustering

Dynamic cluster formation is a methodology in which the vehicles are grouped together according to the scenario. The cluster formation is taken into consideration regarding the vehicle speed, direction, and connectivity degree and mobility pattern. It includes the static agents and the mobile agents. At first, based on the direction and vehicle speed the cluster members are chosen. Then the cluster head is chosen based on the connectivity degree. Once the cluster head is chosen, it predicts the pattern of its members using the mobility pattern. The cluster head informs the member vehicles of the pattern. Depending on the mobility pattern the cluster members reconnect with the cluster head. Agents are the programs that sense the environment and they act upon the environment using its ability. The agents may be single agent or multiagent. Some of the drawbacks include that all the vehicles are considered to be smart. Thus the dynamic clustering is done using the multiagent approach, which is better than the existing cluster system. VANETs have relatively more dynamic nature as compared to mobile ad hoc networks (MANETs), resulting in fast changes in the network topology. The design and implementation of an efficient and scalable algorithm for information dissemination in VANETs are a major issue that should be tackled. Indeed, in this dynamic environment, an increasing number of redundant broadcast messages will increase resource utilization, which would indirectly affect the network performance.

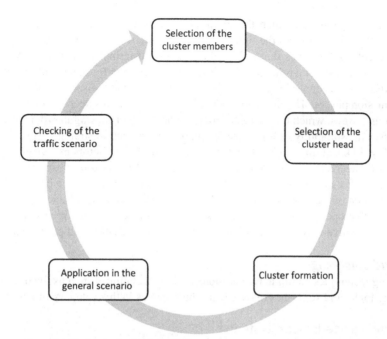

FIGURE 3.2 Cluster Formation in Dynamic Methodologies

Dynamic clustering technique forms cluster structure based on node dynamics like mobility patterns, velocity, and density. Fig. 3.2 depicts the functioning of dynamic clustering.

A multiagent-based dynamic clustering scheme for VANETs is established. The scheme comprises heavyweight static and lightweight mobile agents that form a moving dynamic cluster on a lane between two intersections by considering parameters such as vehicle speed, direction, connectivity degree to other vehicles, and mobility pattern. Initially, cluster members are identified based on vehicle's relative speed and direction for dynamic clustering. CH is selected among the cluster members based on a stability metric derived from connectivity degree, average speed, and time to leave the road intersection. It consists of a set of static and mobile agents. The relative speed difference among neighboring vehicles is the main parameter used for cluster formation. Only the neighbor vehicles traveling in the same direction in a lane are considered. The cluster member with the highest stability metric is regarded as the CH. This scheme also has certain limitations, such as that all vehicles need to have relatively strong computational resources, capable of authenticating and validation of vehicles during dynamic clustering process, which is not practical for current vehicular networks.

3.1.2.2 Passive Clustering

Passive clustering is a clustering mechanism that passively constructs a cluster structure. At any time, a node in a cluster possesses an external or internal state. In passive clustering each vehicle can lower the control overhead in packet flooding by the use of ongoing data packets instead of extra explicit control packets to construct and maintain the clusters. When a node receives data packets, it may change its cluster state based on the state information piggybacked on ongoing data packets. This reduces the number of explicit control packets. Thus a passive clustering mechanism generates significantly less overhead for cluster maintenance than the traditional cluster-based technique because its nodes do not maintain cluster information all the time. Wang et al. proposed a passive clustering aided routing (PassCAR) protocol for VANETs that refines the passive clustering mechanism proposed in which the main goal was to construct a reliable and stable cluster structure for enhancing the routing performance in VANETs. The proposed mechanism also includes the route discovery, route establishment, and data transmission phases. The main idea behind PassCAR was to select suitable nodes to become cluster-heads or gateways, which then forward route request packets during the route discovery phase. PassCAR assesses the suitability of nodes using a multimetric election strategy. This strategy considers link reliability, link stability, and link sustainability as the main factors and quantifies them using the metrics of node degree, expected transmission count, and link lifetime, respectively. Each CH or gateway candidate self-evaluates its qualification for CH or gateway based on a priority derived from a weighted combination of the proposed metrics. The pass CAR designs an efficient passive-clustering-based mechanism that operates at the logical link control sublayer, and the proposed mechanism can easily be associated with any routing protocol to support stable, reliable, and permanent data delivery.

3.1.2.3 Hybrid Clustering

Hybrid clustering techniques combine two or more existing techniques such as the use of artificial intelligence, fuzzy logic, and so forth. Following are the schemes in this category of clustering.

3.1.2.3.1 Intelligence-Based Clustering

Intelligence-based clustering is a distributed and dynamic cluster head selection criteria to organize the network into clusters. CH is selected based on stability criteria, which reflect the relative movement between adjacent vehicles. The vehicle's acceleration is also used in this work to predict its speed and position in the future. However, the decision to accelerate, to decelerate, or to stay at the same speed depends on many factors, such as the distance between the vehicle and its front neighbor, the relative speed between them, the road conditions, and the drivers' behavior. Since the drivers' behaviors and how they estimate the interdistances and other factors are subjective, so triangular fuzzier is used to deal with this uncertainty, using the fuzzy logic inference system. The proposed scheme can achieve a highly stable cluster topology, which makes it more suitable for implementation in VANETs. However, the distributed processing overhead results in a decrease in message transmission efficiency. Kumar et al. proposed an agent-learning-based clustering algorithm (ALCA). Agents are able to learn from the environment in which they operate and perform the task of CH selection. The proposed approach consists of selection of CH, keeping in view the direction of mobility and density of the nodes. The direction of the mobility of the nodes is calculated by the agent in an interactive manner. The agent learns from the direction of motion of the vehicle and traffic flow across different junctions of the road. Agents are deployed at different road junctions for monitoring the activities of the vehicles. Agents perform their action, and accordingly, their actions are rewarded or penalized in unit steps. The density of the vehicles and average speed are used for dividing the time into different zones. These zones are then used for collecting the information about the vehicles that is used as input to the agents for clustering. The learning rate is also defined for the agents to make the adaptive decisions. For each action performed by the agents, the corresponding action is rewarded or penalized, and value of the learning parameter is incremented or decremented. This process continues until the maximum value is reached. The performance of the proposed scheme is evaluated by varying the number of agents with various parameters. The results obtained show that the proposed scheme can be used in future applications in VANETs.

3.1.2.3.2 Cooperative Decentralized Clustering

Cooperative vehicular systems are currently being investigated to design innovative ITS solutions for road traffic management and safety. Through various wireless technologies, cooperative systems can support novel decentralized strategies for ubiquitous and cost-effective traffic monitoring system. Quicksilver is a lightweight distributed clustering protocol that integrates a traditional source routing protocol for intracluster node-centric communication and the construction of a multichannel link for contention-free intercluster data-centric communication. It is a system architecture that provides efficient use of available resources to guarantee that no harmful competition takes place for the channel bandwidth. Quicksilver employs lightweight clustering, in which clusters form and behave in an uncoordinated manner without requiring a cluster ID and there are no CHs. Quicksilver utilizes two radio interfaces that allow vehicles to maintain their intracluster connectivity and at the same time look for intercluster contact opportunities. Cluster formation and maintenance is done by building a cluster formation and management list of neighbors at each node. It focuses on the creation of stable links.

3.1.3 DRIVER BEHAVIOR-BASED HYBRID CLUSTERING

Vehicles are nowadays provided with a variety of sensors capable of gathering information from their surroundings. In the near future, these vehicles will also be capable of sharing all the harvested information, with the surrounding environment and among nearby vehicles over smart wireless links. They will also be able to generate alerts at regular intervals for emergency services such as in case of accidents. Blum et al.proposed a clustering for open intervehicle communication (IVC) networks (COIN) algorithm. In COIN, CH selection is based on vehicle dynamics and drivers' intentions as input for clustering instead of any conventional parameter like vehicle ID, relative mobility, or other parameters that are used in a classical clustering method. Further, COIN attempts to preserve CH for a longer duration and uses mobility information for clustering. Cheng et al. proposed an innovative car-society clustered network based on an imaginative classification scheme. The proposed scheme forms clusters by including vehicles that have the same interest and are operating in the same communication range. The aim of the proposed approach is to increase the lifetime of the interest group, and to increase throughput in vehicle-to-vehicle (V2V) environments. The proposed scheme develops the interesting ontology of cellular automata clustering by using zone of interest for mobicast communications in VANET environments.

3.1.3.1 Secure Clustering

VANETs can support applications and services for safety and comfort for the passengers on the road and assist in improving the efficiency of the road transportation network. However, several serious challenges remain to be solved before efficient and secure VANET technology becomes available. One of these challenges is an efficient authentication of messages using cryptographic techniques. Solutions for secure clustering in VANETs require efficient clustering algorithms in terms of complexity, scalability, availability, and reachability. Several algorithms have been proposed in the literature based on public key infrastructure (PKI) for enabling communications security in vehicular environments. These are based on a trusted third party called a certification authority (CA), which is responsible for certifying the public keys of vehicles. Several research schemes have been proposed for distributing the responsibility of the CAs among a set of nodes in the network, using mobility as a metric to select the vehicles that will assume the role of CA.

3.1.3.1.1 Predictive Clustering

In predictive clustering, the cluster structure is determined by the current geographic position of vehicles and its future behavior. This vehicle traffic information helps to associate priorities, which then assist in cluster formation. The future position and the intended destinations of vehicles have been used in the literature to form clusters in VANETs.

3.1.3.1.2 Position-Based Clustering

Position-based clustering is a technique of forming clusters on the basis of the geographic position of the vehicle and cluster head. A new position-based clustering algorithm (NEW-ALM), which is an improvement to the existing ALM algorithm is established. The cluster structure is determined by the geographic position of the vehicle and the cluster-head (CH) is selected based on priorities associated with each vehicle. A hash function based on the estimated travel time is used to generate this priority for the vehicle. The stability of the system is improved by selecting the vehicles having a long trip as the cluster-heads. Although this solution gives a stable cluster structure, its performance is not tested in sparse and jammed traffic conditions, which are very frequent in dense urban regions. Wang et al. proposed another position-based clustering algorithm. It is a cross-layer algorithm-based on hierarchical and geographical data collection and dissemination mechanism. The cluster formation in this protocol is based on the division of road segments. However this protocol incurs more overheads for V2V and vehicles-to-infrastructure (V2I) communication. Thus its performance is affected based on the availability of an infrastructure. Fan et al. proposed a clustering scheme where a utility-based cluster formation technique is used by extending the definition of spatial dependency, which was initially proposed. In the utility function, position and velocity, closest to a predetermined threshold value, are used as the input parameters. The threshold is computed based on the previously available traffic statistics. A status message is periodically sent by all the neighboring vehicles. After receiving this information, each vehicle chooses its CH based on the results produced by the utility function. The node with the highest value is chosen as the CH. This scheme attempts to enhance the classical clustering algorithms by taking into considerations the characteristics particular to VANETs. However it still applies many fixed weights and parameters like fixed cluster formation interval, which implies a synchronous formation of clusters. This scheme fails to adapt to traffic dynamics and is also not applicable for effective cluster reorganization.

Position-based clustering solutions are the key for clustering in VANETs. In the past few years, many clustering protocols have been built by considering the various characteristics. Out of these proposals, the protocols based on the vehicle positions are most adequate to VANETs due to their resilience in handling the nodes' position variation. The table provides the relative comparison of these protocols with respect to key parameters that influence position-based clustering. Since the aforementioned clustering protocols primarily rely on the position of the vehicle, the range of values for vehicular density and vehicle speed exhibits a variation for every protocol. However, the value of the cluster convergence rate is low even if the vehicle density and cluster dynamics increase, which indicates a better cluster stability for these schemes. The variation in cluster size also affects performance in terms of mean cluster diameter and threshold for position-based clustering. The value of transmission efficiency, which ultimately effects packet delivery ratio, is also on the lower side. Hence, it can be concluded that transmission overhead and cluster connect time needs further analysis for improving the overall efficiency of clustering. The high values of cluster connect time and transmission overhead indicate the need for further analysis and improvement so that position-based clustering schemes can be efficiently utilized for VANETs.

3.1.3.1.3 Destination-Based Clustering

Destination-based clustering technique takes into account the current location and speed, relative to the final destination of vehicle, for cluster formation. The destination is known by using the navigation system. Various proposals in this category are described as follows: Farhan et al. proposed an algorithm for improving the accuracy of GPS devices called location improvement with cluster analysis (LICA). Vehicles are able to collect real-time data and relay the information to other vehicles, guiding the drivers to reach their destination safely. To measure distance, time of arrival and RSS techniques are used. LICA uses a modified tri-alteration technique in which multiple measurements can be taken for which the average value is used as the final distance measurement resulting in a set of possible refined *xy* coordinates on which a cluster analysis is applied, allowing more weight given to accurate data, which results in an improvement in nodes' location estimation. By using accurate distance measurements, the location error is reduced in LICA and thus gives better performance. Tian et al. presented a clustering method based on a vehicle position and moving direction. The clustering method is based on Euclidean distance, which uses the position information as well as the moving direction to divide the vehicles into clusters. Each vehicle broadcasts the beacon message that includes its ID latitude, longitude, direction, and time to the whole network. The receiving vehicle will first check the beacons' hop count value and if the number of hops is larger than the maximum value, it will discard this beacon. The sender vehicle then updates its topology table by calculating the distance between the vehicles. The cluster heads are generated by selecting the vehicle with minimum distance parameter as the cluster-head. The remaining vehicles are then divided into clusters.

3.1.3.1.4 Lane-Based Clustering

Lane-based clustering forms the cluster structure based upon the estimation of vehicle lane with respect to certain parameters. Some of the proposals in this category are explained as follows: Fan et al. proposed broadcasting-based distributed algorithm (BDA) to stabilize the existing clusters that require only single-hop neighbor knowledge and incur minimal overhead. This approach attempts to improve the performance of classical clustering algorithms by making them aware of the vehicle's movement. However, all nodes attempt to reevaluate their condition by computing utility values at the same time, which may cause traffic overhead and therefore consume more bandwidth.

The developer has also theoretically analyzed the message and time complexities of BDA. BDA gives maximum priority to leadership duration for cluster formation, which is difficult to compute and may result in large overhead by a node before it joins a cluster. A lane-based clustering algorithm based on the traffic flow of vehicles is developed. The proposed algorithm is based on the assumption that each vehicle knows its exact lane on the road through some lane detection system and in-depth digital street map that includes lane information. It also uses GPS combined with wheel odometer for lane detection of a vehicle. The authors use the same general idea as the utility algorithm but implement different set of rules. Each vehicle computes and broadcasts its cluster head level (CHL) along with its speed and other parameters. The vehicle with the highest CHL will be selected as the CH. CHL is determined on the basis of the network connectivity level of vehicles and average velocity of traffic flow. The proposed algorithm creates CH that has a longer lifetime as compared to lowest node degree for MANETs.

3.1.3.1.5 K-Hop Clustering

In multihop or K-hop clustering, cluster structure is controlled by the hop distance. Each cluster has one of the nodes in the cluster as the CH. The distances between a CH and the members of the cluster are within a predetermined maximum number of hops, which can be one or more hops. Some of the research proposals in this category are explained as follows: Zhang et al. proposed a multihop clustering scheme based on the mobility metric for representing N-hop mobility. A vehicle is allowed to broadcast beacon messages periodically and a vehicle calculates relative mobility based upon two consecutive beacon messages received from the same node in the N-hop distance. Each vehicle node then calculates the aggregate mobility value, which is the sum of relative mobility values into weight value for all the neighboring nodes in N-hops. The vehicle nodes then broadcast their aggregate mobility value in the N-hop neighborhood and the vehicle with a smaller aggregate mobility value is selected as the CH and the other vehicle nodes work as cluster member nodes. The vehicle node joins a cluster if it receives the beacons broadcast from the CH node. When a vehicle node receives multiple beacon messages, it will select the CH, which is the closest one in terms of number of hops. If several CHs have the same hops, the vehicle node joins the cluster which has the lowest relative mobility.

3.1.4 MAC-BASED CLUSTERING

Several medium access control (MAC)-based clustering techniques have been proposed for cluster formation in VANETs. These techniques use IEEE. MAC protocol to generate clusters. Some popular MAC-based protocols are discussed as follows:

- IEEE 802.11 MAC-based clustering: Su et al. proposed a cluster-based multichannel communication scheme that integrates clustering with MAC protocols (CB-MMAC). The proposed scheme mainly consists of three core protocols called Cluster Configuration Protocol that group all vehicles traveling in the same direction into clusters.
- The Intercluster Communication Protocol dictates the transmissions of real-time safety messages and nonreal-time traffics among clusters over two separate IEEE. MAC-based channels respectively.
- Intracluster Coordination and Communication Protocol that employs Multichannel MAC algorithms for each CH vehicle for collecting/delivering safety messages from/to cluster-member vehicles using the upstream time-division multiple-access (TDMA)/downstream-broadcast method and allocating available data channels to cluster member vehicles for non-real-time traffics. The proposed scheme requires the use of two transceivers, one used for delay-sensitive communication within the cluster, while the other is used for intercluster data transfer.

A cross-layered clustering scheme for fast propagation of broadcast messages that is called dynamic backbone–assisted MAC (DBA-MAC) scheme may be considered an extension of the MAC scheme described. A dynamic virtual backbone infrastructure is established through a distributed proactive technique. The backbone formation process considers the current distance between candidate backbone vehicles and the estimated lifetime of the wireless connection between neighboring backbone member.

The authors have compared the proposed solution with three similar proposals, a simple MAC flooding scheme where each vehicle receives an alert message and then broadcasts it by using the standard IEEE Back-Off scheme. A Fast broadcast protocol is proposed and the static backbone such as roadside infrastructure system is used, with nodes placed at the maximum distance to preserve the connectivity. DBA-MAC has been shown to be compliant with IEEE. DCF systems, and its performance shows advantages in performance, reliability, and overhead reduction.

3.1.5 TDMA-BASED CLUSTERING

The process of assigning time slots can be scheduled using a TDMA technique in which slots are assigned for data transmission. Some of the proposals in this category are described as follows: Biswas et al. proposed Vehicular Self-Organized MAC (Ve-SOMAC) protocol based on a self-configuring TDMA slot reservation protocol, which is capable of intervehicle message delivery with short and deterministic delay bounds. To achieve the shortest delay, vehicles determine their TDMA time slot based on their location and movement on the road. Also, the TDMA slot assignment is designed to be in the same sequential order with respect to the vehicle's physical location. The process of assigning time slots is performed without using infrastructure or virtual schedulers such as a leader vehicle. However, this assumption of forwarding messages without processing time or propagation delay is unrealistic. In reality, if the message needs to be delivered from the tail to the head of the platoon, it will need a time frame for each hop.

3.1.6 SDMA-BASED CLUSTERING

In SDMA-based protocols, the road is subdivided into fixed length segments, and a segment is divided into a fixed number of blocks. Each block is assigned a time slot representing the allowed time for a vehicle to transmit data. SDMA is known to have better performance in a dense network where practically all slots are used, but performance decreases proportionally with density. Hence, in sparse networks, SDMA gives poor performance. This is due to the data collection time and number of time slots increasing linearly at approximately constant rate of SDMA. The SDMA mechanism also affects clustering overhead in terms of packet delivery ratio. The vehicle density also influences the message transmission time and results in lower cluster stability. SDMA based schemes also have larger cluster connect time due to re-clustering frequency being high. The throughput and number of transmissions also have an impact on cluster dynamics. These protocols also need to be investigated to improve vehicular parameters such as cluster stability and cluster dynamics. The cluster time and vehicle density affects the performance of SDMA-based clustering schemes.

3.2 VEHICLE PLATOONING

Vehicle platooning is a technique where the highway traffic is organized into groups of close-following vehicles called platoon or convoy. The most widely studied platoon configurations in transportation is the column, also known as road trains, although other types of formations can also be considered. Platooning enables vehicles to drive closer (maintain a smaller headway) than normal vehicles with the same speed, which improves traffic throughput as well as homogeneity. Additionally, safety is enhanced due to small speed variation and relative low impact velocity in collisions. Platooning is not only a promising way to improve traffic efficiency and safety, but can also reduce fuel consumption and emissions due to air drag reduction. Platooning can be regarded as an eco-driving strategy and is most effective for heavy-duty vehicles (HDVs). It is considered as a promising solution to reduce fuel consumption in HDVs, and is getting increasing attention from private fleets and commercial carriers. Last but not least, platooning facilitates more efficient information dissemination and sharing among vehicles in the same platoon. While platooning is originally designed for an automated highway system (AHS), the improvements in wireless communication and vehicle control technology make platooning feasible for partial automated

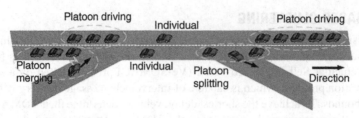

Platoon driving   Individual   Platoon driving

Platoon
merging   Individual   Platoon
splitting   Direction

FIGURE 3.3 Platoon Formation in VANET

vehicles, such as cooperative adaptive cruise control (CACC) vehicles. Close-following ability of CACC vehicles enable them to drive in tight platoons, and consequently increase highway throughput. While the technical feasibility of platooning has been analyzed worldwide under various projects, the details of the platooning vary among projects since there are different goals and motivations for doing platooning. Although platooning offers a lot of benefits, it requires cooperation between vehicles with the help of a platoon management protocol. Fig. 3.3 depicts the platooning model.

A well-developed platoon management protocol is important to ensure good CACC platooning performance and should be verified before using in real-world applications. When traveling on a highway, a group of consecutive vehicles can form a platoon, in which a nonleading vehicle maintains a small distance from the preceding vehicle.

In the literature, it has been shown that there are many benefits to driving vehicles in platoon patterns. First, since adjacent vehicles are close to each other, road capacity can be increased, and traffic congestion may be decreased accordingly. Second, the platoon pattern can reduce energy consumption and exhaust emissions considerably because the streamlining of vehicles in a platoon can minimize air drag. Third, with the help of advanced technologies, driving in a platoon can be safer and more comfortable. To facilitate platoons, two important technologies have been introduced in the past decade, specifically, autonomous cruise control (ACC) and VANETs. The ACC system with laser or radar sensors can obtain the distance to the preceding vehicle and regulate the movements of individual vehicles in a platoon. On the other hand, VANETs not only help form and maintain a platoon but also enable a vehicle to exchange traffic information with neighboring vehicles or infrastructures, which may improve traffic safety, efficiency, and comfort. In the past few years, a lot of studies have been conducted on such VANET-enabled platoons, which can be classified into two categories. In the first one, studies mainly address VANET issues, such as VANET connectivity, data dissemination protocol and routing techniques, MAC scheduling, and so forth, based on an existing platoon. In the second category, most studies are about traffic dynamics control and performance optimization by managing and controlling platoons with the help of an existing VANET. In this hypothesis, we assume that a VANET has already been set up, and we will investigate the dynamics of a VANET-enabled platoon system. Specifically, we investigate the dynamics of a VANET-enabled platoon under traffic disturbance, which is a common scenario on a highway.

3.2.1 DISTURBANCE-ADAPTIVE-PLATOON ARCHITECTURE

Here, we first propose a general disturbance-adaptive (DA)–platoon architecture. We then specify one particular instance to be investigated.

3.2.1.1 DA-Platoon Architecture

Although there are many existing studies on the platoon dynamic system under disturbance, we note that there are still many open issues, including the impact of platoon dynamics on VANET behaviors and how to mitigate negative effects due to traffic disturbance. To address these important issues, we propose a new DA-platoon architecture, where we jointly consider VANET requirements and traffic dynamics requirements under disturbances. In this architecture, vehicles can communicate through the VANET. Vehicles of one platoon share a unique DA-platoon ID. According to the spatial position and functionalities, members in a platoon can be classified into four roles, namely, leader, relay, tail, and member. Fig. 3.4 depicts its functionalities.

- *Leader:* The leader is the leading vehicle in the platoon. It is responsible for creating and managing the platoon, for example, identifying and periodically broadcasting the DA-platoon ID, deciding whether a vehicle can join the platoon and then assigning a role to the vehicle, and determining whether a platoon shall be split or whether two platoons shall be merged into one.
- *Tail:* The tail vehicle locates at the end of a platoon. It is responsible for communicating with the following vehicles, particularly the leader of the next platoon.
- *Relay:* The relay vehicles act as data-forwarding nodes in a multihop VANET environment. In this way, the information from the leader can be efficiently disseminated to all vehicles in a platoon.
- *Member:* Other member vehicles are regular vehicles that receive information from the relay and shall follow a specified driving strategy.

In such a design, the topology of the VANET becomes simpler because a backbone is formed by the leader, relays, and tail. Moreover, the few relays can efficiently determine the transmission schedule of each vehicle in the platoon, which can significantly improve the reliability of VANET communications. We consider our design a platoon management strategy. Therefore, we can apply existing platoon management protocols to facilitate the implementation of the management strategy. With the development of the automobile industry and urbanization, more and more vehicles are on the highway linking adjacent cities. It is estimated that currently there are more than a billion registered motor vehicles worldwide, and that the number will be doubled within the next two years. As a result, a series of critical issues are becoming more serious in modern transportation systems, such as traffic congestion, traffic accidents, energy waste, and pollution. For instance, in the United States alone, traffic congestion costs

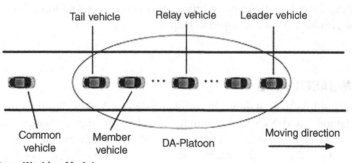

FIGURE 3.4 DA Platoon Working Model

drivers more than 2$ billion annually due to wasted fuel and lost time. Moreover, vehicle emissions caused by traffic congestion are also regarded as the key contribution to air pollution and are a major ingredient in the creation of haze in some large cities. Although the investment in road construction can alleviate traffic congestion to some extent, it is not sustainable because of the huge construction cost and limited availability of land.

To deal with these issues, an effective approach is to change the driving pattern from individual driving to a platoon-based driving. In general, the platoon-based driving pattern is a cooperative driving pattern for a group of vehicles with common interests, in which a vehicle follows another one and maintains a small and nearly constant distance to the preceding vehicle, forming platoons. In the literature, it has been shown that the platoon-based driving pattern can bring many benefits. First, since vehicles in the same platoon are much closer to each other, the road capacity can be increased and traffic congestion may be decreased accordingly. Second, the platoon pattern can reduce the energy consumption and exhaust emissions considerably because the streamlining of vehicles in a platoon can minimize air drag. Third, with the help of advanced technologies, driving in a platoon can be safer and more comfortable. Last but not least, a platoon-based driving pattern facilitates the potential cooperative communication applications (e.g., data sharing or dissemination) due to the relatively fixed position for the vehicles within the same platoon, which may significantly improve the performance of vehicular networking. Clearly, a platoon's adaptive cruise control (ACC) system can use sensors to detect the distance between adjacent vehicles and autonomously maintain the speed and/or distance. Meanwhile, more advanced driverless cars are being developed and several states in the United States have legalized the use of self-driven cars.

In addition to the technologies applied individually, platoons can be facilitated by utilizing modern wireless communication technologies, which have greatly promoted the development of ITS. Particularly, by integrating the wireless communication interface on board, known as onboard unit (OBU), a running vehicle can collect information from its neighbors or the roadside infrastructure, known as RSU, which facilitates a safer and more comfortable driving experience. In practice, vehicles with communication capability can dynamically form a mobile wireless network on a road, called a VANET, which as a promising technology can offer two types of wireless communications: V2V communication and V2I communication. Such a complex system tightly integrates computing, communication, and control technologies. Therefore, it can be considered as a platoon-based vehicular cyber-physical system (VCPS), in which all vehicles communicate via vehicular networking and are driven in a platoon-based pattern, with a closed feedback loop between the cyber process and physical processes. A complex physical system. As shown in Fig. 3.5, drivers must act cooperatively to control and manage the platoon, including formation, merging, splitting, maintenance, and so forth. Over the past decade, many new technologies have been developed to help drivers.

3.2.2 PLATOON-BASED VCPS

In this section, we first briefly explain basics of platoon-based VCPS. We then highlight important applications of platoon-based VCPS. And finally, we describe the methodologies on a platoon-based VCPS. In conception, generally, a platoon-based VCPS can be characterized by the tight coupling between vehicles' physical dynamics (mobility) and the behaviors of vehicular networks.

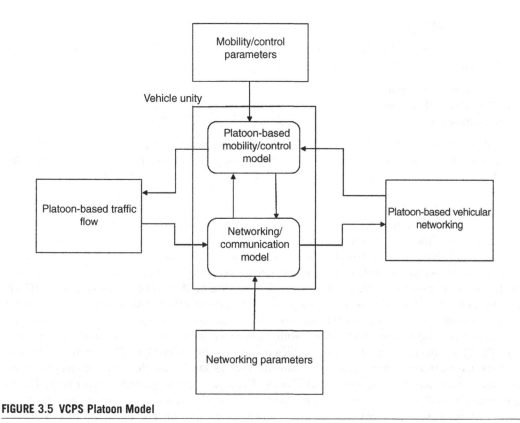

FIGURE 3.5 VCPS Platoon Model

As illustrated in Fig. 3.5, a platoon-based VCPS consists of two planes, a physical plane and a cyber-plane. The physical plane describes the platoon mobility under the constraints of traffic environment, while the cyber plane describes the behaviors of vehicular networks formed by adjacent vehicles. Due to the tight interactions between the physical plane and the cyber plane, the impact of platoon mobility must be taken into account when analyzing the performance of vehicular networking. Meanwhile, the performance of vehicular networking, such as packet loss and transmission delay, can also significantly affect the behaviors of platoons. Therefore, tight integration of computing, communication, and control technologies is required to achieve stability, performance, reliability, robustness, and efficiency of the platoon-based VCPS. It shall be noted that there are in general two types of VCPS: intravehicle CPS and intervehicle CPS. For an intravehicle CPS, the main concern is to improve the kinetic performance of a single vehicle by combining and coordinating all of its components, such as sensors, actuators, and field buses, into a tight system. For intervehicle CPS, the main objective is to optimize traffic performance or vehicular networking from a CPS design standpoint. In this chapter, we mainly address intervehicle CPS, where the vehicles are considered as mobile nodes running on roads.

3.2.3 APPLICATIONS

The typical platoon-based VCPSs are illustrated in Fig. 3.5, and can be classified into three categories from the point of view of the application:

1. Traffic flow optimization
2. Traffic green and economics
3. Infotainment service

Traffic Flow Optimization: The primary objective for vehicle platooning is to reduce traffic congestion and improve traffic flow throughput. To this end, many platoon-related projects have been implemented in the past decades. The most famous one is the California Partners for Advanced Transit and Highways (PATH) project, which commenced in 1986 and aimed to improve traffic throughput by deploying platoons in the highway. Another project is the Grand Cooperative Driving Challenge (GCDC) where multiple teams tested their CACC vehicles and benchmarked them to the CACC vehicles of other competitors. The aim of the GCDC is to promote the development, integration, and deployment of cooperative driving systems based on the combination of vehicular communication and state-of-the-art sensor fusion and control. The recently emerging vehicular networking technologies facilitate vehicles platooning on roads and promote smoothness of traffic flow. The EU-sponsored SARTRE program ran from 2009 to till date deploys a platoon on highway with a lead vehicle (typically truck) followed by a series of cars driven autonomously in close formation. The experiments showed that the platoon can drive at speeds of up to 90 km/h with a gap between the vehicles of no more than 6 m.)

Traffic Green and Economics: Another critical issue for platoon-based VCPS is to improve traffic efficiency and promote greener traffic environments, such as saving traveling time, cutting down on fuel consumption, and reducing exhaust emissions. The representative project called Energy ITS in Japan aimed at reducing CO emissions from automobiles, which includes two themes: an implementation of an automated truck platooning system and an evaluation method of effects of ITS-related systems and technologies for the CO emission reduction. In, the decentralized platoon lane assignment was proposed to decrease travel time and enhance traffic capacity. The robust H infinity control method was introduced to design platoon velocity profile, taking into consideration fuel consumption, road inclinations, emissions, and traveling time. Wireless communications also boost various infotainment applications in vehicular networking, such as vehicle-platoon-aware data delivery among vehicles, platoon-based drive-through Internet access, cooperative local service, and so forth.

3.2.4 METHODOLOGIES

Clearly, common knowledge regarding VCPS is the cornerstone to support platoon-based VCPS, which mainly involves two general aspects in terms of the taxonomy, networking related issues that mainly include vehicular networking standards and architecture to support V2V and V2I communication, and traffic dynamics that include traffic flow distribution and vehicle mobility models. To meet the requirements of platoon-based VCPS implementation, there are several specific issues. On the one hand, in a platoon-based VCPS, vehicles are supposed to guarantee the platoon-based driving pattern. To achieve this goal, some fundamental issues, such as platoon management (i.e., how to regulate the actions of platoon formation, maintenance, and splitting), platoon attributes (e.g., stability) analysis, and cooperative platoon driving need to be addressed. In addition, it is critical to design suitable protocols or algorithms to facilitate data delivery within the platooning system. On the other hand, the platoon-based driving pattern reshapes the whole traffic flow distribution into intraplatoon and interplatoons, compared to the individual driving pattern, which can significantly affect the vehicular networking and communication in the VCPSs. Therefore, it is essential to reevaluate the communication performance (e.g., connectivity of V2V and V2I) of vehicular networking under the specific platoon-based driving pattern.

3.2.5 CHALLENGES AND OPEN ISSUES

In this section, based on the existing studies on the fundamental issues in platoon-based VCPSs, we discuss some open issues for future research.

3.2.5.1 Deployment of Platoon-Based Driving Pattern

Although vehicle platooning has been widely accepted as the future promising driving pattern, it is still challenging to implement this on our highways. Many factors may affect the incentive to form platoons for each individual vehicle, such as different destinations for each vehicle, heterogeneous vehicle types, or even the driver's distrust of the platoon-based driving pattern. Technically, the current platoon-based cooperative driving is vulnerable to unreliable vehicular communications. In view of the cyber process of VCPSs, the status of vehicular networking is dynamic, that is, the performance metrics such as packet reception ratio and transmission delay are changing within a certain range. This one critical issue is how to adaptively control the platoon-based cooperative driving system in such a dynamic vehicular networking. For example, most of the presented control systems assume that to achieve the control performance, a constant minimum sampling frequency is desired. However, a variable sampling frequency seems more suitable for occasional disturbance in traffic flow: lower sampling frequency is adopted for stable traffic flow and higher sampling frequency is required when a traffic disturbance occurs.

The local situation awareness is considered as a prerequisite for most of decentralized platoon-based VCPSs design. However, the practical imperfect communication channel with packet loss and transmission delay impairs the accuracy of the local situation estimation and accordingly has a negative impact on the system performance. Therefore, it is still a challenge to accurately and timely estimate the local traffic condition under imperfect vehicular networking environment. In addition, platoons are normally assumed to have unified system parameters, such as the same intervehicle distance within the platoon and the same model parameters (acceleration, actuator parasitic delay, etc.) for all vehicles. The further work is expected to pay attention to the heterogeneity platoon-based cooperative driving, which is closest to the practice.

It shall be noted that the accuracy of the relative position parameters is very critical for vehicle platooning implementation, especially for the communicated-GPS-only platoon system. Many related studies have focused on improving the GPS precision. However, the information from the GPS is unavailable under some conditions, for example, when vehicles run under tunnels or bridges. To achieve the accurate position parameters in such cases, the integrated GPS with onboard sensors (such as radars or infra sensors) as well as the sensor data fusion should be taken into account. Multimetrics optimization on the platoon-based driving is also an open issue, in which not only the platoon stability is regarded as the primary control objective, but also the traffic efficiency such as travel time and energy saving is involved.

3.2.5.2 Communication for Vehicular Platooning

As we stated previously, the current IEEE .p-based vehicular communications meet many challenges, for example, the lower packet reception rate, especially in the case of a highly mobile and dense deployment.

Although various solutions have been proposed in the past few years, the future DSRC evolutions are expected to further improve the performance of vehicular communications. Some potential enhancements may include: adopting more advanced PHY technologies such as multiple-input multiple-output (MIMO) support (IEEE .n) and multiple stream support (IEEE .ac), more flexibility in channelization, and better MAC congestion control protocols. In addition, the extended vehicle to pedestrian communications could enhance safety for pedestrians and cyclists. Moreover, vehicular communication protocols dedicated for platooning application need to be further investigated. For example, under the platoon-based driving pattern, traditional V2V and V2I communications are transferred to intra/interplatoon and the platoon to RSU communications. In this case, it is important to develop more effective protocols for data dissemination. To facilitate individual vehicles forming into the platoon, the standardization for platooning application is also essential. The envisioned protocols should specify cooperative platoon behaviors among vehicles, such as platoon merging and splitting. Another critical issue is cyber security, which has attracted more concerns with the large-scale deployment of vehicular networks. Specifically, the cooperative platoon-based driving pattern is more vulnerable to vicious attacks, which may lead to traffic chaos and even car crashes on the road. In such a platoon-based VCPS, one vehicle may suffer the potential attacks from infrastructures or other vehicles. The typical attacks include the fake message (e.g., BSM) and the poisoning of the map database locally stored on vehicles. The mitigation techniques mainly require the setup of an authentication system and a misbehavior detection system.

3.2.5.3 Platoon-Based Traffic Flow and Vehicular Networking

Vehicle platooning has been regarded as a promising technology to deal with transportation challenges, for example, to mitigate traffic congestion and to reduce vehicle emissions. However, it is not yet clear how and to what extent current traffic flow is influenced by this type of cooperative driving pattern. In other words, can the platoon-based traffic flow be characterized or modeled? In addition, due to the increasing market penetration rate of autonomous cars, both platoon-based driving and individual driving could coexist on the road for a period of time. It is also crucial to investigate how this coexistence has impacts on road safety, traffic flow efficiency, road capacity, and fuel economy. Some recent work has started to investigate these issues. For example, a platoon-based macroscopic model was proposed that verified that platoon-based driving behavior of intelligent vehicles enhances the stability of traffic flow with respect to a small perturbation. However, the research on this issue is expected to go further. Likewise, vehicular communication may also be affected by the platoon-based driving pattern. However, due to the limited number of vehicle experiments implemented on the road, it is not yet clear what is the network performance under large-scale deployment of V2V communication, such as network connectivity and throughput. Research into this performance, the first large-scale field trials on V2V communication, for example, the Ann Arbour Safety Pilot in the United States and the simTD project in Germany, are in progress. In addition, a more realistic highway traffic simulator is needed through which these platoon-based driving scenarios can be run to evaluate the actual effects on traffic flow and VANET performance.

3.2.6 PLATOON MANAGEMENT FRAMEWORK

A platoon is composed of a platoon leader, which is normally the first vehicle in the platoon, and one or more followers that drive closely behind each other. In many experimental studies, due to safety reasons, the platoon leader is driven by a trained professional driver. The following vehicles are driven fully automatically, allowing the drivers to perform tasks other than driving, such as using a mobile phone. In a study, it is shown that vehicles in the platoon are CACC-capable and participate in information-sharing and cooperative driving through VANET communications. CACC system is basically an enhancement of adaptive cruise control (ACC), which incorporates wireless V2V communication to access rich preview information about the surrounding vehicles. This leads to tighter following gaps and faster response to changes than ACC. The CACC control logic is incorporated in the regulation and physical layer of each vehicle.

3.2.7 PLATOON MANAGEMENT PROTOCOL

The platoon management protocol supports three basic or elementary maneuvers: merge, split, and lane change. In merge, two platoons, traveling in the same lane, merge to form one big platoon; in split, one platoon (with at least two vehicles) separates at a specific position to form two smaller platoons; while lane change permits a one-vehicle platoon (free agent) to change lanes. We can deal with more complex platooning scenarios using the aforementioned basic maneuvers. For instance, platoon follower leave can be performed using a sequence of split, lane change, and merge. Due to the distributed control design, each maneuver is coordinated by exchanging a sequence of micro-command messages between platoon management protocols in different vehicles. In total, we have defined a set of 17 micro-commands in the module. Wireless V2V communication is achieved using DSRC, which has been standardized in IEEE 802.11p. DSRC operating at 5.9 GHz is designed to support a large variety of applications. It supports high data rates, and has a transmission range of two meters, which makes it suitable for information dissemination and sharing among vehicles in a platoon. Although DSRC has been the prominent IVC technology in ITS context, the performance of DSRC broadcasting may raise some reliability concerns. The platoon management protocol uses a centralized platoon coordination approach where all communications are coordinated by the platoon leader. Followers take orders and send requests from/to the platoon leader. We believe that centralized platoon coordination is fast, scalable, and does not make the platoon leader a bottleneck since the frequency of platooning decisions is low (every minute). Moreover, only the platoon leader stores and manages the platoon configuration. This enhances privacy in situations where followers should not have access to the platoon configuration, since they dynamically enter and exit the platoon.

Consider an example in which vehicle A relinquishes control and joins a platoon. The platoon begins its journey on the highway and performs necessary maneuvers. Eventually, as vehicle A approaches its destination, it leaves the platoon. In the centralized platoon coordination, all the necessary platoon configuration data are stored in the platoon leader and are kept hidden from the followers. Vehicles A does not need to know the platoon size, type and destination of other vehicles, and so forth. Sharing of platoon configuration data is done only when the platoon leader leaves, in which case the old leader passes all the necessary data to the new leader.

3.3 VEHICULAR CLOUD

This research proposes an intelligent transportation concept framework, Firstly, a transportation cloud-based service platform is constructed using the virtualization and cluster computation features of cloud computing to provide safe, convenient, flexible, and diverse cloud-based software development and storage services. Then, telematics, navigators, and vehicle data recorders are integrated with cloud computing services. The cloud-based platform can facilitate the collection, exchange, and integration of transportation related energy conservation information and provides in-car information such as streaming video, eco-driving route navigation, driving behavior pattern analysis, and so forth. Additionally, it can also develop visualization software as a supplementary option for eco-driving. In this chapter, we focus on cloud- and Internet-assisted V2I communication for emerging nonsafety applications, which require the quality of service (QoS) up/downloading of large amounts of data, such as podcast subscriptions of audio/video programs, digital map downloading/updating, Web surfing, advertising applications and opportunistic vehicular assisted content delivery applications. In fact, it is expected that these bandwidth-demanding applications will have a significant impact on the commercial success of vehicular cloud computing (VCC) and will contribute to accelerate its implementation and deployment. However, in order to continue to guarantee higher priority to the traffic flows generated in downlink by the Service Providers, hard upper bounds must be imposed on the tolerated instantaneous rate of packet collision among the backbone traffic (that is, the primary traffic) and the access traffic (that is, the secondary traffic). Several recent studies (see, e.g, and references therein) about the mobile computation offloading in real-life cloud-assisted scenarios point out that the usage of wi-fi-based traffic offloading in place of G-assisted one may reduce the average energy consumption of current smartphones by about 40%.

About the spectral crowding of current vehicular networks, the communication traffic flows typically generated by safety applications and routed in downlink over the available backbones are of a burst-type. Hence, these flows present interarrival gaps of no negligible time durations, which can be opportunistically exploited by VCs equipped with cognitive radio (CR) smartphones to accede to the serving RSUs through wi-fi connections. Therefore, motivated by the aforementioned considerations, in this work we consider the V2I CR-based access scenario where multiple car smartphones equipped with heterogeneous cognitive capabilities and energy budgets play the role of secondary users and compete for acceding to the serving RSUs by opportunistically exploiting the time and frequency holes of the traffic flow generated by the service provider (that is, the primary user of the Internet backbone). The pursued twofold objective is the joint maximization of the aggregate access good put of the overall network, and the average per-client access rates.

With respect to the technical contribution of the work and the novelty of the idea, the target of the work is to optimize the access throughput of the secondary user of the vehicular networks, while respecting the QoS requirements of the primary users, expressed in terms of maximum tolerated collision rate with the secondary users. From this point of view, the work proposes a new optimized MAC protocol, able to maximize, under some assumptions detail in subsequent sections, the average aggregate throughput of the system.

Vehicular networks are in the progress of merging with the Internet to constitute a fundamental information platform, which is an indispensable part of ITS. This will eventually evolve into all vehicles connected in the era of the Internet of Things (IoT). By supporting traffic-related data gathering and processing, vehicular networks are able to notably improve transport safety, relieve traffic congestion, reduce air pollution, and enhance driving comfort ability. It has been reported that, in Western Europe, the percentage of deaths due to car accidents could be reduced by deploying safety warning systems at highway intersections. Another example is that real-time traffic information could be collected and transmitted to the data center for processing and, in return, information could be broadcasted to the drivers for route planning. City traffic congestion is alleviated and traveling time is reduced, leading to greener cities. A variety of information technologies have been developed for intelligent vehicles, roads, and traffic infrastructures such that all vehicles are connected. Smart sensors and actuators are deployed in vehicles and roadside infrastructures for data acquisition and decision. Advanced communication technologies are used to interconnect vehicles and roadside infrastructures, and eventually access to the Internet. For instance, DSRC is specifically designed for V2V and vehicle-to-roadside (V2R) communications.

The IEEE.802.11p, called Wireless Access in Vehicular Environments (WAVE), is currently a popular standard for DSRC. Besides, the LTE, LTE-advanced, and CR are all fairly competitive technologies for vehicular networking. Despite the well-developed information technologies, there is a significant challenge that hinders the rapid development of vehicular networks. Vehicles are normally constrained by resources, including computation, storage, and radio-spectrum bandwidth. Due to the requirements of small size and low-cost hardware systems, a single vehicle has limited computation and storage resources, which may result in low data-processing capability. On the other hand, many emerging applications demand complex computations and large storage, including in-vehicle multimedia entertainment, vehicular social networking, and location-based services. It becomes increasingly difficult for an individual vehicle to efficiently support these applications. A very promising solution is to share the computation and storage resources among all vehicles or physically nearby vehicles. This motivates us to study the new paradigm of cloud-based vehicular networks. Recently, a few research works are reported to study the combination of cloud computing and vehicular networks. In the reports, the concept of autonomous vehicular clouds (AVC) is proposed to exploit the underutilized resources in VANETs. A platform as a service (PaaS) model is designed to support cloud services for mobile vehicles. The work is proposing architectures of VC, vehicles using clouds (VuC), and hybrid clouds (HC). Vehicles play as cloud service providers and clients respectively in VC and VuC, and as hybrids in HC. In this chapter, we propose a hierarchical cloud architecture for vehicular networks. Our work is different from previous researches in three main aspects. First, we aim to create a pervasive cloud environment for mobile vehicles by integrating redundant physical resources in ITS infrastructures, including data center, RSUs, and vehicles.

The aggregation of these sporadic physical resources potentially composes massive and powerful cloud resources for vehicles. Second, we propose a three-layered architecture to organize the cloud resources. The layered structure allows vehicles to select their cloud services resiliently. Central clouds have sufficient cloud resources but a high rate of delays in end-to-end communications. On the contrary, roadside cloud and vehicular cloud (VC) have limited cloud resources but satisfying communications quality. Third, we emphasize the efficiency, continuity and reliability of cloud services for mobile vehicles. As a consequence, efficient cloud resource management strategies are elaborately proposed. Countermeasures to deal with vehicle mobility are devised.

3.3.1 VEHICULAR CLOUD

In a VC, a group of vehicles share their computing resources, storage resources, and spectrum resources. Each vehicle can access the cloud and utilize services for its own purpose. Through the cooperation in the group, the physical resources of vehicles are dynamically scheduled on demand. The overall resource utilization is significantly enhanced. Compared to an individual vehicle, a VC has many more resources. Due to vehicle mobility, VC implementation is very different from a cloud in a traditional computer network.

3.3.2 GENERALIZED VEHICULAR CLOUD CUSTOMIZATION AND SPECIFIED VEHICULAR CLOUD CUSTOMIZATION

In generalized vehicular cloud customization (GVCC), a cloud controller is introduced in a VC. A cloud controller is responsible for the creation, maintenance, and deletion of a VC. All vehicles will virtualize their physical resources and register the virtual resources in the cloud controller. All virtual resources in the VC are scheduled by the cloud controller. If a vehicle needs some resources of the VC, it should apply to the cloud controller. In contrast to GVCC, specified vehicular cloud customization (SVCC) has no cloud controller. Fig. 3.6 describes the VC framework.

A vehicle will specify some vehicles as candidate cloud sites, and directly apply for resources from these vehicles. If the application is approved, the corresponding vehicles become cloud sites, which will customize virtual machines (VMs) according to the vehicle demand. These two strategies, GVCC and SVCC, are quite different. With respect to resource management, GVCC is similar to a conventional cloud deployment strategy in which cloud resources are scheduled by a controller. A vehicle is not aware of the cloud sites where the VMs are built up. The cloud controller should maintain the cloud resources. During a cloud service, if a cloud site is not available due to vehicle mobility, the controller should schedule a new site to replace it. In SVCC, since there is no cloud controller, a vehicle has to select other vehicles as cloud sites and maintain the cloud resources itself. In terms of resource utilization, GVCC is able to globally schedule and allocate all resources of a VC. GVCC has higher resource utilization than SVCC. However, the operation of the cloud controller will need extra computation. Therefore, SVCC may be more efficient than GVCC in terms of lower system overhead. A roadside cloud is composed of two main parts: dedicated local servers and RSUs. The dedicated local servers virtualize physical resources and act as a potential cloud site. RSUs provide radio interfaces for vehicles to access the cloud. A roadside cloud is accessible only by the nearby vehicles, that is, those located within the radio coverage area of the cloud site's RSU.

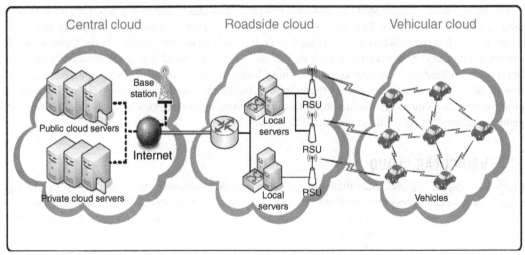

FIGURE 3.6 Vehicular Cloud Framework

This fact helps us recall the concept of a cloudlet. A cloudlet is a trusted, resource-rich computer or cluster of computers that is connected to the Internet and is available for use by nearby mobile devices. In this chapter, we propose the concept of a roadside cloudlet. A roadside cloudlet refers to a small-scale roadside cloud site that offers cloud services to passing vehicles. A vehicle can select a nearby roadside cloudlet and customize a transient cloud for use. Here, we call the customized cloud a transient cloud because the cloud can serve the vehicle only for a while. After the vehicle moves out of the radio range of the current serving RSU, the cloud will be deleted and the vehicle will customize a new cloud from the next roadside cloudlet in its direction of travel. When a vehicle customizes a transient cloud from a roadside cloudlet, it is offered by virtual resources in terms of a VM. This VM consists of two interacting components: the VM-base in the roadside cloudlet and the VM-overlay in the vehicle. A VM-base is a resource template recording the basic structure of a VM, while a VM-overlay mainly contains the specific resource requirements of the customized VM. Before a cloud service start, the vehicle will send the VM-overlay to the roadside cloudlet. After combining the VM-overlay with the VM-base, the roadside cloudlet completes the customization of a dedicated VM. During a cloud service, as the vehicle moves along the roadside, it will switch between different RSUs. For the continuity of cloud service, the customized VM should be synchronously transferred between the respective roadside cloudlets. This process is referred as VM migration.

3.3.3 CENTRAL CLOUD

Compared to a VC and a roadside cloud, a central cloud has much more resources. The central cloud can be driven by either dedicated servers in vehicular networks data center or servers in the Internet. A central cloud is mainly used for complicated computation, massive data storage, and global decision. There already exist mature open source or commercial software platforms that could be employed for the deployment of a central cloud. Open stack is an open source cloud platform using infrastructure as a service (IaaS) model. Other potential commercial platforms are Amazon Web Services, Microsoft Azure, and Google App Engine.

3.3.4 PROMISING APPLICATIONS OF CLOUD-BASED VEHICULAR NETWORKS

With powerful cloud computing, cloud-based vehicular networks can support many unprecedented applications. In this section, we illustrate potential applications and explain the exploitation of a VC, a roadside cloud, and a central cloud to facilitate new applications.

3.3.4.1. Real-Time Navigation With Computational Resources

Sharing in a real-time navigation application, the computational resources in the central cloud are utilized for traffic data mining. Vehicles may offer services that use resources that are outside their own computing ability. Different from traditional navigation which can only provide static geographic maps, real-time navigation is able to offer dynamic three-dimensional maps and adaptively optimize routes based on traffic data mining.

Vehicle A is using real-time navigation during its travels. It will first request cloud service from the central cloud and the roadside cloud. Then, a VM cluster and a VM are established in the central cloud and the roadside cloud, respectively. The VM cluster-A in the central cloud is in charge of traffic data mining and will suggest several routes based on the current traffic conditions. Once a route is selected by A, real-time navigation starts. VM-A in the roadside cloud acts as an agent to push messages to vehicle A, updating the driver with traffic conditions on the road. As vehicle A moves on, VM-A will migrate to different roadside cloud sites. During the entire travel, VM cluster-A in the central cloud will keep updating the route information based on real-time traffic condition. Once there is an unexpected event, for example, traffic congestion, VM cluster-A will report the situation timely and compute a new route.

3.3.4.2 Video Surveillance With Storage Resource Sharing

Video surveillance is an important application that utilizes shared storage resources. Currently, many buses in a city have installed High-Definition (HD) camera systems to monitor in bus conditions. A very large-volume hard-drive is needed to store video content for a couple of days. This video storage scheme has several disadvantages. First, to save HD video content for days, the hard-drive should have very large storage, which leads to high cost and big size. Second, video content can be checked only in an off-line manner, the department of transportation is not able to make timely and proper decisions immediately after an accident. In cloud-based vehicular networks, a new distributed storage paradigm can address this problem. The storage capability of in-bus video camera systems is significantly extended. In a Bus network VM-A exploits the roadside cloud to facilitate storage in an in-bus video surveillance content. Specifically, the bus applies to cloud services and receives a VM in the roadside cloud. The video content is uploaded to the guest VM-A in the roadside cloudlet in a real-time manner. When the bus moves along the road and is located in the coverage area of the roadside cloudlet, VM-A will be migrated accordingly. As a result, the video content is divided into several segments and separately stored in different roadside cloudlets along the road. The video segments in the roadside cloudlets will be transmitted to a data center on demand. When an accident is reported, the department of transportation can request roadside cloudlets to send video back to the data center.

3.3.4.3 Cooperative Download/Upload With Bandwidth Sharing

Cooperative downloading and uploading services are interesting applications that share bandwidth resources. Many new applications involve large-volume data uploading or downloading. Typical examples include in-vehicle multimedia entertainment, location-based rich-media advertisements, and large email services. Due to limited wireless bandwidth and vehicle movement, it is very difficult to download an entire large file from a specific RSU. While the vehicle drives by, there is not enough time to complete the download of large amounts of data. Here, we illustrate that the use of a VC will make such applications feasible. Vehicle A is going to download a large file from the roadside infrastructure. The cooperative downloading has two phases. In the first phase, vehicle A observes neighboring vehicles B and C and then sets up a VC for cooperative downloading. Then, a guest VM will be constructed in both B and C. The file downloading will be carried out by the VC that consists of vehicle A and the two VMs on B and C. Since the file is downloaded by three vehicles in a parallel manner, the total transmission rate becomes much faster. In this way, vehicle A has a high possibility to finish downloading before vehicle A moves out of the range of the roadside infrastructure. In the second phase, the VMs in B and C will further cooperatively transmit two separated segments of the file to A. Since only V2V communications are involved, the second phase can be performed without the roadside infrastructure. After that, A will reassemble the file segments into an entire file.

3.4 **HYBRID SENSOR–VEHICULAR NETWORKS**

Both VANETs and wireless sensor networks (WSNs) are subjects of ongoing research activities. However, the characteristics of VANETs and WSNs are very different. Nodes in sensor networks are highly miniaturized, mostly static, very resource and energy constrained, and usually have good sensing capabilities. In contrast, VANETs have very dynamic topologies and the vehicles do not suffer from significant energy constraints. The vehicles could be equipped with sensors themselves. However, the sensor coverage cannot be guaranteed, as vehicles are not present everywhere and at all times and some kinds of events cannot be reliably detected by moving entities. We introduce the new concept of hybrid sensor–vehicular networks so that both network types can benefit from the strengths of each other while compensating the weaknesses. We use a WSN deployed in or near roads as a sensor grid with constant availability and dense coverage in contrast to the V2V network, which might have only sparse coverage. The sensor network constantly communicates its sensor data to the vehicles driving on the road, delivering them with accurate and up-to-date sensor information. Vehicles communicate to disseminate this information to over comparatively long distances. There, the vehicles deliver this data back the sensor network where it is stored for future retrieval by other vehicles. This relieves the sensor network from the energy-consuming task to transfer the data hop-by-hop inside the WSN itself, as shown in Fig. 3.7.

Such hybrid sensor–vehicular networks are suited for all applications where a stationary WSN collects sensor data that is disseminated on only a small scale within the WSN, then delivered to vehicles that transfer it to other regions by multihop routing or vehicle movement and either hand it to interested vehicles or to remote WSN nodes that store the data and deliver the content to approaching cars under certain conditions. We use an example for further explaining this concept. The application implements a dangerous road condition warning, where drivers are warned about potentially dangerous road conditions such as an icy road. First, a WSN node detects ice on the road and shares this information with neighboring nodes inside a small region. When vehicle A enters this region, the WSN triggers a vehicle-present event and the information is transmitted to the car. This way, the driver of vehicle A would receive a short-term warning and can react accordingly. Vehicle A forwards the information via the long-range VANET to vehicle B. A relevance function determines that vehicle B is in a good position to feed the information back to the WSN for further availability. As the road splits at position B, the icy road information would otherwise become unavailable to vehicles approaching from the lower road. So B transfers the information back to the WSN and the nodes distribute it in a small neighborhood for redundancy purposes. A and B leave this road segment and are out of communication range,

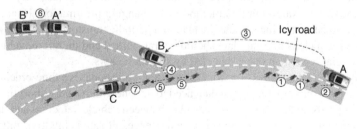

FIGURE 3.7 Hybrid Sensor Vehicular Network

when vehicle C approaches the intersection and still receives the warning information from the WSN. The vehicle displays a warning to the driver, who has plenty of time to adapt his driving style to the approaching danger.

There are two important observations here:

1. Vehicle C is never in direct reach of the other cars. So a vehicular sensor network composed only of the vehicles would never deliver the warning to vehicle C.
2. There is a significantly lower number of mote transmissions compared to cases in which the motes try to deliver the information hop-by-hop from the source to the position of vehicle C. A lot of mote energy is saved and the lifetime of the WSN nodes is prolonged.

3.5 INFORMATION DISTRIBUTION

Within hybrid sensor–vehicular scenarios, different ways of disseminating information can be distinguished: Information can be exchanged within the WSN, by data transition from WSN to VANET, by dissemination within the VANET, through information injection from VANET to WSN, and in the form of physical data transport by moving vehicles.

3.5.1 DISTRIBUTION INSIDE THE WSN

When events are captured by the WSN these events are about to be reported to mobile nodes. A central idea in our perspective on such scenarios is that the WSN and the VANET are coupled directly, and hence, certain wireless sensor nodes that transmit WSN data to vehicles have to be chosen. These gateways are distinct from the reporting nodes, which are mainly responsible for event detection and multihop routing. As we rely on information transport using a VANET, the sensors do not form one huge WSN. Instead, we propose a dynamic decomposition of the sensor nodes in many small to midsize sensor networks in which data are reported to gateway sensors. Further spatial coverage of events is reached using VANET message dissemination. After an event has been detected or sensor data have been collected, this information needs to be reported to a gateway sensor, which can be realized by standard WSN source-to-sink techniques like spanning trees. To equalize energy consumption, the gateway role will change periodically.

3.5.2 DATA TRANSITION FROM WSN TO VANET

As illustrated, gateway sensors interact directly with mobile nodes, and basically two questions are of particular interest when examining this method of exchanging information. Hence, one might ask when information is to be sent to the vehicle. Instead of a periodic transmission, we propose a triggered scheme: Once a new vehicle is present, data should be transmitted and therefore, vehicle presence can be regarded as a special type of an event detected by special sensors.

Once triggered, the actual transmission from sensors to mobile nodes is a time-crucial task: As sensor nodes have a limited transmission range, the data need to be sent within a very short time. Vehicles may move with relative speeds up to 40 m/s, and as a delay between vehicle detection and data transmission exists, the time frame left may be lower than a second. Hence, all data being transmitted must fit compactly into one or very few frames in order to improve the probability of success for the transmission.

3.5.3 **VANET MESSAGE DISSEMINATION**

The main task of the vehicular network in our approach is to disseminate messages picked up from a local gateway sensor. The primary goal is of course to inform approaching vehicles about a potential hazard that was measured by a local WSN. However, for the hybrid sensor–vehicular network, the purpose of the vehicular part is also transporting messages to remote locations for reinjection into a WSN. This way, information becomes time stable and does not rely on the presence of vehicles. Geocast is a well-known primitive in the VANET domain that is suitable for this kind of information dissemination.

3.5.4 **INFORMATION INJECTION**

Once information has been distributed over the VANET, it can be stored back from the vehicle to the WSN. While at first glance this might look like an unnecessary gimmick, we argue that this mechanism is a key feature of hybrid sensor–vehicular information distribution: It might happen that the VANET loses connectivity if vehicles move out of range. In this case, messages cannot be distributed to other vehicles using the VANET itself, although cars approaching the current node's position later in time might be interested in this information, for example, if it is a warning notification. In this case, the warning message can be stored to the WSN, where it is kept until other vehicles pass by and retrieve this information again. Similarly, this mechanism could be further utilized for other tasks like gateway notifications.

3.5.5 **PHYSICAL DATA TRANSPORT**

Besides the vehicles' interconnection, their spatial movement can be utilized for data dissemination as well. If the vehicle density is sparse, data sampled from the WSN will be cached by vehicles. Based on the relevant function's results, the information is injected back to the WSN.

3.6 **INTERNET OF VEHICLES**

The Internet of Vehicles (IoV) is an integration of three networks: an intervehicle network, an intravehicle network, and vehicular mobile Internet. Based on this concept of three networks integrated into one, we define an IoV as a large-scale distributed system for wireless communication and information exchange between vehicles (vehicle, road, human, and Internet) according to agreed communication protocols and data interaction standards (examples include the IEEE 802.11p WAVE standard, and potentially cellular technologies). It is an integrated network for supporting intelligent traffic management, intelligent dynamic information service, and intelligent vehicle control, representing a typical application of IoT technology in ITS. The convergence of technology encompasses information communications, environmental protection, energy conservation, and safety. To succeed in this emerging market, acquisition of core technologies and standards will be crucial to securing a strategic advantage. However, the integration of the IoV with other infrastructures should be as important as the building of the IoV technologies themselves. As a consequence of this, the IoV will become an integral part of the largest IoT infrastructure with its completion. Here, it must be emphasized that collaboration and interconnection between the transportation sector and other sectors (such as energy, health care, environment, manufacturing, and agriculture, etc.) will be the next step in IoV development.

3.6.1 IoV TECHNOLOGY LEADS THE INDUSTRIAL REVOLUTION

The convergence of technology encompasses information communications, environmental protection, energy conservation, and safety. To succeed in this emerging market, acquisition of core technologies and standards will be crucial to securing a strategic advantage. However, the integration of the IoV with other infrastructures should be as important as the building of the IoV technologies themselves. As a consequence of this, the IoV will become an integral part of the largest Internet of Things (IoT) infrastructure with its completion. Here, it must be emphasized as primary, that collaboration and interconnection between the transportation sector and other sectors (such as energy, health-care, environment, manufacturing, and agriculture, etc...) will be the next step in IoV development. As human ability and experience evolve, future vehicles will have to be able to address a growing list of pertinent issues, which affect an automotive society including road safety, energy consumption, environmental pollution, and traffic congestion. IoV technology is designed to address and solve many of these issues through promoting a goal of "minimum accidents, low energy consumption, low emissions, and high-efficiency" through the development of automobiles and the transportation system. IoV technology will facilitate the concordant unification of humans, vehicles, their roads, and the environment. By promoting the integration of the IoV technologies with vehicles through manufacturing and industry, great contributions to economic growth and improving the global infrastructure will be made. IoV technology is a driving force that will make major transformations to the automotive industry thanks to its role in expanding human ability, experience, safety, energy, environment, and efficiency issues inherent in living in an automotive society. There is a huge gap between the automotive and information technology industries in terms of culture, institutions, and product development processes. The IoV technology in automobile factories is relatively underdeveloped, far from the speed and experience requirements of innovative applications. However, the IT industry updates too quickly and is too open to ensure reliability and safety when relevant products are used in vehicles. The collision and fusion of the automobile industry and IT industry is an inevitable trend of IoV and even of the whole automobile industry.

3.6.2 OPPORTUNITIES AND CHALLENGES OF IoV

Research and development, as well as the industrial application of IoV technologies will promote the integration of automotive and information technology. The integrated information services of vehicles, vehicle safety, and economic performance will contribute to a more intelligent urban transportation system and advance social and economic development. The IoV will have far-reaching influence on the consumer vehicle market, consumer lifestyle, and even modes of behavior. The future IoV market will see rapid growth in the Asian-Pacific region. The McKinsey Global Institute has reported in June that the IoT has the potential to launch around $1 trillion in new global economic value annually by 2020. Seventy percent of all manufacturers will apply IoT technology by then, leading to potential economic impact of $1 trillion for the global manufacturing industry. According to the data on APEC website, the member countries share approximate 60 percent of world GDP. In other words, APEC members will be growing by $1 trillion in GDP and manufacturers of the economies will embrace $1 trillion growth in the meanwhile.

The application of IoV technology in providing information services, improving traffic efficiency, enhancing traffic safety, implementing supervision and control and other aspects will enable millions of people to enjoy more comfortable, convenient, and safe traffic service. Large concentrations of vehicles, for example, in city parking facilities during business hours, can also provide ad-hoc computational resources that will be of interest to those in the IT fields. Complementary efforts should be made for developing and enhancing middle-ware platforms, which will enable analytic and semantic processing of data coming from vehicles. Lack of coordination and communication is the biggest challenge to IoV implementation. Lack of standards make effective V2V (vehicle to vehicle) communication and connection difficult and prohibits ease in scaling. Only by adopting open standards can the current, closed, and one-way systems be integrated into an effective system for the smooth sharing of information. Dreams of intelligent transportation and even automatic drive systems can come true through an effective IoV. Both technological innovation and business model innovation in the Internet era depend on partnering across traditional boundaries. While maintaining a plan for improving products, services and experiences, we should make joint efforts to break barriers, stay open and inclusive, and to build a healthy and sustainable ecosystem. Therefore, the whole industrial chain can achieve joint development. One of the possible projects could be creating a trusted environment for cross-border document circulation. We see opportunities for cooperation in this area. Legally significant trust services could become one of the IoV services.

3.6.3 SOCIAL INTERNET OF VEHICLES

The emergent technological developments in the field of information technology have made smart cities a thing of the near future. This increasingly intelligent information would provide safe and appropriate surroundings through increased interconnection and interoperability, which is also termed the IoT. Hence in the vast area of the IoT, vehicles play a significant role for safe and convenient travel that leads to the IoV. The number of vehicles has increased intensely in modern times. Almost all major cities experience heavy traffic during peak hours. Observant suggestions from the neighboring vehicles could be vital to provide improved safety to the vehicle users. State-of-the-art vehicles are equipped with cutting-edge technologies that facilitate them to communicate with adjacent vehicles by forming VANETs. There has been growing interest in building a vehicular social network (VSN) where passengers can engage in entertainment-, utility-, and emergency-related data exchanges. This type of social network belongs to the mobile social network (MSN) category where mobile users share user-centric information with each other using mobile devices. In contrast, the emerging Social Internet of Things (SIoT) where things become the social entity rather than their owners, which aligns very well with the vision of smart cities. Fig. 3.8 depicts the Social Internet of Vehicles.

Here, smart things establish connection with other smart things (e.g., vehicle–vehicle, home multimedia devices, etc.) and exploit social network relationships to solve various interest groups' necessities. From the IoV perspective, this new paradigm raises a valid question, "What are the key differences between the human social network (HSN) and the social network of vehicles, where human and vehicles are social entities respectively?" The analysis shows a comprehensive difference in terms of a dynamic nature, social interactions, topology, privacy, and usage. As a result, it is important to describe the social network of vehicles from the SIoT perspective, too, rather than the MSN view only, which introduces the SIoV. A description of SIoV in which vehicles are smart and interactive social objects is discussed.

3.6.3.1 Figure Architecture for SIoV

The proposed SIoV system leverages existing VANETs technologies such as V2V, vehicle-to-infrastructure, and vehicle-to-Internet communications and presents a vehicular social network platform following cyber-physical architecture. The cyber-physical SIoV system uses social relationships among

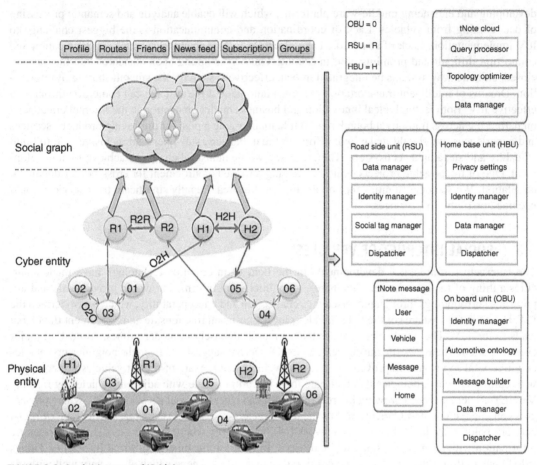

FIGURE 3.8 Social Internet of Vehicles

physical components to encourage different types of communications and stores the information (e.g., safety, efficiency, and infotainment messages) as a social graph. The social graph is distributed in various layers of communications and it can provide near real time or offline use cases for the ITS. The near real time applications offer safe and efficient travel of the vehicle users, and the offline data ensures smart behavior of the vehicles or Big data analysis for the transport authorities. We envision that social interactions based IoV would be an integral part of the future ITS.

The contributions of this chapter are identification of social structures and related interactions of the IoV components, mapping of VANETs components with the IoT architecture reference model, and details of communication message structure that corresponds to the IoV social graph. We also provide implementation details of the proposed system, related experimental analysis and various application scenarios. We have described SIoV using already established acronyms in the VANETs model such as OBU and RSU. OBUs represent the vehicles on the road and RSUs represent the roadside infrastructures that are interconnected using the Internet. OBUs use LTE/G type technology for Internet connections and wireless ad-hoc networking for direct message (safety and nonsafety) exchange with the surrounding or with the RSUs. SIoV is a cyber-physical application on top of the original physical vehicular network of WAVE (IEEE .p) communication model. Every physical entity has its corresponding twin cyber (i.e., virtual) entity and operations can be directed from cyber to- physical or vice versa while entities are in physical/cyber peer-to-peer (e.g., OO, RR, HH) connections. The one-to-one network connection of physical to virtual entity is pervasive and interactions can ubiquitously travel either physical-physical or physical-cyber-cyber-physical path based on convenience or availability. The interaction data of physical or cyber layer is accumulated in the Social Graph cloud, where every entity represents a node and the data exchanges are represented using links. In the following sections, we describe the relationships and the interactions of SIoV components, their detailed architectures and privacy-security issues from the physical end, which will be similar from the cyber end as well.

3.6.4 SIoV RELATIONS AND INTERACTIONS

It is assumed that every vehicle belongs to a household and there exists a home base unit (HBU) to which all the vehicles and other household devices are connected to form the IoT. In the SIoV, there are different classes of social structures along with various types of relationships and interactions, which are depicted in the subsequent sections.

3.6.4.1 Structures and Relationships

SIoV consists of both dynamic (OBU) and static (RSU and HBU) types of nodes and changes the network topology continuously. In the first scenario, a vehicle (OBU) is parked at the owner's residence and forms a social network with the respective HBU. Since both OBU and HBU are static in this scenario, we consider it as static SIoV, which can extend to neighboring OBUs and HBUs. For example, all the vehicles parked in an apartment's basement or in the parking lot can form SIoV with the building's HBU. In the second scenario, an OBU creates relationships with remote HBUs using HBU–HBU or OBU–HBU communication. For example, a traveling OBU can be in a relationship with the owner's office HBU or an OBU can share usage data with a mechanic's HBU. These are examples of somewhat static relationships. The third scenario is highly dynamic, where an OBU is on the move on a roadway and in a dynamic peer-to-peer relationship with surrounding OBUs and RSUs to exchange safety and nonsafety information. These physical-physical or physical-cyber-cyber-physical communications have short life spans and are represented as data edges in the social graph.

3.6.4.2 Internet of EV: Internet of Electric Vehicles

Over the past few years, the automotive industry has introduced a variety of new electric vehicle models that have drastically expanded the customer choices. The main drivers that shape the EV adoption include the size of the battery packs (usually varies between 16 to 56 kWh) and the duration to recharge the vehicle. The battery pack determines the all-electric range of the vehicle and therefore is an important criterion in handling any anxiety about range. Charging duration, however, depends on the employed charger technology, and it becomes a critical element in the competition against the gas-powered counterparts. For instance, during a charging period of 30 mins, level II single, and three-phase, and DC fast charge can enable a Nissan Leaf model to drive 5.5, 11 and 83.4 miles, respectively. The charging standards may vary from country to country. Moreover, the popularity of each charging type will greatly be determined by the housing demographics. For instance, in the early EV adopter cities, a substantial portion of the population lives in multiunit dwellings and EVs in these locations will likely use public fast-charging facilities. Furthermore, several studies are conducted by different organizations to forecast EV penetration rates. Depending on the assumptions made, prediction results may diverge, but nevertheless there is a consensus that EVs will represent a sizable portion of electrical consumption in the next decades.

The US national grid includes three distinct geographic interconnections, namely the Eastern Interconnection, the Western Interconnection, and the Electric Reliability Council of Texas. The transmission network comprises 1,70,000 miles of transmission lines rated at 200 (kV) and above, delivering the power generated at 5,000 power plants. Over the last two decades, the transmission network acts as an open highway, which connects wholesale electricity markets to with end users. The primary goal of the network operators, on the other hand, is to make sure that transmission lines operate efficiently and reliably as the grid delivers the minimum cost generation to end users.

3.6.5 OPPORTUNITIES

The introduction of bidirectional chargers enables electric vehicles to transfer energy back to the grid (VG) or to other electric vehicles (V2V). The utilization of such ancillary services can aid transmission operations, mainly by reducing congestion during peak hours. For example, a group of vehicles can sell back part of their stored energy to other EVs who are in urgent need. This way, energy trading via V2V will eliminate the need to draw power from bulk power plants and hence the associated power losses in transmission will be minimized. For instance, studies present a mathematical framework to model the interaction of energy trading in a V2V scenario, where the groups of EVs determine the amount of energy to exchange and negotiate on unit price. Moreover, EVs can transport their stored energy from one location to another, which can support the grid via VG applications. For example, literature provides a transmission network based on the capability IoV to transfer energy to regions of high-energy consumption. This way, the required upgrades will be deferred and occur gradually over time.

3.6.6 DISTRIBUTION NETWORK

The distribution network is the final portion of the power grid that interfaces with the consumers. It is responsible for reducing the high voltage carried by transmission lines to appropriate levels for end users with the use of transformers typically rated between 2 to 40 kV. Over the past decade, the distribution network has been running up against its operating limits. In the United States national grid, almost 7% of the electrical energy is lost (mostly in the form of heat) between generation units and end users and distribution network is mostly responsible for this. The distribution system is the most interruption-prone component of the power grid. According to the survey, more than three-fourths of service interruptions originate in the distribution level.

3.6.7 IMPACT OF THE EV PENETRATION

Whether charged at stations supplied in parking lots or at a customer's premises, most electric vehicles will be attached to an electrical distribution grid. Uncontrolled EV charging could stress the grid and cause system failures, such as transformer and line overloading and can deteriorate power quality (e.g., large voltage deviations, harmonics, etc.). Considering the fact that EV penetration is going to be geographically clustered, negative impacts will be more severe in certain regions. For instance, the US distribution grid is designed to meet three to five houses per transformer. Since charging of one EV doubles the daily load of a typical house, further challenges will be faced by the additional load introduced by EVs. If just two level chargers are used concurrently, the local transformer is going to be overloaded. The frequent occurrence of such events will increase power losses and voltage deviations, and decrease transformer lifetime (high loading leads to high operating temperature). A comprehensive study on the impacts of a variety of EV charging scenarios for required transformer upgrades and transformer efficiency is discussed. Such frameworks require both parties (EVs and the grid) to communicate. According to a framework, controlling EV charging can reduce the number of congested (overloaded) network components, which need to be replaced, hence eliminating the need for costly upgrades. It is further shown that controlling EV charging can reduce the cost of energy losses by 20% when compared to uncontrolled charging. In addition, EVs can be seen as distributed-energy storage mediums that are very essential for ancillary smart grid applications like integration of renewable energy resources and frequency regulation applications.

3.7 **CHAPTER SUMMARY**

Vehicular networks are formed using wireless network via data exchange, and are the key component of ITS. In this chapter cluster-convergence-based vehicular networks andclassification are discussed, leading to a consideration of vehicle platooning which allows vehicles (which are as close as a few inches) to follow a leading vehicle by wirelessly receiving acceleration and steering information. VC is addressed as one of the solutions for traffic management and road safety by offering instant use of vehicular resources, along with hybrid sensor vehicular networks and the IoV.

CHAPTER SUMMARY

EVALUATION OF VEHICULAR NETWORK MODELS

4

4.1 DATA DISSEMINATION IN VEHICULAR NETWORKS

Intelligent transportation systems (ITS) can provide efficient solutions for road traffic problems by combining technology and improvements in communication, information systems, and advanced mathematical models with the existing world of surface transportation infrastructure. Vehicular ad hoc networks (VANETs) represent a major component of ITS because of their potential to enable various applications to improve road safety and travel comfort. VANET enables participating vehicles to communicate cooperatively for exchanging information about road conditions and travel situations, by providing a self-organizing network environment, without requiring a fixed infrastructure or centralized administration. With the increasing number of vehicles being equipped with communication capabilities, large-scale VANETs are expected to be available in the near future. The novelty of VANETs with respect to other ad hoc networks has been recently highlighted, and detailed VANET requirements are specified. The literature shows that rapid changes in the network topology are difficult to predict and manage. Moreover, the network is prone to frequent fragmentation leading to high variability of the connectivity. In addition, redundancy should be limited. For these reasons, providing scalable data dissemination in VANETs is a challenging task.

Existing VANET dissemination techniques can be classified into three models: push, pull, and hybrid. In the push model, data is disseminated proactively using periodic broadcast, while in the pull model, data is disseminated on-demand, where a routing pro tool carries data to relatively faraway distances. Such protocols also rely on broadcasting for data dissemination at each hop. There are a few schemes that combine both dissemination models together so as to support different types of applications. The push-based model is often preferred for safety applications, when an immediate response is required, while the pull-based model is used for delay tolerant applications, such as seeking a free parking slot or detecting congestion on the faraway road. Compared to push-based model, pull model often requires less overhead, with less latency constraints. In delay-tolerant applications, the requester usually sends a query to the broadcast site, and gets a reply message from there. In such applications, users can tolerate more delays, as long as a response eventually return.

It is a major concern to optimize dissemination caused by blind data flooding in VANETs, which is the simplest dissemination style. Blind flooding suffers from a high percentage of redundant data that wastes the limited radio channel bandwidth. Moreover, packet collisions may lead to a broadcast storm problem since a large number of vehicles in the same vicinity may rebroadcast the same data nearly simultaneously. In pull-data dissemination, further optimization is required to cache data locally by participating vehicles, in order to increase dissemination efficiency by improving the probability of finding a query answer with reduced delay. Despite the proven performance of caching in VANETs, research efforts in this direction are still limited. There is no standard approach for performance evaluation of data dissemination in VANETs. Most of the designed dissemination techniques are verified via simulation results, and few are analyzed using a mathematical model. To model dissemination in a VANET for performance analysis, the major challenge is to provide a sufficient level of details to ensure realistic traffic scenarios and driving behavior. Three different models are to be considered: the road layout model, the mobility model, and data dissemination model.

4.1.1 DATA DISSEMINATION TECHNIQUES

Different data dissemination techniques for VANETs are proposed to fit different applications. Basically, two major applications are heavily research in this area: traffic safety and travel comfort. Traffic safety applications are low data-rate, confined to a limited number of neighborhoods with strict latency constraints. While travel comfort applications are known as delay-tolerant applications with more relaxed time constraints, vehicles are expected to require data transmission spanning relatively faraway distances.

With the assistance of vehicular communication systems, traffic safety applications can be employed to considerably lower the accident rates and decrease the loss of life on the road, mainly by providing warning systems such as intersection collision, lane change assistance, overtaking vehicle, emergency vehicle, wrong-way driver, collision risk, hazardous location, and signal violation. On the other hand, driver comfort applications can significantly improve our everyday lives, by enabling the delivery of traffic data in addition to announcements and advertisements, such as the congestion status of a faraway road, the available parking slots at a parking place, the estimated bus arrival time at a bus stop, sale information at a department store, and the meeting schedule at a conference room. Only clients around the access point (AP) can directly receive the information, since the broadcast range is limited. However, drivers and passengers who are far away may receive these data. For example, a driver may want to query some department stores to decide where to go. A passenger on a bus may query several bus stops to choose the best next stop for bus transfer. Such queries may be issued tens of kilometers away from the broadcast site. Within a VANET, the requester can send the query to the broadcast site and may tolerate more delay as long as the reply eventually returns.

There are three basic models for data dissemination in VANETs: push, pull, and hybrid. In the push model, data is disseminated proactively using periodic broadcast, while in the pull model data is disseminated on demand. There are a few hybrid schemes that combine both models together to support different applications. The push-based model is often preferred for safety applications, when an immediate response is required, while the pull-based model is used for delay-tolerant applications with the aim of improving traffic efficiency and travel comfort. There are three basic models for data dissemination in VANETs: push, pull and hybrid. In the push model, data is disseminated proactively using periodic broadcast, while in the pull model data is disseminated on-demand. There are a few hybrid schemes that combine both models together to support different applications.

4.1.2 PUSH MODEL

A push model is generally preferred for safety messaging systems, such as collision warning systems, emergency message dissemination systems, and information systems specified for hazardous road conditions like ice, water, or snow. Nevertheless, other approaches also exist to support other types of applications such as arrival time estimation, speed expectation, and congestion detection. In this section, a preventative technique is provided for each of these applications.

4.1.3 SAFETY MESSAGING SYSTEM

The data push model is a method in context of the "Traffic View" vehicular information dissemination system. The study differentiates between the vehicle's own data and the stored data about other vehicles. Three propagation models were compared: same direction, opposite direction, and bidirection. In the same-direction model, a vehicle periodically broadcasts both its own data in addition to its stored data in a single packet, which is propagated "backward" by vehicles moving in the same direction. In the opposite-direction model, vehicles traveling in the same direction broadcast only their own generated data, which are aggregated and propagated backwards by vehicles moving in the opposite direction. These two models are combined together with the bidirection model, in which the vehicles' generated and stored data are propagated backwards by vehicles moving in the same direction, and stored data only is propagated by vehicles moving in the opposite direction. Simulation results indicate that traffic densities in both directions of the road significantly affect the performance of the data dissemination model. Such a simple strategy poses the problem of a great amount of overhead because all vehicles traveling in the desired direction participate in broadcasting, while it could be sufficient to broadcast data by only a subset of the vehicles.

4.1.4 HAZARDOUS ROAD CONDITIONS WARNING

Inside, two dissemination protocols for VANETs are proposed in the context of the Life Warning System (LIWAS) research project, which is a traffic warning system that aims at providing drivers with information about hazardous road conditions such as ice, water and snow. The first protocol is called the "zone flooding" protocol. This protocol proposes three different optimization techniques to limit the forwarding of packets. The first technique is "hop count," which aims to ensure the maximum number of hops before discarding a packet. The second technique is "sequence list," which ensures that a certain packet can be forwarded only once. The "zone flooding" concept is also introduced to further limit the dissemination of packets.

The second protocol is called the "zone diffusion" protocol, which is a data-centric protocol that is based on data aggregation. This protocol assumes that every node maintains an environment representation (ER) for the surrounding environment. ER is updated whenever data is received from sensors, and data are periodically broadcast to neighbors. Simulation results prove that these two protocols are robust to changes in network mobility and density. However, the three simple techniques utilized for dissemination optimization are not sufficient to mitigate broadcasting overhead under high densities.

4.1.5 ARRIVAL TIME ESTIMATION

An example of estimating arrival time to vehicles' destinations is proposed in, where the road map is divided into areas in which vehicles can measure the time required to pass through each area. A sufficient number of vehicles is required in each area in order to keep accurate traffic information statistics continuously. Each vehicle periodically broadcasts area passage time to share with neighboring vehicles. The time required to pass through a certain area can be estimated by each vehicle locally, by averaging the area passage times collected from neighbors. The proposed approach is evaluated with realistic traffic flows on realistic road system and proved to achieve the traffic information sharing at a practical level. This approach was proposed to be improved based on a message-ferrying technique in data dissemination. Broadcasting is not optimized in this approach, and the network could be easily flooded with data under high densities.

4.1.6 SPEED EXPECTATIONS

A speed expectations example approach is proposed in which vehicles are enabled to build their own local traffic maps of speeds experienced on visited roads and share them with other vehicles. This allows a vehicle to build a map of expected speeds even on nonvisited roads, which indicates traffic changes through the network. This approach was applied on a simple Manhattan grid network map, and data is exchanged only on areas of unexpected traffic, by using a distributed clustering algorithm that does not require constant network connectivity. This approach performs well in a sparsely connected dynamic network, but is not evaluated in large-scale scenarios.

4.1.7 CONGESTION DETECTION

The congestion detection is presented based on disseminating and propagating traffic data using received message dependent protocol (RMDP). Most of the vehicles can acquire the head of traffic jam in a short time using RMDP. A simple communication strategy is considered, in which a vehicle broadcasts its own information to its surrounding vehicles that are traveling in the opposite lane. As shown in Fig. 4.1, the proposed approach can be presented as follows: Assume that a moving vehicle A disseminates its locally stored information to vehicle B moving in the opposite direction lane. B moves forward and re-disseminates A's information to a vehicle C moving in the same direction as A. In this case, C can know the head of the traffic jam and may decide to change its route. From this simple illustration, it can be concluded that RMDP has a limited scope since it focuses on the congestion on the road directly ahead.

4.1.8 PULL MODEL

The pull model techniques often follow the request-response paradigm for data dissemination. Compared to the push-based model, the pull model often requires less overhead, with less latency constraints. In the pull-based approach, the requester usually sends a query to the broadcast site, and gets a reply message from there. In such applications, users can tolerate more delays as long as a response eventually returns. Pull-based techniques often target travel comfort applications such as service discovery and delay-tolerant systems.

4.1.8.1 Service Discovery

Address-based service resolution protocol (ABSRP) integrates a pull-based technique to discover services in VANETs. When a vehicle needs a service, it creates a service request with the specification of the type of service and the desired service area, and then transmits it to the nearest roadside unit. The receiving roadside unit checks if it has proactively learned about the service provider. If it is aware of the service provider's IP address, it forwards the service request to the target service provider.

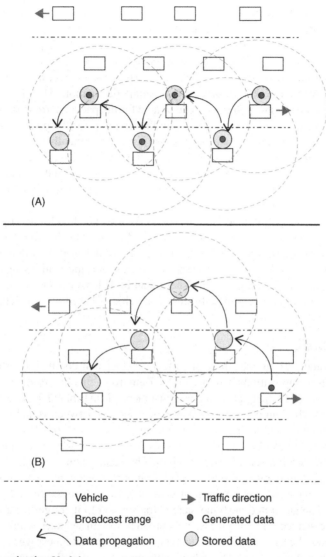

FIGURE 4.1 Data Disseminating Model

(A) The same direction. (B) The opposite direction.

Otherwise, it broadcasts the service request destined to the target service provider over the backbone network. In the case of service discovery, the request received by the roadside unit is broadcasted to the two nearby units. After receiving the request, the target service provider creates a service response and transmits it to the originating vehicle. A roadside unit can transmit a service request to the target service provider over the vehicle network or backbone network. In the former case, broadcasting can rapidly flood a congested vehicular network with data packets, since no optimization is proposed in ABSRP.

4.1.8.2 Delay-Tolerant Systems

Vehicle-assisted data delivery (VADD) is another pull-based approach for data dissemination in VANETs. When a vehicle issues a request to a certain fixed site, VADD proposes techniques to efficiently route the packet to that site and receive the reply within a reasonable delay. Involved nodes carry the packet when routes do not exist and forward it to the new receiver that moves into its vicinity. As shown in, vehicle A has a packet to forward to a certain destination. The optimal direction of this packet is assumed to be north. Two contacts are available for the packet carrier: B moving south and C moving north. Thus, A has two choices for selecting the next hop for the packet. Both choices aim at forwarding the packet north. B may be selected because it is geographically closer toward the north and provides better possibilities to exploit the wireless communication (e.g., B can immediately pass the packet to D, but C cannot). C may also be selected because it is moving in the packet forwarding direction. These two choices lead to two different forwarding protocols: Location First Probe (L-VADD) and Direction First Probe (D-VADD).

VADD makes use of the predictable mobility in a VANET, which is limited by traffic pattern and road layout. Extensive experiments were designed for performance evaluation. Results show that the VADD outperforms existing solutions in terms of data packet delay, packet-delivery ratio, and protocol overhead. Nevertheless, VADD is designed specifically for applications in sparsely connected networks, and did not resolve communication issues under high densities. Dense networks may require the selection of the next forwarding vehicle from sets of vehicles based on some criteria.

4.1.9 HYBRID MODEL

Along with the push and pull models, there are a few schemes that combine both models in order to support different types of applications within a VANET environment. An information transfer protocol for vehicular computing (VITP) supports the establishment of distributed service infrastructure over VANETs, by specifying the syntax and the semantic of messages between vehicles. VITP uses both of the information dissemination models. For safety messages such as alerts about emergencies or hazardous traffic conditions, a push-based technique is used, while a pull-based technique is proposed to retrieve information by location-sensitive queries issued by vehicles on demand. The push-based technique proposed by VITP disseminates alert messages among vehicles moving into the affected area. Whenever a vehicle detects such a condition, it generates an alert message and transmits it via the underlying VANET. The generated push message is transported to its target location area using geographic routing. Once arrived, the push message is broadcast to all vehicles within the target location area. On the other hand, the use of pull-based technique to disseminate messages is issued on demand in a context of service provision scenario, such as estimating the traffic-flow condition in a target location. When a vehicle initiates such a request, it submits that request to the target area, assuming that there is a connection from the requesting vehicle in that area through the VANET.

The propagation of such a request is done through intermediate nodes using geographic routing, in a way that is similar to transporting a push message. The semantics of the query determines the way to treat it once it arrives at the target location area, where vehicles construct a virtual ad hoc server (VAHS) to provide a reply message. The request message propagates through the virtual server until a certain return condition is satisfied. The vehicle that detects such a return condition immediately creates a reply message, and posts it toward the source area, where the requesting vehicle is located. Simulation results have proven the feasibility of VITP in the VANET environment. However, there is a high drop rate for queries, which grows substantially with increasing query distances, and with decreasing vehicle densities. That's why optimization techniques are required to enhance the performance of VITP.

4.1.9.1 Issues and Challenges

VANET applications impose diverse requirements on the supporting technologies. This diversity leads to a number of challenges. This section addresses the main research challenges to be considered for data dissemination in VANETs. These include scalability, security and trust, quality of service, node cooperation, and simulation issues.

4.1.9.2 Scalability

As we have previously mentioned, high VANET density scenarios can lead to broadcast storm problems. VANET researchers continue to focus on scalable data dissemination, by trying to reduce data redundancy. Novel solutions should be developed to detect traffic density such that scalability issues can be addressed.

4.1.9.3 Security and Trust

In travel comfort applications, security issues are not often considered because cooperative driving is typically assumed. During safety data dissemination, integrating security mechanisms are highly necessary within VANETs. Warning systems will not be accepted by customers if trust, security, and reliability are not provided. The establishment of trust by providing trustworthy applications is considered as the most crucial security issue within a VANET. However, integrating security schemes into VANET applications will increase the delay of message arrival.

4.1.9.4 Quality of Service and Traffic Characterization

Quality of service (QoS) and traffic characterization are additional important issues to be addressed by dissemination methods in VANETs, since different types of applications are expected to have different QoS requirements. QoS metrics for VANET are not yet well defined.

4.1.9.5 Node Cooperation

The majority of VANET dissemination protocols assumes that nodes are willing to cooperate and allow the use of their resources to provide connectivity for other nodes. However, this assumption might not always be valid. In addition, some nodes might exhibit selfish behavior and make use of services available by other nodes while not allowing similar use of their resources by the same nodes. Efficient reward, punishment, debit, and credit mechanisms would have to be enforced by the corresponding protocols and systems.

4.1.9.6 Simulation

The cost and complexity of implementing VANET data dissemination schemes and applications in large test-bed system forces such an implementation to be within a simulated environment. Three major challenges can be addressed in the context of VANET simulation. First, the credibility and feasibility of simulation systems require reliable and standardized simulation parameters so that verification techniques can be applied. Second, mobility models should address sufficient levels of complexity to simulate realistic traffic scenarios and realistic driving behavior. Third, the scalability of simulation represents a huge challenge in this context. Specifically, it is currently impossible to simulate the full stack of very large networks.

The need of humans to be connected has led to rapid growth in wireless communications technology. VANETs are an emerging part of this trend. These networks can be used to disseminate information such as weather, traffic conditions, and commercial information, such as restaurant and gas station locations. The many VANET applications can be divided into two main categories: safety and nonsafety. Safety applications include spreading an alarm or warning with the aim of avoiding danger and reducing risk. Nonsafety applications include information about a new product or business, the closest restaurant or gas station, or the shortest path to a destination. This information may be transmitted in response to a request. Since this information may include multimedia content, the message size can be considerably greater than that of safety messages. Roadside units (RSUs) must therefore distribute messages of varying sizes and content, and this must occur according to time, current policy, traffic conditions, and so forth.

The applications mentioned previously are just the beginning of the flood of applications anticipated for VANETs. As with other types of networks, VANETs have their own advantages and disadvantages. VANETs are a subset of mobile ad hoc networks (MANETs) with restricted node behavior. Vehicle (node) velocity and their limited ability to change direction are two significant differences between MANETs and VANETs. Due to their highly dynamic and restricted characteristics, VANETs are more vulnerable to the fragmentation problem. This means that the delivery of a message to an arbitrary vehicle can be very difficult. One of the proposed methods for mitigating this problem is store–carry–forward (SCF). Every RSU broadcasts messages based on time, policy, or network-specific criteria. Vehicles approaching an RSU receive these messages, and they should be decoded and a decision made before passing the RSU. For example, suppose a multimedia message, that contains the location of a gas station location is being transmitted. A vehicle looking for a gas station should decode this message before the corresponding RSU is encountered. In other words, the vehicle must be given sufficient time to make a decision, safely reduce speed, and possibly change direction. Every message has a validation period, after which it is replaced with another message according to the corresponding policy.

The distance between a vehicle with a message and the source of that message is called the decoding distance. In this chapter, the decoding distance is increased by combining rate less coding with the SCF technique. The trade-offs between vehicle speed, broadcast interval, number of lanes, and decoding distance are examined. Due to buffer limitations, we employ a buffer management mechanism. The impact of this mechanism is investigated.

The effect of an RSU changing its messages, and the ability of vehicles to sense these changes, is also examined. Finally, message dissemination patterns around each RSU is determined. This shows the effectiveness of the proposed approach.

4.1.10 SCALABLE DATA DISSEMINATION IN VEHICULAR AD HOC NETWORKS

VANETs provide local vehicle-to-vehicle (V2V) and vehicle-to-infrastructure (V2I) communications to support ITS applications. Example applications are emergency electronic brake lights, slow vehicle indication, wrong-way driver warning, stationary vehicle warning, lane change assistance, and so forth. The technology used to enable such ad hoc networking is called IEEE. This is an amendment to the IEEE. Standard that contains several enhancements to improve performance under vehicular conditions. Examples are increased output power, dedicated channel, and reduced channel bandwidth to account for the influence of Doppler spread. In contrast with other ad hoc networking use cases, VANET communication in general does not focus on unicast transmissions. Instead, the emphasis is put on the dissemination of information to all nodes located in a certain region. Typically, this functionality is achieved by combining media access control (MAC) level broadcasting with geographic-aware forwarding schemes on the networking layer.

In general, two different kinds of information messages are used: cooperative awareness messages (CAM) and decentralized environmental notification messages (DENM). The former is utilized to continuously exchange status information such as location, heading, and speed with the other vehicles in the immediate environment. Hence, CAM beacons are restricted to single hop broadcasts. The latter is applied when some specific piece of information regarding the environment, for example, tail of traffic jam, slippery spot, obstacle on the road, and so forth is to be communicated to all vehicles within a given area. Therefore, DENM messages are multihop broadcasts in the VANET. An important challenge in the VANET domain is the scalability of data dissemination, which has been identified in numerous independent studies. The goal of this work is to realize a solution that overcomes this challenge, enabling scalable data dissemination in V2V and V2I communication. Note that next to the VANET scalability issue, there are also other VANET networking challenges to be overcome (e.g., IP session connectivity, which relies on intelligent link-layer, and IP-layer handovers as demonstrated. Here, we focus on the VANET scalability challenge for data dissemination.

Under dense traffic conditions, the large number of communicating vehicles can easily result in a congested wireless channel. As a result, delays and packet losses increase to a level where the VANET cannot be applied for safety applications anymore. In the hidden node problem is identified as one of the main drivers behind the performance decrease. The IEEE .p MAC relies on a technique called carrier sense multiple access with collision avoidance (CSMA/CA) to coordinate transmissions on the wireless channel in a distributed manner. In short, a node can only transmit a packet if it has sensed that the wireless channel is idle for a sufficient amount of time.

If it overhears the transmission of another node on the channel, it defers its transmission attempt until that transmission has finished. A hidden node (H) however, is not aware of a concurrent transmission because it is out of the range of the sender (S) but in the range of the receiver (R). Therefore, it is possible that the hidden node will start sending its own data and interfere with the concurrent transmission between S and R. To solve this problem, the technique of request-to-send (RTS) and clear-to-send (CTS) was developed. In this case, node S first broadcasts a short RTS message. The receiver node R replies with a CTS message, indicating the duration of the planned transmission. Because the hidden node is within reach of the receiving node, it will receive the CTS message and can derive the appropriate time to wait before attempting any transmission by itself. However, because there is no receiver defined in broadcast mode, IEEE. does not support RTS/CTS when broadcasting. As depicted in Fig. 4.1, this leads to a high sensitivity of the VANET to the hidden node problem, since for a given node S, a relatively large hidden node area (annotated gray) can be identified. This sensitivity is further increased by the fact that broadcasting has also resulted in the omission of MAC acknowledgment and retransmission techniques.

Another cause of the VANET scalability problem is the consecutive freeze process (CFP). It refers to the situation where a station that has just completed a transmission chooses zero as its initial backoff time and hence starts transmitting immediately after a distributed coordination function (DCF) interface space. This gives other stations no chances to back off. As discussed in literature, CFP occurs more frequently in broadcast situations, leading to high end-to-end delays. A final VANET challenge is the rapid variation of the channel at vehicular speeds. This results in increased packet loss when using a standard channel estimation scheme for IEEE 802.11p. Hence, when targeting reliable VANET solutions, there is a need for solutions that enhance the packet success rate (PSR) at rising speeds while maintaining full compatibility with the IEEE 802.11p standard. Several techniques have been researched to tackle the VANET scalability problem. These are situated on all layers of the Open Systems Interconnection (OSI) protocol stack. In general, previous studies focused on applying a single technique, identifying the optimal parameter configuration, and indicating the VANET performance gain.

However, recent work has pointed out the need for a more holistic approach, where different techniques are combined to effectively solve the VANET scalability problem. However, this is not as straightforward as it may seem: techniques that perform well independently might very well result in mutual compensations, ruling out each other's performance gains. An example is the work of Baldessari et al., which came across such difficulties when combining a transmit power and rate control algorithm. In this paper, a holistic solution to the VANET scalability problem is established. We name this solution scalable data dissemination in VANETs or scalable data dissemination in vehicular ad hoc network (SDDV). It is composed of several techniques spread across the different layers of the protocol stack.

These techniques are characterized by a low level of complexity. This approach makes the solution more straightforward to implement, debug, and maintain. Simulation results are presented that illustrate the severity of the scalability problem when applying common state-of-the-art techniques (Section 4.2). Starting from this baseline solution, optimization techniques are gradually added to SDDV until the scalability problem is entirely solved. The next Section determines the performance characteristics of the final SDDV configuration through extensive simulations. As the final part of our research, Finally, Section 4.2 validates the simulation results by comparing the performance of the baseline solution and SDDV.

4.2 MOBILITY MANAGEMENT: IPv6-BASED INTERNET

As a new type of vehicle communication network, vehicular networks achieve multihop wireless communication between vehicles and between vehicles and roadside infrastructures. With the development of vehicular networks and the emergence of a variety of new applications, it is urgent to connect vehicular networks to the IPv6-based Internet in order to meet the increasing service demands. As a special type of MANET, a vehicular network has its own characteristics, such as high speed, a large number of nodes, a large coverage area, and so forth. The IP-based Internet has many advantages, such as mobility support, abundant address resources, good scalability, and so forth. Therefore, the IPv6-based vehicular networks become the ideal solution for satisfying the service demands. The IEEE Working Group proposes the framework for the IPv6-based vehicular networks. Due to the differences between the architecture of the IPv6 network and the one of the vehicular network, this framework has the following limitations on achieving address configuration, routing, and mobility management:

1. In the address configuration, this framework does not support DAD.
2. In the routing, the framework does not support multihop communication.
3. During the mobility handover process, a vehicle must acquire a new care-of address. Since a vehicle moves at a high speed, the frequent change of a vehicle's care-of address increases the packet loss rate and reduces the communication quality.

In order to overcome these limitations, this work proposes a mobility management solution that is based on address configuration and routing algorithm, and it has the following contributions:

1. The architecture based on vehicle domains is proposed in order to reduce the mobility handover frequency and delay.
2. Based on the architecture, a distributed address configuration algorithm is proposed. In the algorithm, a vehicle acquires a unique IPv6 address from a neighbor node without DAD.
3. Based on the architecture and an address configuration algorithm, a vehicle can establish a routing path reaching the nearest AP and achieve the multihop communication with the Internet through the routing path.
4. Based on the address configuration algorithm and routing algorithm, the intra-VD (vehicular domain) mobility management algorithm and inter-VD mobility management algorithm are proposed. During the mobility process, a vehicle is always identified by its home address, so the algorithm does not perform the care-of address configuration. Moreover, the handover process in the network layer (L) is performed before the one in the link layer (L), so both the handover delay and packet loss rate are reduced. Particularly, while the inter-VD handover is performed, a vehicle can receive data packets from the same AP. As a result, the packet loss rate is significantly reduced.

IPv6 address structure is also created as shown in Fig. 4.2. In the scheme, DAD for a cluster member's address is performed in the corresponding cluster, and the address configuration for cluster members in different clusters is carried out at the same time, so the address configuration cost is reduced and the delay is shortened. The proxy-based address configuration scheme adopts the random ID and

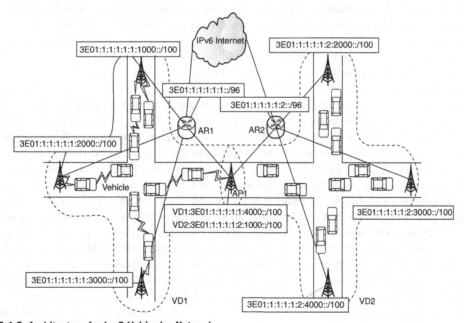

FIGURE 4.2 Architecture for Ipv6 Vehicular Network

time stamp to identify a new node. If multiple nodes with the same ID and time stamp send an address request message to a proxy node simultaneously, then the proxy node is unable to distinguish between these nodes and to properly perform the address configuration. In the scheme, neighbor solicitation (NS) and neighbor advertisement (NA) are used to perform the communication between a new node and a proxy node, while REQ and REP are employed to achieve the communication between a proxy node and a gateway node. Therefore, a proxy node has to store the mapping between different kinds of messages, so the address configuration performance is potentially reduced. In the tree-based dynamic address autoconfiguration protocol T-DAAP, the network is organized in the tree topology and includes three kinds of nodes: normal node, leader node, and root node.

A normal node acts as a relay. A leader node has a disjoint free address pool and is responsible for assigning an address for a new node. Only one root node is included in the network, and it stores the information on all leader nodes in the network. In this way, a leader node can acquire the status of another leader node through the root node. The root node is also responsible for address reclamation and network merging, so it becomes the bottleneck of the entire system. While an AP is equipped with a DHCP server and can assign an address for a vehicle, it does not record the address assignment status. All the address assignment states are managed by a balanced server (BS), which is also responsible for reclaiming the address resources released by parking vehicles. A border access (BA) point is employed for reclaiming the address resources released by vehicles moving out of the serving area. Then, a BS/BA returns the reclaimed address resources to the corresponding APs. An AP has an address recovery buffer. If the buffer of an AP is full, then the AP cannot reuse the recovered address resources. As a result, the address resource loss is incurred. If an AP's buffer is empty, the AP requests the address space from a BS. In the situation, the address configuration is performed through a central server, so the address configuration delay is prolonged. Yuh-Shyan Chena et al. propose an address scheme for vehicular networks. When a vehicle is going to leave the serving area, it passes its IP address to an intermediate vehicle that remains in the serving area in order to extend the address lifetime.

During the extended address lifetime, a vehicle that is entering the serving area can acquire the address through multihop relays from the intermediate vehicle. If a leaving vehicle is unable to communicate with an intermediate vehicle in the serving area, then an entering vehicle acquires an address from the remote DHCP servers. In this situation, the address configuration delay is prolonged. Moreover, a vehicle broadcasts a message within multihop scope according to time to live (TTL), so the address configuration delay is potentially increased. The each node maintains a specific address space. If a node moves out of the network, its address space is reclaimed. However, when a node leaves or fails without alerting, the address space loss can be caused. In this situation, the scheme employs the periodic-flooding query mechanism to reclaim the address space, so the address configuration performance is weakened. In the location-based address configuration scheme, a node gets its location information from the global positioning system (GPS) and then it acquires an address based on the location information. A node performs DAD to ensure the uniqueness of its address, so the address configuration delay is increased. This work proposes a distributed address configuration algorithm where a vehicle acquires a unique IPv6 address from a neighbor node without DAD. In the algorithm, a network is divided into multiple grids according to location coordinates. Each node's address includes its location coordinates. When one node wants to communicate with another node, it launches the routing establishment process according to the location coordinate of the destination node. Movement prediction-based routing (MOPR) uses link stability metrics to predict the link lifetime and route lifetime. It assumes that each vehicle can acquire neighbor vehicles' information such as speed, location, and direction, and can use this information to predict the connection interval.

However, this protocol does not support mobility handover. The proposed position-based routing protocol relies upon the extraction of a static street map from an external service such as geographic information systems (GIS) to construct a spatial model for routing. It has some recovery strategies to route packets. The greedy perimeter coordinator routing algorithm GPCR takes advantage of the fact that city streets form a natural planar graph. In this way, a restricted greedy algorithm can be followed as long as the nodes are on the street. In GPCR, the routing decisions are taken only at street junctions. A source node establishes multiple disjoint routing paths reaching a destination node through one routing discovery process, and then ranks the multiple routing paths based on the link cost. The routing path with the minimum link cost is the primary path. If the primary path fails, then the second optimal routing path is selected to continue routing the data. The scheme effectively reduces the frequency of reestablishing the failed routing paths, but maintaining multiple disjoint routing paths increases the network resource consumption and degrades the network performance. The connectivity-aware routing (CAR) protocol is a position-based routing that maintains routes between source and destination pairs. CAR predicts the positions of destination nodes to improve the routing performance. It can repair routes as nodes' positions change. W. Sun et al. propose a routing protocol that uses digital map and position information of each vehicle to discover a network route with the best stability.

This protocol divides the map into grids, and uses the mobility characteristics to determine the route stability. A vehicle sends an RREQ message to the destination grid to launch the routing establishment process. When a vehicle is moving toward the destination the broken routes can be restored. However, during repairs of the broken routes, the packet loss is increased. Based on the proposed address configuration, this work proposes a multihop routing algorithm in order to reduce the packet loss rate. The Internet engineering task force (IETF) has proposed various IP-based mobility management protocols, such as MIPv6 and PMIPv6, in order to provide communications continuity when a node moves between different IP domains. However, most of these protocols are unsuitable for vehicular networks because of considerable packet loss and long delays. In the situation, researchers have proposed some mobility handover schemes for vehicular networks. Gerla M et al. have discussed the development trend of vehicular networks in the future, and have addressed the key issues of mobility management for vehicular networks. In addition, Gerla M et al. have also analyzed the reasons why the existing technology cannot solve these key issues. The proposed scheme reduces both the mobility handover cost and tunnel establishment cost, but it depends on the dispatch types to determine the source or destination of a packet. As a result, intermediate nodes forwarding a packet have to identify all Dispatch types in order to determine the next hop, so the mobility handover delay is increased and the network scalability is also limited.

Moreover, a header structure is added between the adaptation layer and IP layer, and also increases the transmission delay. Sensor Proxy Mobile IPv6—SPMIPv6 presents the network architecture and message formats for the mobility handover process, and also evaluates the mobility handover cost and energy consumption. The analytical results show that SPMIPv6 reduces the energy consumption significantly. The mobility handover process is achieved in the link layer, so that the mobility handover delay and cost are reduced. A mobility management scheme for integrating MANETs into the Internet using multiple mobile gateways (MGs) and foreign agents (FAs) is elaborated. The scheme extends ad hoc on demand distance vector (AODV) and MIP to achieve the integration, and the simulation results show that the use of multiple MGs and the hybrid gate discovery mechanism enhance the network performance. The protocol provides the localized mobility management in mesh networks, and it achieves the low mobility handover delay through the multipath routing. However, this solution requires some special signaling costs when it deals with mobile terminals, so the delay is prolonged to some extent. Chiu K et al. propose a cross-layer fast handover scheme where the physical layer information is shared with the link layer in order to reduce the handover delay in vehicular networks. This scheme operates based on WiMAX mobile multihop relay technique, which allows intervehicle communications to access the Internet via a relay vehicle. However, the scheme does not discuss the IP mobility.

The scheme uses an intermediate-mobile access gateway (iMAG) to perform the mobility handover for vehicular networks. iMAG must be geographically located between the home domain and foreign domain, so the scheme cannot support a global mobility management. In addition, iMAG needs to store the information on all roadside units, and maintaining the information on roadside units consumes a lot of network resources. Prakash et al. propose a vehicle-assisted cross-layer handover scheme to help relay packets of a handover vehicle. The vehicular clusters are employed so that cluster heads are in charge of IP mobility for other vehicles. Xiaonan Wang et al. propose a mobility handover scheme for IPv6-based vehicular networks. The scheme adopts the tunnel technology to achieve the mobility handover. During the mobility handover process, a vehicle can keep the connection with its current associated AP, so the packet loss rate is reduced. However, the tunnel increases the mobility handover cost and delay to some extent. Mun-Suk Kim et al. enhance PFMIPv6 and propose an enhanced PFMIPv6 (ePFMIPv6) for vehicular networks. In ePFMIPv6, the serving mobile access gateway (MAG) preestablishes a tunnel with multiple candidate MAGs. In this way, when the serving MAG performs the mobility handover, the packets can be forwarded to the next MAG. ePFMIPv6 shortens the mobility handover delay and lowers the packet loss to some extent, but it increases mobility handover cost.

This work proposes a mobility management solution where a vehicle does not need a care-of address in order to shorten the handover delay and lower the packet loss. The mobility management solution is based on the address configuration and routing, but the existing schemes only discuss one issue. Therefore, this work proposes a complete mobility management solution where the issues of the address configuration and routing are also addressed.

4.2.1 IPV6 ADDRESS CONFIGURATION: ARCHITECTURE

A vehicular network is made up of access routers (ARs), APs and vehicles. The communication range of an AP is more than the one of a vehicle. An AR is connected to the Internet backbone and an AP is connected to two ARs. The area enclosed by APs and connected to an AR is called a VD, so an AP belongs to two VDs. A vehicle has the routing and forwarding function and achieves the communication with the IPv6 Internet through the nearest AP, as shown in Fig. 4.2.

4.3 A SEAMLESS FLOW MOBILITY MANAGEMENT ARCHITECTURE FOR VEHICULAR COMMUNICATION NETWORKS

VANET is a rising subclass of MANETs, which provide wireless communication among vehicles as well as between vehicles and roadside devices. In VANETS, each vehicle can have multiple radio interfaces, thus being able to simultaneously connect to different domains and radio access network technologies. Although these vehicles can connect to these different network technologies simultaneously, nowadays vehicles are limited to choosing a default interface for sending and receiving information. This limitation is related to the current model of multiple interface management, where several interfaces are attached to the operating system. Usually, operating systems use configuration files from the user, or consider the types of applications to select a default network interface to send and receive data. To allow the use of more than one network interface simultaneously, the IETF has developed the technology of IP flow mobility, which can divide IP flows among multiple links according to application requirements and user preferences.

There are some groups of the IETF, such as the IETF mobility extensions for IPv6 (MEXT) and IETF-based network mobility extensions (NETEXT), which have been working on the development and elaboration of a protocol that allows the use of more than one interface simultaneously. The MEXT has standardized a host-based IP flow mobility in Mobile IPv6, enabling flow bindings for the mobile node (MN) with multiple interfaces. This method has an air waste resource problem, such as establishing IP-in-IP bidirectional tunnel over the air interface and exchanging mobility-related layer (L) signaling messages via the wireless link. To avoid overloading the wireless network, the NETEXT discusses the use of a network-based IP flow mobility in Proxy Mobile IPv6 (PMIPv6). This solution has a limitation because the flow mobility of the MNs should be initiated and controlled only by network-side entities. Moreover, there exist some limitations with flow mobility support. In order to contour these limitations and to enable the dynamic movement of individual flows according to the flow control, we propose a new mobile-initiated seamless IP flow mobility mechanism, developed over the network-based mobility management architecture. In this work we propose and evaluate a seamless flow mobility management architecture (SFMMA) in vehicular communication networks.

The proposed architecture deals with different network interfaces at the same time, seeking the maximization of the network throughput and keeping low latency and low packet loss rate. To achieve this, our scheduling considers that applications are divided into three classes, according to the general goals of vehicular network applications: safety, comfort, and user. Moreover, this model considers that vehicles are moving into a city or on a highway, and that person in the vehicles is running more than one application class at the same time.

4.3.1 PROTOCOL

The IEEE 802.11 provides a standard to assist the implementation of vertical handovers, and it is a recent effort to allow the transfer and interoperability between heterogeneous network types. The goal of IEEE 802.11 is to improve and facilitate the use of MNs, providing uninterrupted transmission in heterogeneous networks. The most important task of the IEEE 802.11 is the discovery of new networks in the environment and the selection of the most appropriate network for a given need. The network discovery and process selection are facilitated by network information exchange that helps the mobile device to determine which networks are active in its neighborhood, thus allowing the mobile device to connect to the most appropriate network, based on its own policies.

The core of the methodologies is the Media Independent Handover Function (MIHF). The MIHF has to be implemented in all devices compatible with the IEEE 802.11 (in hardware or software). This function is responsible for communicating with different terminals, networks, and remote MIHFs, and also for providing information services to the higher layers. The MIHF defines three different services: Media Independent Event Service (MIES), Media Independent Command Service (MICS), and Media

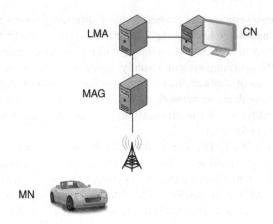

FIGURE 4.3 PMIPv6 Framework

Independent Information Service (MIIS). These services allow obtaining and storing relevant information about the network status such as loss, throughput, and what are the subnets. Part of this information is found on the information elements IE_CONTAINER_NETWORK and IE_CONTAINER_POA of the protocol architecture, which are used in the context of this particular work.

4.3.2 PROXY MOBILE IPV6

PMIPv6 provides network-based mobility management to hosts connecting to a PMIPv6 domain. PMIPv6 introduces two new functional entities, namely the Local Mobility Anchor (LMA) and the Mobility Access Gateway (MAG). The MAG is the first layer three hops detecting mobile node attachment and providing IP connectivity. The LMA is the entity assigning one or more Home Network Prefixes (HNPs) to the MN and is the topological anchor for all traffic from/to the MN. The fundamental foundation of PMIPv6 is based on MIPv6 in the sense that it extends MIPv6 signaling and reuses many concepts such as the home agent (HA) functionality. The LMA and the MAG establish a bidirectional tunnel for forwarding all data traffic belonging to the MNs. The network-based localized mobility support provided by PMIPv6 was designed for hosts, so a mobile host can freely roam within the PMIPv6 domain, without changing its IP address. Fig. 4.3 shows a simple topology of the PMIPv6 protocol. We have a MN, a MAG connected to a wireless AP, and an LMA. We also have an LMA connected to a corresponding node (CN), which can be any node on the Internet or in the LMA that communicates with the MN.

4.4 A SEAMLESS FLOW MOBILITY MANAGEMENT ARCHITECTURE

The proposed (SFMMA) considers a common infrastructure for multiple access technologies in a transparent way. We created a multiaccess wireless network architecture using the Wi-Fi, vehicular, WiMAX, and LTE technologies, providing a continuous and transparent connection for the vehicular applications. The objectives of the architecture are to maximize network throughput and to keep latency and packet loss within the minimum requirements for vehicular applications. To accomplish this, the proposal creates a flow mobility management based on the application classes of vehicular network and on the status of each active network on the environment. Our architecture differs from other architectures for vehicular networks because it considers the needs of each application class, such as throughput, delay, and packet loss. Moreover, it uses the state of the currently active network to perform the division of the flow. Another difference is that not only the LMA can take the decision to split the flow, but also MAG and MN can take action in the flow divisions.

4.4.1 MOBILITY MANAGEMENT SCHEME

In this section, our mobility management solution for vehicular networks is proposed. In general, vehicles are divided into different clusters and each cluster is considered as a mobile network. Intracluster communication is allowed to reduce the handoff latency and minimize the packet loss ratio.

4.4.1.1 System Architecture

In a vehicular network, according to different functions, there are two kinds of nodes: mobile vehicles and APs. Adapting the conception of network mobility to the vehicular networks, all of the vehicles can be divided into different clusters according to the geographical distance and related velocity. Each cluster constructs a mobile network. The system architecture is illustrated in Fig. 4.4.

In this sample scenario, there are three mobile networks. The movement direction of the mobile network is shown as the arrow. The question of how to divide vehicles into different clusters and how to maintain the dynamic clusters efficiently is not considered in our paper. We assume that there is an efficient clustering scheme to generate and maintain clusters under the help of other physical equipment's such as GPS, and so forth. If we consider each cluster as a mobile network, the network mobility management can be used to implement the mobility management scheme for vehicular networks. Unfortunately, using the network mobility management the user will spend a long time period to complete the handoff process, which would be more than 10 s. Therefore, the author propose a solution to reduce the handoff latency using intracluster communications.

In our scheme, vehicles in a cluster are divided into four types of nodes: cluster head nodes, cluster tail nodes, cluster center nodes, and general cluster nodes. The cluster center node is the vehicle, which provides the mobile router (MR) function. In a cluster, all of the vehicles access Internet through the cluster center node. In Fig. 4.4, vehicles A, B, and C are cluster center nodes. These nodes connect to the APs on the roadside. The communications among the vehicles in the same cluster can be implemented by an ad hoc routing protocol. The cluster head node is the vehicle that is in the front of the cluster, and conversely the cluster tail node is the vehicle that is at the end of the cluster. For mobile network A, the vehicle A2 is the cluster head node because it is in the front of the mobile network A respect to the movement direction of the whole mobile network and vehicle A1 is the cluster tail node of the mobile network. Because the cluster is mobile and velocities of vehicles are different, the cluster head node and the cluster tail node will be changed dynamically. Any other vehicles in the cluster that do not have any specific functions of mobility management, such as A3, A4, are general cluster nodes. The cluster head node and the cluster tail node are determined according to the vehicles' geographical locations and their related velocities. And the cluster center node is determined according to the vehicle's function. Therefore, it is possible that one vehicle would be the cluster tail node and the cluster

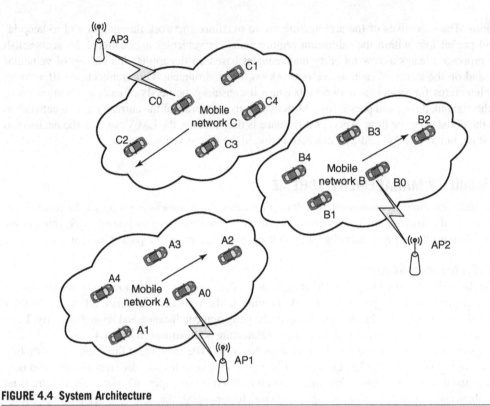

FIGURE 4.4 System Architecture

center node at the same time. A special case is that there is only one vehicle in a cluster, and that vehicle would serve all roles, as the cluster head node, the cluster tail node, and the cluster center node.

4.4.1.2 Mobility Management Services

Sustainable urban mobility management is recognized by the European Commission as one of the key ways to reach the EU objectives of combating climate change. In this section, an overview of the current approaches of mobility management services is presented. Only services that are addressed in the MobiTraff project are described. Their main objective is to improve bus service quality. This includes (1) minimization of travel time of buses and harmonization of their headways, (2) minimization of stop-and-go driving, and (3) provision for passengers of hassle-free/cost-effective dynamic guidance throughout their trips. Finally, the concept of congestion pricing is introduced. It is an important mobility-management technique, aiming at reducing travel demand.

4.4.1.3 Bus Priority (Transit Signal Priority)

Regularity is the main performance criterion for high-frequency bus services. It is defined by headway time gap between the arrival times of a bus and the bus in the front of a cluster. Differential priority in urban environments provides a higher level of priority to buses with headways much higher than scheduled. Recently, it has been shown that a priority strategy for a bus should not be based only on the headway of the bus itself (classical approach) but should also consider the headway of the bus behind.

Currently, the architecture for bus priority management is composed of the following centralized entities: Automatic Vehicle Location Centre (AVL), responsible for monitoring of bus locations; UTC; and traffic signal controller. These entities are linked by infrastructure-based communication systems to exchange information. The infrastructure-based priority management techniques differ in the location of the entity determining priority request, priority request method, and location of priority control. The estimation of dwell time (expected delay of buses at bus stops) is a significant component of priority request, allowing efficient prediction of link journey times for buses.

4.4.1.4 Real-Time Passenger Information

Modal shift toward public transport in the EU's Action Plan on Urban Mobility acknowledges the role of providing consumers with better travel information. A trip has two phases: pretrip and on-trip. Conventional RTPI systems are based on a centralized AVL Centre and aim at providing real-time information.

Personalized navigation systems (PNS) are the next-generation RTPI systems. They go one step further by providing passengers (through their mobile devices) with on-trip personalized navigation cues. The systems proposed in the literature assume the existence of a centralized back-office responsible for itinerary calculations. Communication with back-office is provided by cellular networks. Maritime is a PNS deployed in Japan. It uses client-server architecture. Location awareness is based on GPS and cellular-based positioning. It requires an Internet connection between the server and the client; hence it is costly, especially to roamers. Computing tasks (computation of the best itineraries) are distributed among servers and mobile phone clients.

The ENOSIS system integrates wireless and web-based communication technologies: its services are offered through the Internet, a voice portal, and information kiosks located in the city. The system involves several stakeholders. Recently introduced Navi proposes to base location awareness of passenger on the electronic (RFID-based) ticketing system already developed in public transport. The system assumes near-field communication capability to be present in mobile phones. The web interface of the service is provided over the Internet of via kiosks. Trip computation is provided by back office. The results of the computation are provided to travelers by means of the short message service (SMS). The on-trip assistance is triggered by the validation of the electronic ticket. The One Bus Away system provides real-time departure information only about nearby stops (it does not take into account the entire trip).

4.4.1.5 Congestion Pricing

Congestion pricing allows surcharging of users of private vehicles in periods of peak demand. The charges are related to the negative external costs (impact on the environment and congestion) that each vehicle creates, and hence can easily be justified on equity grounds. Congestion pricing reduces traffic congestion consumers have incentives to prioritize trips, that is, avoid marginal value trips or to switch to other modes of transport. Cost-based fees (basis for congestion pricing) have high transaction costs. However, the arrival of wireless communications technologies allows implementing charging schemes, according to which consumers bear the costs they individually impose. Efficient congestion pricing assumes that "charges should reflect as closely as possible the marginal social cost of each trip in terms of the impacts on others" and "charges should vary smoothly over time."

4.4.2 TRAFFIC MANAGEMENT SERVICES

Dynamic changes in traffic lights schedules (e.g., due to priority at lights received by buses) or traffic incidents change the optimal behavior of vehicles (i.e., selection of the optimal speed and route). Vehicles should regularly reevaluate and adapt their driving strategies using the available traffic information. Services described later have the following objectives: (1) to optimize traffic flows in a distributed, infrastructureless way, (2) to provide vehicles with a green light speed advisory system allowing them to adapt speeds to traffic lights and road conditions.

4.4.2.1 Collaborative Routing in Nonrecurring Congestion

Collection, storage, and exchange of traffic information is only the first step in improving traffic efficiency. For instance, in case of sudden traffic breakdowns, informed drivers will most likely make the same routing decisions to typically select the route with the shortest traveling time, which can spawn new traffic congestion. This is referred to as flash crowd effect (FCE) or "similar advice" problem. Although CTISs proposed in the literature provide vehicles with real-time traffic information, they do not consider how routing choices are made by the vehicles.

Hence, they do not address the FCE. One of the challenging issues in the FCE is the conflict between "user" and "system optimality" in individual route selection. The question of optimality is related to the problem of prediction of traffic patterns, commonly addressed using network traffic equilibrium models (similar to the Nash equilibrium in game theory). Wardrop's first principle of equilibrium refers to "user optimality" according to which each vehicle selects its best route. Hence in "user equilibrium" (UE) flows, all routes have an equal journey time. The consequence of such a routing is that the average traveling time might be far from the optimal one. It is the logic of the situation absence of traffic regulation by some central authority and self-regarding users that traps them in the inefficient outcome (social dilemma). System (or social) optimum (SO) flows (described by Wardrop's second principle) assume that vehicles choose routes in order to maximize the efficiency of the whole road system. However, due to self-regarding preferences of users, reaching system optimum even if vehicles are provided with traffic information, in-vehicle navigation guidance, and methods for communication with other road users is not feasible, unless additional measures like variable congestion pricing (VCP) are applied. According to VCP, charges are related to the negative external costs of the individual vehicle, and depend on the actual traffic conditions. Nevertheless, due to higher transaction fees comparing to lump-sum payments, deploying VCP is not efficient using current technologies.

The inefficiency of a system with self-regarded users (UE flows vs. SO flows) can be measured by the concept of the Price of Anarchy.

4.4.2.2 Cooperative Traffic Signal Schedule Advisory

A GLOSA system advises drivers with the optimal speed they should maintain when approaching a signalized intersection. Access to traffic light schedules was recognized by US and European transport agencies. The integration of short-range antennas into traffic lights is foreseen in the future. Until recently, only costly, infrastructure-based systems (roadside message signs wired to traffic lights) were proposed. The authors propose a cooperative approach for collection and dissemination of information about traffic lights schedules using smartphones mounted on car dashboards. The information is derived from the images captured by the phone cameras. System participants collectively derive timing of traffic lights. Infrastructureless exchange of the information between devices is performed using wireless ad hoc communication (IEEE .g). In a GLOSA system tested in Berlin by Audi, vehicles receive information about signal schedules from a central server using cellular networks. In the future, schedule information will most likely be available via cooperative traffic information systems based on VANETs. In such systems traffic-related information is collected individually by vehicles and exchanged among them using wireless networks. Two communication patterns in VANETs are suitable for a GLOSA system: V2V communication between nearby vehicles, and V2I communication between vehicles and roadway infrastructure. Traffic lights equipped with wireless communications technology will be able to transmit signal phasing and timing (SPaT) data to vehicles. Several projects have already investigated the use of V2V and V2I communication for GLOSA.

The top-down overview of the problem and potential solutions are tackled in the MobiTraff project. The services aiming at reaching mobility and traffic efficiency objectives given in the previous sections are highly dependent. For instance, dynamic prioritization of public transportation (e.g., changes in traffic lights schedules) will modify traffic flows. This will have an influence on speed advisory and personalized navigation services. Therefore, it is a correlated optimization process. Public transport receives prioritized treatment, which optimizes its performance. This implies that the optimal behavior of vehicles and passengers might have changed. Thus they should recalculate the driving strategies. The literature, for example, acknowledged behavioral complexities of system users (drivers and bus passengers) as a factor that should influence traffic assignment methods. However, the availability of VANET-based information combined with an advisory system allows shifting from descriptive to prescriptive services.

4.4.2.3 Joint Architecture for Mobility and Traffic Objectives

Cooperative traffic and mobility management system: The services covering the defined objectives can rely on BUS-ITS. It extends the emerging concept of CTIS with new types of information and services. In particular, BUS-ITS is responsible for collection, storage, and dissemination of information regarding traffic conditions, public transport, and Spat data. Each bus stores the information in its knowledge base (KB). In addition, buses provide traffic- and mobility-related services. A city is divided into zones, while zones are further divided into road segments. The main actors of the system, public buses, are used as "information ferries" serving as an information hub. Since the buses belong to the same authority, they are used to guarantee security and privacy by provided services. The second actor is all remaining vehicles (belonging to different authorities), which are used as traffic sensors and message relaxers. The third actor is passengers with pre- and on-trip phases, who communicate with the system to obtain personalized navigation services and to register bus-stop demands. The fourth actor is traffic lights.

All actors are assumed to be equipped with wireless communication capabilities. Within each zone traffic information is collected and exchanged between all vehicles using V2V communication. Between segments, the information is exchanged only between buses using long-range communication links.

4.4.2.4 IP Mobility Management for Vehicular Communication Networks: Challenges and Solutions

The emergence of new applications designed for vehicular environments has triggered an interest in conducting research on VCN. These applications were initially designed for safety-oriented communications, but the role of infotainment applications has rapidly taken an important place. One example of applications on the safety-oriented side is the notification of emergency situations (e.g., car accidents or bad weather conditions). On the other hand, examples of infotainment applications go from using V2I communications for driver assistance services or for traditional Internet-based applications (e.g., up-to-the-minute traffic reports, assisted parking, and the download of music and video files), to using V2V communications for distributed games that are played among passengers in neighboring vehicles. Although the primary objective of VCN is to increase safety for drivers and passengers in vehicular scenarios, the infotainment applications are likely to generate a faster adoption of the required equipment and supporting infrastructure. Therefore, it is very critical to guarantee seamless, reliable, and ubiquitous communications that provide a satisfactory user experience to the early adopters. As a result, it becomes necessary to have protocols that facilitate not only the intelligent and secure flooding of information, but also the mobility management of mobile networks such as buses, trains, or cars providing connection to their passengers. VCN is constituted of in-car (on-board units; OBU) and on-road (roadside units; RSU) devices with communications, positioning, and computing capabilities. Both the OBU and the RSU incorporate the stack of protocols defined for vehicular communications.

The stacks proposed by various standard development organizations include a special set of protocols to handle safety and emergency communications while they include a parallel stack to handle IP-based applications. In this way, general IpV6 traffic and Internet-based applications are also supported in the VCN. In addition to the inclusion of IpV6, the IP mobility has been suggested to be managed by the IETF standards: Mobile IpV6 (Map) and NEMO BS. NEMO BS is meant to provide continuous network connectivity to a group of nodes that are moving together, that is, a mobile network. The mobile network is managed by a MR that provides connection to the group of nodes [the mobile network nodes (MNN)]. Similar to Map, NEMO BS uses the concept of a fixed IpV6 prefix [the mobile network prefix (MNP)] to provide global reachability to the mobile network. When the MR connects to an AR in a visited network, it acquires a topologically valid IP address [care of address (CoA)], followed by a registration of this CoA with the HA. Then, the HA creates an entry that directs the traffic destined to the mobile network to be routed to the newly assigned CoA. In this way, NEMO BS establishes a bidirectional tunnel between the MR and the HA, which is used every time a MNN communicates with any Correspondent Node (CN). Although NEMO BS seems to fit well in the context of terrestrial transport systems, it has not been designed to support the dynamics and special characteristics of VCN.

The current version of NEMO BS, as defined in the standard, does not incorporate a route optimization (RO) mechanism, as its counterpart Map does, and that affects its performance in vehicular scenarios. In addition, vehicles roaming along heterogeneous access networks (i.e., IEEE. p, Imax, Wi-Fi, G/LTE), as well as multihued vehicles connecting simultaneously to more than one access network, pose additional challenges to the IP mobility management. Therefore, in this chapter we examine the specific requirements of VCN in terms of IP mobility, survey, and evaluate the existing approaches to improve the performance of NEMO BS by means of RO mechanisms in vehicular scenarios, and outline the emerging challenges. Other surveys in RO for NEMO BS exist, but to the best of our knowledge, none of them focuses on vehicular scenarios.

4.4.3 OVERVIEW OF THE IP MOBILITY IN VCN

In vehicular scenarios, similar to any IP-based scenario that involves mobile networks, a mechanism is required to handle the change of point of attachment to the IP network. With this mechanism, session continuity is provided and the changes are transparent to end-users. However, the special characteristics in VCN create unique requirements for IP mobility mechanisms. Some characteristics are high velocities, nonrestricted power, and processing resources (as opposed to regular MANET), extended area of coverage (citywide, countrywide, and worldwide), and heterogeneous access networks (e.g., coverage may be provided by G/LTE, IMAX, or Wi-Fi, with some or all of them constituting different administrative domains). Moreover, the combination of MNs (e.g., passengers' mobile devices) and MRs, with independent stacks of protocols and IP mobility mechanisms, and with ability to communicate in ad hoc or infrastructure-based fashion, makes the IP mobility in VCN a challenging task. NEMO BS, on the other hand, is a potential candidate for providing IP mobility in VCN. However, it is designed to use the tunnel MR-HA every time a MNN communicates with any CN. This can affect the performance of certain applications, especially delay-sensitive ones such as voice-over IP, due to the added delay when the two peers use a nondirect path. The suboptimality of the protocol appears when the distance between CN-MR is smaller than the distance MR-HA. An example is a NEMO-enabled VCN.

For instance, when MNN communicates with CN, the data packets are transmitted first to HA MR and HA MR, instead of going directly through the path MR-AR-MR-CN. The problems of NEMO BS are fully documented in RFC. However, an optimized version is not yet standardized. The optimization of NEMO BS is currently addressed by the IETF working group Mobility Extensions for IpV6 (MEXT WG), which evaluates RO mechanisms for different contexts of application. In general, an IP mobility mechanism should meet the following requirements.

- Reduced transmission power at end devices: The end devices' proximity to the MR allows them to use less power-consuming interfaces, reduced handover events.
- The MR should hide the changes of the attachment point from the group of MNNs, that is, reduced complexity.
- The MNNs should not be required to run their own IP mobility protocol. In this way, the complexity of end devices can be reduced, and finally, reduced bandwidth consumption.
- The MR should cluster the signaling required to keep the nodes globally reachable, therefore consuming less bandwidth resources.
- Even map-enabled nodes should benefit from the stable CoA configured from the MNP. On the other hand, regardless of the adopted technique to provide RO for the IP mobility mechanism, the technique should efficiently utilize the network resources and improve the network performance, that is, end-to-end delay, susceptibility to link failures, and data efficiency (overhead/payload relation). In the particular case of vehicular scenarios, an additional set of requirements to be addressed by NEMO BS and the RO technique are summarized as follows
- Minimum signaling: The RO technique must carry the least possible amount of signaling messages.
- Reparability: The MR must determine if the RO strategy is enabled in a per-flow basis and according to predefined policies. Any information about the CN's location could be relevant to define such policies
- Security: There must be mechanisms to validate the MNP and Coast ownership claimed by the MR that sends the binding update (BU).
- Binding privacy protection: The content of BU (Coast, MNP) must only be revealed to the entities involved in the tunnel establishment.
- Multihoming: The MR must be able to simultaneously connect available egress interfaces to multiple access networks.
- Switching HA: The MR must be able to switch its registration to the closest HA (when available). This is very important given the aforementioned areas of coverage that are possible in vehicular networks.

Furthermore, a vehicle's OBU is likely to have more than one network interface, which means it is able to connect to more than one access network at the same time, as well as to switch between different technologies in order to achieve seamless communications. This heterogeneous nature at the infrastructure side of the VCN pose additional challenges to the IP mobility management mechanism. On one hand, there is still a lack of full integration between IP-based and cellular networks, in terms of the entities and signaling employed to provide IP mobility. For example, in traditional G networks, a proprietary protocol named GTP is used as part of the IP mobility. In the case of LTE network architecture, there has been efforts to adopt Internet standards in order to comply with the concept of all-IP networks; however, the gap between the protocol elements defined by LTE and the entities defined by Map/NEMO BS has not yet been resolved. On the other hand, for a vehicle roaming at high speeds along dissimilar radio access technologies, the vehicular scenario imposes stricter requirements on the handover latency, especially for fleeting network connectivity such as that offered by Wi-Fi access. In the following section, we classify the suboptimality problems of NEMO BS and the RO techniques proposed to solve them. They are evaluated and compared in the context of vehicular scenarios. We also present a survey about RO solutions for NEMO BS that are dedicated to vehicular scenarios and introduce the ongoing research along the line of IP mobility in heterogeneous vehicular access networks.

4.4.3.1 Mobility Management for Vehicular Ad Hoc Networks

With the availability of DSRC (dedicated short-range communication) technology, multichip ad hoc networks will become a key technology in vehicular environments.

In VANETs, vehicles are able to communicate locally without relying on any infrastructure or base stations controlling medium access. An example is the Fleet Net communication system, a radio communication technology based on UTRA TDD for ad hoc networking between vehicles. In order to achieve multichip communication, the forwarding of data to the targeted vehicle in VANETs typically uses a location-based ad hoc routing protocol instead of IP addresses. VANETs are very important for the development of vehicular-centered applications such as floating car data where vehicles generate and collect local information, distribute this information locally and consume local information received from neighboring vehicles. These applications are not necessarily limited to intervehicle communication. In VANETs, Internet gateways (IGWs) installed at the roadside can provide temporary Internet access, which opens up the Internet for the VANET and vice versa. This communication scenario is illustrated in Fig. 4.5, where an IGW provides Internet access for the passing vehicles organized in a VANET. This way, vehicular applications can also consider information from the global Internet.

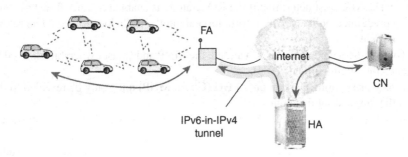

FIGURE 4.5 MMIP Architecture

An example could be information about the current road and weather conditions along the trip, which can be used for an optimal route guidance. However, the Internet access requires a respective mobility management to handle the mobility of the vehicles on the Internet. It therefore has to ensure that the requested data from the Internet is always delivered via an appropriate IGW to the vehicle. Vice versa, the vehicles must be able to discover the IGWs within the VANET even when they are multiple hops away.

This work proposes MMIP, a highly optimized mobility management protocol for VANETs. The following section specifies the requirements for the mobility management of VANETs and gives an overview of related work for the mobility management of multichip ad hoc networks. Section introduces MMIP, which is evaluated in section. MMIP In order to handle the mobility of vehicles, we developed a mobility management protocol called MMIP. MMIP is based on the principles of Mobile IpV6, but was designed to support IpV6-based MNs organized in ad hoc networks. In contrast to related approaches, MMIP was developed with respect to VANETs, that is, the protocol mechanisms take into account the requirements for the mobility management of VANETs described in the previous section.

4.4.3.2 Protocol Overview

Like Mobile IpV6, MMIP uses an agent-based system with a HA representing a vehicle in the home network (Fig. 4.5). However, MMIP is completely different in the basic concept, the addressing, and the protocol mechanisms being deployed. MMIP reintroduces FAs, such as in Mobile IpV6, which are located at the IGWs.

The FA represent the vehicle located in the VANET; this way, it hides the multichip capability of the VANET and the vehicles appear as "common" MNs. A very important feature is that MMIP relies on globally routable and permanent IpV6 addresses to identify the vehicles. With the use of FAs, all vehicles participating in the VANET form one logical Ipv6 subnet, where the IGWs act as transition points between the VANET and the Internet. The IPv6 addresses can be assigned statically to each vehicle, that is, they are preconfigured in the communication hardware shipped with the vehicles. In contrast to Mobile IpV6, a vehicle does not receive a valid IpV6 care-of address when entering a foreign network. MMIP avoids link-local addresses when a vehicle is located in a foreign network. This supersedes the automatic (stateless or stately) address configuration of IpV6, which conserves bandwidth in the VANET. Communication in this scenario works as follows: If a correspondent node (CN) in the Internet wants to send IP packets to a vehicle v, it always transmits them to the v's home IpV6 address. This way, IP packets are routed via the Internet to the home network of v.

- The HA in the home network accepts the IP packets on behalf of v and tunnels them to the FA that v is currently registered with. Therefore, MMIP uses IpV6-in-IpV6 tunneling as the Internet is still based on IpV6 technology.
- The FA on the IGW unpacks the encapsulated packets and forwards them to v using the VANET routing protocol. Conversely, a vehicle that wants to send IP packets to a CN in the Internet first transmits them to the FA. Then, the FA tunnels the IP packets back to the HA, which itself unpacks the IP packets and routes them through the Internet to the CN. In MMIP, the VANET routing protocol has to determine the delivery of data. If the receiver is a vehicle or located in the VANET and can be reached via multichip communication, the VANET routing protocol has to deliver the IP packets locally. Otherwise, the data will be delivered to the FA that the sending vehicle vs. is currently registered. This decision process comprises two aspects: As the VANET forms one logical IpV6 subnet, it can be determined in a first step whether or not the receiver

is a vehicle within the VANET or whether it is a CN in the Internet by comparing the subnets addressed. And second aspect optimizes communication in case or its addressed cannot be reached with multichip communications.

In this situation, the location-based ad hoc routing protocol cannot resolve the position of vs resulting in the following communication path: Vehicle vs delivers the IP packets to its FA, denoted as FA (vs), which tunnels the data back to HA (vs). As the global IpV6 address of each vehicle belongs to a home network on the Internet, HA (vs) forwards the data to HA (vr) of the targeted vehicle vr. In turn, HA (vr) tunnels the data to FA (vr), the FA vr is currently registered with. Finally, FA (vr) forwards the data to or over the VANET. In order to handle the interoperability with the IPv6-based Internet, MMIP is integrated into a proxy-based communication architecture. This way, an IPv6-based vehicle is able to access IPv6-based CNs on the Internet.

The FA discovery in MMIP is based on a proactive service discovery protocol optimized for large-scale multichip VANETs. The key concept of this service discovery protocol is that FAs do not wait for solicitation messages from vehicles requiring Internet access. Instead, they announce their service periodically. In order to avoid a flooding of the overall ad hoc network, the service announcements are restricted locally to the so-called service area. This can be achieved, for example, by a hop-limited broadcast or by specifying a recast region using the recast capabilities of VANET routing protocols. Vehicles looking for an FA assume a passive role, that is, they do not discover the FAs actively. Our discovery protocol also supports the selection of the most suitable IGW if several IGWs are available simultaneously.

Therefore, we implemented a fuzzy-based approach, which considers available information about the gateways. When a vehicle v moves into the service area of a new IGW the situation is depicted. In the first step, v receives the service announcements of the FA and may decide to handoff. In this case, it initiates the registration procedure, where v registers itself through the new FA with its HA. The registration procedure is based on two messages, a registration request and a registration reply. After receiving a service announcement from the IGW in step, v sends a registration request to the FA to initiate the registration (step). The FA processes this request, updates its internal visitor list, and relays the registration request to the HA of the vehicle (step). The HA also processes the registration request by updating its mobility bindings and responds with a registration reply message to the FA to grant or to deny the request (step). Finally, the FA processes the reply message and relays it to the vehicle (step). The registration procedure is similar to the one specified for Mobile IpV6, but requires modified message formats and at different processing in FAs and HAs. Similar to the original Mobile IpV6, registrations have a lifetime in MMIP, which is specified in the registration request. Before this time expires, the vehicle has to renew its registration with the FA.

MMIP dynamically determines the lifetime by estimating the time a vehicle travels through the service area of an IGW. In order to avoid vulnerabilities by nonauthorized vehicles, registration requests and registration replies can be authenticated. Therefore, each vehicle, FA, and HA support a mobility security association similar to the concept specified for Mobile IpV6.

4.4.3.3 Modeling the Impact of Mobility on the Connectivity of Vehicular Networks in Large-Scale Urban Environment

Urban VANETs are recognized as a significant component of the future ITS. Valuable information can be exchanged through the VANETs to ensure driving safety and traffic efficiency, as well as to promote new mobile services, such as content sharing applications (e.g., advertisements, entertainments) to the public. Emerging vehicular applications range from emails and voice messages to emergency operations, such as responses to natural disaster and terrorist attack, and so forth. Equipped with wireless communication devices, vehicles can transfer data with each other or with fixed roadside infrastructure. Because vehicles typically depend on multihop communication paths to transfer data in a VANET, the connectivity of the network is of great importance in determining the network's achievable capacity, and mobility is one of the most important factors that influence the network connectivity.

More specifically, the dynamic network topologies caused by the mobility of vehicles impose challenging radio propagation environments. By exploring the relationship between connectivity and mobility of networks, we can better understand the characteristics of spontaneous vehicular networks. This in turn will enable us to design better VANETs in order to achieve reliable and low-latency communications. Consequently, there have been continuous investigations recently to study vehicular mobility characteristics from various perspectives, and different mobility models have been proposed. For example, on one hand, the studies consider the problem in microscopic dimension by describing the acceleration or deceleration behavior of each individual vehicle. On the other hand, the work focuses on macroscopic description modeling by considering the vehicles as a traffic flow instead of distinct entities. Based on these works, some conclusions have been drawn about the effects of diverse microscopic and/or macroscopic parameters. Additionally, the studies analyze the problem under different road assumptions, ranging from highway environments to urban environments. Furthermore, a new concept of network topology has been introduced to study the mobility characteristics in VANETs. With the concept of network topology, researchers can analyze the mobility characteristics of a vehicular network from a network perspective.

For example, the empirical studies have investigated the instantaneous topology of a large-scale urban vehicular network. More specifically, Nabulus et al. have studied the availability, connectivity, and reliability of urban vehicular networks. Due to the lack of real-world vehicular mobility datasets, however, the study is conducted based on a synthetic vehicular dataset, which is far from a real-world situation and cannot reflect the real vehicular behaviors in urban scenarios, leading to a potentially inaccurate analysis. Lou et al. present the characteristics of Shanghai trace, which involves taxis, in their study, and they use this real-world vehicular dataset in simulation to discuss the connectivity and network performance, including link duration, average hops, and connection rates. They find that more than 70% taxis can be integrated into a single ad hoc network in certain time periods if communication range is over 200 m, which can provide a good network performance. The metrics selected in their study benefit the network analysis but this study only describes the key mobility characteristics rather than discovering which underlying factors can affect them.

Currently, we still lack quantitative and fundamental understanding of the connectivity and how other key factors can influence it in a large-scale urban scenario. This is despite the fact that there exist many studies investigating the potential impacting factors of the connectivity, including factors such as topology, traffic signals, and vehicle traffic, For example, Mafia et al. focus on stop-and-go behavior of traffic to study how it can cause network congestion and affect the connectivity. Artily et al. investigate connectivity in VANETs and examine how the relative velocity as well as the number of lanes impact on the connectivity. However, among various potential factors that influence the connectivity, mobility is of great importance. Some studies do aim to explore the relationship between connectivity and mobility. However, all these works either study this relationship in general wireless network or analyze the problem in a theoretical way, thus there still exists no study that reveals the fundamental relationship between mobility and connectivity in large-scale urban vehicular networks. In this contribution, we employ the real-world mobility traces from taxis recorded for over 1 month in Shanghai for analysis. Compared to the studies based on synthetic traces or analytical tools, this brings great advantages because the large-scale real-world vehicular motions recorded in these traces can reflect the real situations in large-scale urban environments to a greater degree. Moreover, to the best of our knowledge, there is no existing work studying how the mobility of a vehicular network impacts its connectivity, as measured by the topology metric known as component size, based on real experiments. Thus we are the first to unveil the fundamental relationship between mobility and topology of large-scale urban vehicular networks. We emphasize that the connectivity can be studied based on some fundamental topology characteristics, in particular, a key metric referred to as component size.

A larger component size indicates that more vehicles are connected together successfully with multihop communication, and the connectivity is therefore better. Moreover, the connectivity can be judged by the number of vehicles linked to a certain vehicle. Thus for the sake of clarity, we consider the connectivity of a large-scale urban vehicular network in the view of network topology characteristics and we endeavor to reveal the relationship between the mobility and topology. In this way, we discover that when the component speed is larger than a threshold, which is between and 200 m/s in our study, there is a power law relationship between the component speed and the corresponding component size, while when the component speed is smaller than this threshold, the relationship between the component size and speed changes into a uniform distribution. This dichotomy in the relationship of component size and speed indicates that mobility destroys the connectivity when speed is larger than a threshold, and otherwise it has no apparent influence on the connectivity.

4.5 VEHICULAR-DELAY TOLERANT NETWORK

Wireless networks have evolved at a very fast rate and are applicable to several contexts and different communication solutions. In the automobile industry, many wireless solutions have been proposed to improve safety-related and data communication between vehicles and between vehicles and infrastructure. These proposals form the ITS field, which aims to improve the efficiency and security of transportation using vehicular networks (VNs). Although, VNs make use of VANETs for V2V communication, the concept of VN expands VANETs by adding V2I as well as cellular communication. Sometimes, VANETs are considered a subset of MANETs. However, the high speed of the nodes in a VANET, and the presence of obstacles like buildings, produce a highly variable network topology, as well as more frequent partitions in the network. Therefore, typical MANET protocols do not adapt very well to VANETs since a complete connected path between sender and receiver is usually missing. Under these conditions, delay-tolerant networks (DTNs) are an alternative able to deal with VANET characteristics, and are applicable to VN for ITS. DTNs originated as a proposal for interplanetary networks (IPNs) to provide communication between satellites and base stations. DTNs allow information to be shared between nodes even in the presence of high delays, which are typical in spatial communications.

In DTNs, when a message cannot be routed to its destination, it is not immediately dropped but is instead stored and carried until a new route becomes available. Messages are removed from the buffer when their lifetime expires or for buffer management reasons. This mechanism cannot be applied only to IPNs but also to VNs, taking advantage of their high degrees of mobility. DTNs have been standardized by the Delay-Tolerant Network Research Group (DTNRG) to ensure network interoperability. The research community has been very active over recent years, proposing new protocols and applications for Vehicular Delay Tolerant Networks (VDTNs). This diversity may overwhelm the inexperienced researcher. Our aim in this survey is to provide the reader with a broad view of the different proposals for VDTNs. We classify them according to their main routing metric, showing their relationships and evolution. We also present the applications where VDTNs can be applied, and evaluate the suitability of different protocols for each application. There have been other works to survey DTN routing proposals and opportunistic routing for VNs but, as far as we know, this is the first survey to specifically focus on VDTNs and how Opportunistic DTN protocols have evolved into VDTN protocols. Before VDTN became a hot research topic, the researchers developed a framework to classify DTN routing algorithms and protocols. Their framework described routing protocols based on (1) routing objective, (2) proactive routing versus reactive routing, (3) source routing versus per-hop routing, and (4) message splitting. To classify routing algorithms they defined several knowledge oracles, called Contacts Summary Oracle, Contacts Oracle, Queuing Oracle, and Traffic Demand Oracle, which gradually increase the knowledge available at the nodes. Based on the knowledge of the nodes they mathematically formulated the DTN routing problem as several resource management problems and proposed mathematical algorithms to solve them. A survey of the most representative DTN protocols for MANETs is briefly discussed.

They distinguished between (1) deterministic routing, (2) epidemic and random routing, (3) link forwarding probability estimation, and (4) the model-based approach. Most of the modern routing VDTN protocols we survey in this work may have been included in the last category. They also included "node movement control-based" algorithms, which allow the routing protocol to control the movement of certain nodes, and "network coding" methods. The earlier types of algorithm clearly do not apply to vehicular networks where vehicles move freely. In a more recent work, the authors presented a survey on VANET routing protocols that included a small section devoted to DTN protocols. This section was insufficient and summarized only some of the characteristics of VAAD and Gepps. An extensive survey of DTN architectures, analyzing the bundle protocols and its advantages and disadvantages is discussed.

They did not classify DTN routing protocols, but instead presented some mechanisms generally applicable to any DTN routing protocol and listed several protocols that use them. Their work provides a broad view of the DTN routing problem, without considering the special characteristics of VDTNs. Position-based routing surveys have been previously published. Although some works referred to in this work match the definition of "position-based routing," our analysis focuses on the DTN characteristics of the protocol, while previous papers focused mainly on their pure geographic characteristics. The authors performed an analysis of certain DTN routing protocols in vehicular networks. We consider the scope of their work to be limited, as they consider only a dozen protocols while in this survey we consider different contributions. More recently, a detailed DTN survey with more than mutiple referred papers focused only on opportunistic DTN protocols and, therefore, they did not cover most of the protocols we analyze in this survey. Their classification of DTN routing protocols was one of the bases of this work and we encourage the reader to read their chapter in order to obtain a broader perspective of the DTN routing protocols universe. As far as we know, this is the first survey to have focused on VDTNs and their applications. Moreover, this survey is not limited to protocol descriptions: focusing on reproducibility and repeatability of experiments, we include a review of the evaluation methods used by VDTN researchers.

4.5.1 ARCHITECTURE AND STANDARDS TO SUPPORT THE HETEROGENEITY OF DIFFERENT NETWORKS

The DTN architecture is designed to run as an overlay network over the network layer (IP in the case of the Internet). To do so, two new layers are added: The bundle layer, and the convergence layer. The bundle layer encapsulates application data units into bundles, which are then forwarded by DTN nodes following the bundle protocol. The convergence layer abstracts the characteristics of the lower layers to the bundle layer. The convergence layer does not need to run over the Internet protocol stack, thus allowing for the implementation of DTNs over any type of network.

4.5.2 THE BUNDLE PROTOCOL

The bundle protocol stores and forwards bundles between DTN nodes. Instead of end-to-end forwarding, the bundle protocol performs hop-by-hop forwarding. To deal with network disruption, the bundle protocol can store bundles in permanent storage devices until a new transmission opportunity appears. The concept of reliable custody transfer ensures that a DTN node will not remove a bundle from its buffer until another node has taken custody of it. The bundle protocol operation depends on contacts. A contact occurs when a connection between two DTN nodes can be established.

The contact type depends on the type of operating network: it may be deterministic, as in interplanetary networks, opportunistic, as in VN, or persistent, as in the Internet. Where the size of a bundle exceeds the maximum transferred data of contacts, the bundle protocol must perform fragmentation. Fragmentation is supported in two different schemes: proactive, where a DTN node may fragment an application message into different bundles and forwards every bundle independently, and reactive, where bundles are fragmented during transmissions between nodes.

4.5.3 VDTN PROTOCOLS FOR VANETS: TAXONOMY

In this section, DTN protocols are classified according to different parameters. First, they must be grouped together according to the objective of the protocol: (1) protocols whose objective are to disseminate messages to all the nodes in the network (dissemination) and (2) protocols whose messages have a specific destination that can either be a vehicle or a roadside unit (RSU) (unicast). Second, they are grouped together according to the amount of control information required by each protocol. Inside the dissemination protocols group, we distinguish between the epidemic approach and a group of protocols that uses geographic information to estimate connectivity of nodes (geoconnectivity). Inside the unicast group, we distinguish between zero knowledge protocols, those that do not require any knowledge about the vehicles status or the environment, and utility-based protocols.

Utility-based protocols try to estimate the benefit of each transmission (i.e., how a transmission improves the probability of reaching the destination) to determine the best forwarding node among neighbors. Each protocol estimates this utility using a predefined metric. We have divided these utility-based proposals into five different categories, according to the type of knowledge they need: (1) contact history and social relationships, (2) geographic location, (3) road map, (4) hybrid protocols, and (5) online protocols. The "online" subcategory includes protocols that, besides combining several simpler protocols, require information on the current state of the road network or use sophisticated metrics that do not fit into any other category. Fig. 4.6 summarizes this classification. For each category, we first list the different protocols forming part of it before describing those protocols and, finally, explaining their advantages and disadvantages.

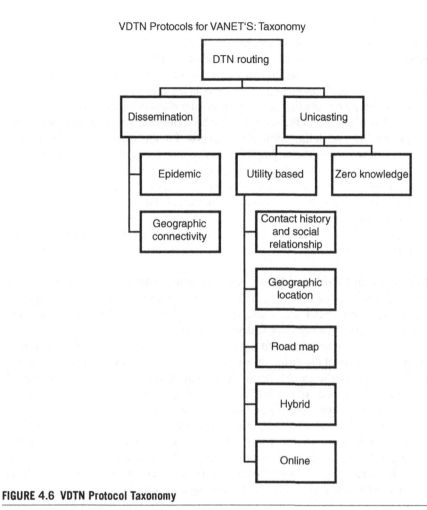

FIGURE 4.6 VDTN Protocol Taxonomy

4.5.3.1 A Formal Model of Human Driving Behavior in Vehicular Networks

The dissemination of traffic information between vehicles provides multiple benefits in terms of road safety and traffic efficiency.

VANETs were then investigated by the research community as an enabling technology for ITS, which allows nearby vehicles to exchange information with each other and with roadside equipment. They can enable a wide range of applications, from road safety (collision avoidance, dangerous road surface), traffic management (intelligent traffic flow control, lane merging assistance, and traffic light optimal scheduling), to comfort and infotainment (Internet access, instant messaging, parking spot locator, visibility enhancer, route guidance). Although the amount of information disseminated through a VANET provides a great opportunity to enhance traffic safety, a study of the behavior of a human driver toward this information remains an important axis to ensure safer roads. To understand the behavior of drivers, researchers propose the use of driving behavior models. These models are of great importance and are expected to support the development of a new generation of assistance systems that offer an adaptive assistance to drivers, hence, allowing the emergence of driver's adapted vehicles. Researches on driving behavior have led to the appearance of a huge variety of models.

These models have different purposes, and differ in terms of strategies and approaches used to capture the driving behavior. Most of the modeling approaches in the literature try to analyze the behavior of drivers to create prototype models that allow them to later classify and identify an observed driving behavior. Other models like those in focus on specific behaviors and propose applications for a driving assistance. A probabilistic modeling approach is proposed in the article, where the authors use a simple Bayesian network to predict the driving behavior in the near future. A recent approach to modeling presented in users concepts from behavioral psychology. The authors consider driving behavior as a result of an optimization process. They formalize their idea within a formal framework of hybrid automata and introduce a theoretical variable to represent the consequences of possible behavior. Although the authors use hybrid automata to model and predict qualitatively distinct driving maneuvers, they do not consider a decision process. The goal of their model is to find an optimal driving trajectory for a given situation. Only a few researchers have investigated the driving behavior in VANET.

A context-aware driver system for driver behavior detection using VANET is proposed were the system combines contextual information about the driver, vehicle and environment. Four types of driver behavior were deduced: normal behavior, drunk, reckless, and fatigued. The system warns the driver and other vehicles when abnormal behavior is detected. In this paper, we try to fill the lack of approaches that address human driving behavior in the context of VANET by proposing a new adaptive modeling method that takes into account the different real-time information and warnings that a driver receives while driving. The idea of our work consists of the construction of a driving behavior model for every driver based on his or her past driving behavior. The main contribution of this work is to define and describe a formal framework for capturing and modeling driving behavior. The framework is described using the formalism of rectangular hybrid I/O automata (RHIOA) with urgent transitions. To gather and encode driving behavior within the proposed model, we propose an approach based on the theory of learning automata (LA). We believe that the proposed model may be important to explain and predict driver behavior in the future, thus being able to prevent unsafe situations. Its use may enable an adaptive and personalized assistance to drivers in different driving contexts.

4.6 FORMAL MODEL OF HUMAN DRIVING BEHAVIOR

Modeling individual human driving behavior plays an important role in the process of development of personalized assistance systems. However, to understand driving behavior, it is important to examine all the components and elements that come into play. Even though the driver is the main actor in driving, the environment in which the driver is moving and the driven vehicle both play important roles in the determination of driving behavior. Driver, vehicle, the environment and their interactions are referred to as the DVE system. This work describes a framework for a driver-centered modeling of driving behavior. In the proposed approach, we try to model the observed driving behavior of an individual driver. The model captures the signals received from the external environment (e.g., traffic signs, collision warnings, traffic information), the signals received from the vehicle (e.g., played music, phone call) and the driving actions performed by the driver. Fig. 4.7 represents the overall framework of

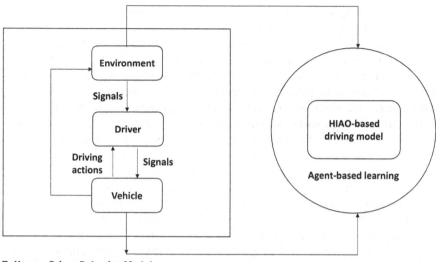

FIGURE 4.7 Human Driver Behavior Model

our approach. The approach that this work relies on combines two well-known modeling formalisms: hybrid input output automata and rectangular hybrid automata.

Hybrid IO automaton (HIOA) is a formal model used to describe discrete and continuous behavior of a system. It is a kind of finite state machine with a set of continuous variables. HIOA has been widely used to describe and analyze different examples of hybrid transportation systems, such as automotive control systems, automated transportation systems, and intelligent vehicle highway systems. Rectangular automata are an important subclass of hybrid automata that was proposed to deal with decidability questions about hybrid automata. Their advantage consists of providing a better analysis of hybrid systems. Our formal model consists of an adaptation of hybrid IO automata and rectangular automata with urgent transitions. Hybrid I/O automata allows us to differentiate input and output actions, while rectangular hybrid automata allows us to define rectangular inequalities over variables. And, we express urgency using the concept of urgent transitions. Urgent transitions are the transitions that occur as soon as their guard becomes true, without any delay.

4.6.1 V2V GEONETWORKING USING WIRELESS SENSOR NETWORKS

Geographic addressing and routing is a networking mechanism that distributes the information to nodes within a physical designated destination area. Traditionally, in WSN technology, geonetworking and geocasting protocols are focused on a static physical infrastructure of the network, with a minimum mobility. However, in wireless communications applied to transport, the mobility is a mandatory feature that is gaining acceptance in most ITS communication architectures. It is based on a combination of routing protocols and GPS positioning that allows optimal information dissemination from a transmitter over multiple hops to every receiver located in the destination area. Each geonetworking node maintains a neighbor location table containing a time-stamped address, position, and speed for ITS stations (nodes) in its vicinity. geonetworking forwarding algorithms use this neighbor location table to make forwarding decisions.

This paradigm is very appropriate for supporting vehicular communications since each vehicle can act as a network node that moves in the geographical space and needs to interact with other vehicles in order to support every kind of ADAS. Each geonetwork node evaluates whether the retransmission of information is required and executes it with proper timing if needed. In this concept, individual node addresses are linked to their geographical position, which is used by forwarding algorithms to transmit data packets toward the destination node. Also, geographical positions are used to define a geographical region that can be linked to nodes, either to address all nodes in the region (geobroadcast) or to address any one of the nodes in a target area (geoanycast). From a safety perspective, vehicular safety applications are expected to rely on communication capabilities for information gathering beyond their immediate environment and line-of-sight vision, and for sharing the necessary safety information. In this context what is relevant is the position of vehicles rather than their identity, as vehicles share their actual positions and anticipated trajectories, coordinate merging maneuvers among sideways neighbors, and instantly notify the vehicle traveling behind of a braking action or warn oncoming traffic of an icy patch.

However, in order to ensure a massive impact of this technology in the vehicle environment, the required standards must be developed so as to guarantee a correct interoperability and performance regardless of the manufacturer. In this way, geonetworking is listed as part of the CALM architecture but is not specified. Therefore, a number of working groups within the European Telecommunications Standards Institute (ETSI) were set up. Thus, the ETSI ITS family standards, which specify the basis for supporting geonetworking in vehicular environments are currently being deployed. Several European research projects, such as CVIS, SeVe-Com, iTETRIS, COMeSafety, COMREACT, or Drive CX include the use of geonetworking in their specifications but are not focused on the communications themselves. They mainly focus on the development of a demonstrator, a set of use cases that assure the feasibility of ADAS: improved GPS systems, creating static sensor networks, emergency services, safe crossings, and the inclusion of the IPv6 protocol in communication standards, and ADAS services supported by vehicular communications. On the other hand, the Genet project was focused on combining IpV6 and geonetworking in a single protocol stack to deliver safety messages among vehicles and to the roadside. Nevertheless, the implementation of this philosophy is presently at an initial stage, where these available developments are based on the IEEE .p, also known as dedicated short-range communication (DSRC) standard, radio modem, Wi-Fi, or cellular. Several pieces of research are being conducted toward the adaptation of IPv6 protocols to support vehicular communications, including geographical routing, but efficient routing algorithms that guarantee network performance and stability are still an open research area.

In fact, some of the proposed solutions have been designed to run offline, their installation in online devices being complex. Thus, in Naumov and Gross an algorithm called CAR is presented that provides a basic position-based routing for VANETs proposed only for simulation, using the connectivity and hop count information as a metric. In, a geonetworking data routing algorithm presented uses the number of hops as a metric to configure the network and a model of infrastructure to estimate connectivity, thereby avoiding beacon transmission. However, this philosophical approach forces us to define specialized network nodes that are in charge of managing its structure, and has been tested only offline in simulation. In fact, due to the limited availability of devices that support geonetworking protocols and the inherent difficulties in developing field trials, the usual testing of protocols and hardware has been carried out through simulations. Thus, the report provides the results of several ITS simulated data using V2V communications. There are also some simulations of massive applications of V2V in large road networks and on specific highways. Finally, the requirements of V2V for tracking neighbors is simulated.

4.6.1.1 *Experimental Equipment*

In order to test the geonetworking algorithms for vehicular communications, two elements must be defined: on the one hand, the chosen communications protocol, and on the other hand, the hardware chosen to support the protocol.

The communication protocol that natively supports mesh communication and includes the modules required to efficiently manage geonetworking. In reference to the communications platform, WSN-supporting hardware uses, GPS positioning and georouting algorithms. Specifically, the network access devices used are Maxfor Inc.'s MTM-CM, based on the TelosB platform. This allows connectivity with any computer platform and acts as a gateway to access the vehicular geonetwork. This device works under the Linux (TinyOS) operating system. In order to access the wireless network at 20 GHz in mesh, it uses the IEEE standard at the physical and link level and a mesh routing protocol, which ensures the desired functionality of the VANET at transmission rates of up to 1000 Kbps in a range of 300 m. The important features of IEEE include real-time suitability by the reservation of guaranteed time slots, collision avoidance through CSMA/CA, and integrated support for secure communications. These devices use the IEEE standard up to the link layer and a novel geonetworking protocol implemented to support the mesh routing. A geonetworking protocol is a network protocol that resides jointly in the Network and Transport layer and is executed in each gateway, specifically in each geogateway. This novel protocol reconfigures the network structure in accordance with the GPS positions of the network nodes. Using this technology the algorithms needed to optimize the message routing in V2V and V2I communications can be developed.

This algorithm can be used as a solution to be applied to other specifically designed vehicular communications technologies when it is available. In the specification of vehicular communications, a requirement for data to be transmitted at a range of between 500 m and 1.5 km, and a normal packet size of bytes. In the case of the system presented the minimum range is from 30 m. This range is not enough to support some kinds of ADAS but is enough to test the behavior of the geonetworking algorithms. The MTM-CM is configured to act as a geonetwork mesh gateway by modifying the internal algorithms and the default protocol stack, connected to a computer, where the data received is saved. Each computer is also connected to a GPS receiver and to the CAN bus of each tested vehicle in order to retrieve the vehicle data in real time. The GPS works in an autonomous mode with a positioning error of 5 m at the most. This error is sufficient to operate the geonetworking for network structure configuration purposes since it is too small to affect the information flow (5 m in a range of 10 m can be considered negligible).

It should be noted that it is possible to acquire speed using the GPS receivers. However, we obtained speed from the vehicle CAN bus when available (Iveco van uses SAEJ) in order to be able to perform the experiments using standard equipment.

4.6.1.2 *Geonetworking Algorithm*

The International Organization for Standardization's (ISO) standard Open System Interconnection (OSI) reference model stack has been modified in order to include the geonetworking functionality by adapting the transport and network levels. The core of the geonetworking is the geocast algorithm in charge of the logical addressing and the route determination that runs at the network level of the ISO model stack. This algorithm can organize the routing in three forwarding schemes: geounicast, where the packets are delivered between two nodes via multiple wireless hops, geobroadcast, where the data packages are distributed by flooding in a determined topographical region, and topologically scored broadcast, where the packets are broadcast to all nodes in an *n*-hop neighborhood from the source.

In our case, the developed algorithm focuses on geounicast communications, and is adapted from the Collection Tree Protocol (CTP) routing algorithm, designed for indoor static mesh networks. The original CTP uses transmission and reception powers to determine the links among network nodes but has the limitation of the impossibility of restricting the data transmission to a limited geographic area. Additionally, it was originally designed for a static network, because there were severe problems for it to run in mobility. These facts have some implications from the point of view of the design implementation of the GCTP, such as defining the beacons, the network update rate, the GPS position, and the time as stamps in every message, and so forth. The data structures of CTP were then reused but the internal algorithm of this protocol has been totally rewritten in order to guarantee geographical addressing, the new protocol being named Geocast Collection Tree Protocol (GCTP).

The aim of this algorithm is to establish the best routing structure for the VANET in a tree architecture, where a node acts as the root and is the destination of every message, ensuring the interconnectivity of every node of the network. The GCTP algorithm uses routing messages (also called beacons) sent by all the network nodes for routing, tree construction, and maintenance, and data messages to report application data between the nodes of the network. The architecture of the mesh network follows a structure of three, where every message from the nodes is routed toward a fixed destination node (root) selected by the user, and uses other nodes as relays in the event of the absence of any direct link. The key to GCTP is the definition of a metric to indicate the "quality" of a node as a potential useful forwarder of a message and use that node to arrive at the node destination in accordance with the potential short way. This metric is the distance expected (DE). We define DE_{ab} as the Manhattan distance in meters between node a and node b. If there is a direct line of sight between node a and node b, there is only one hop in the calculation of the distance and in this case it is named $DEHop_{ab}$.

Thus, this chapter has discussed at length the feasibility of using alternative technologies for vehicular network models, and has also reflected upon different routing mechanisms and principles behind those protocols, while providing a detailed description about mobility management in such vehicular networks. This lays the foundation for cooperative vehicular communication discussed in the next chapter.

COGNITIVE RADIO IN VEHICULAR NETWORK

5

5.1 COGNITIVE RADIO FOR VEHICULAR NETWORKS

The increasing number of vehicles on the road has brought attention to improving road safety as well as in-vehicle entertainment. In tune with this demand, we are witnessing a rise in the development of new applications and services for vehicular environments. Some common examples include applications for collision avoidance, safety and traffic monitoring, multimedia streaming, data collection for smart cities in synergy with wireless sensor networks, vehicle-to-vehicle communication (V2V), and so forth. Consequently, the vehicular ad hoc network (VANET) has emerged as a new technology that can support such emerging vehicular applications. A VANET is defined as a spontaneous ad hoc network formed over vehicles moving on the road. Such a network can be formed between vehicles with V2V communication or between vehicles and infrastructure with vehicle-to-infrastructure (V2I) communication. Such VANETs in which vehicles can communicate with each other and also with roadside infrastructure provide a means to improve road safety by enabling a number of potential applications for driver assistance, collision warning, traffic information, and monitoring.

The availability of various applications will improve road safety and vehicular environment. Dedicated short-range communication (DSRC) is a generic name for short-range, point-to-point communication. It is also the name of the older technology mainly used for vehicle-to-road communication (e.g., at a tollgate). The channels reserved worldwide in the 5.9 GHz band for such communications are known as DSRC channels. The IEEE Dedicated Short-Range Communication Working Group is developing standards for wireless access in vehicular environments (WAVE) and the communication is based on IEEE 802.11p, which is an amendment to IEEE 802.11p Standard in order to support communication in dynamic vehicular environments. IEEE 802.11p standardizes the communication aspects related to physical (PHY) and media access control (MAC). Currently, the US Federal Communications Commission (FCC) has allocated 76 GHz and the European Telecommunications Standards Institute (ETSI) has allocated 76–77 GHz of spectrum for the deployment of intelligent transportation systems (ITS) services. However, a significant rise in vehicular applications, especially in urban environments, may lead to overcrowding of the band and thereby result in degraded vehicular communication efficiency for safety applications. Not only could safety applications be affected, but also growing demand and usage of in-car entertainment and information systems comprising bandwidth demanding multimedia applications (e.g., video streaming) can lead to congested vehicular networks and spectrum scarcity for IEEE 802.11p–based vehicular applications.

In view of this, using cognitive radio (CR) technology in VANETs will enable more efficient radio spectrum usage and, in turn, improve vehicular communication efficiency. Consequently, regulatory agencies, such as the FCC in the United States, which regulates spectrum allocations, have now opened the licensed bands to unlicensed/secondary users (SUs) through the use of CR, to enable more efficient use of the spectrum bands. CR is an emerging technology to improve spectrum usage and alleviate spectrum scarcity by exploiting underused spectral resources through opportunistic spectrum access. Radio cognition (RC) together with dynamic spectrum access (DSA) strategies present promising approaches that allow unlicensed/SUs to opportunistically capture and use the spatial-temporally available licensed spectrum holes as long as licensed/primary user (PU) bands are not perturbed. Though many applications of CR have been proposed for wireless mesh and in ad hoc and cellular networks, employing CR in vehicular (CRV) environments is a relatively novel research subject and some works in that direction have started to appear recently.

CR is an intelligent wireless communication method that is aware of its environment and adapts accordingly to utilize the spectral efficiency. With the increasing demand for wireless resources, there is not much bandwidth left to license, and we are on the verge of spectral scarcity. Research suggests that most of the radio spectrum now is underutilized and is idle for too long. Vehicular networks and vehicular communication can benefit from opportunistic spectrum usage with CR technology. CR for vehicular ad hoc networks (CR-VANETs) is a fast-emerging application area of CR technology. CR-enabled vehicles can use additional spectrum opportunities in TV bands according to the quality-of-service (QoS) requirements of the applications. However, the research solutions proposed for general-purpose CR networks cannot be directly applied to CR-VANETs. This is because the unique features of vehicular environment such as high mobility and cooperation opportunities need to be taken into account while designing the spectrum management functions for CR-VANETs. Unlike static CR scenarios, in CR-VANETs, multiple cooperating vehicles (during busy hours) can exchange spectrum information to get information on the spectrum availability. This enables other vehicles to know the spectrum characteristics of the road to be traversed in advance and they can take proactive adaptive measures .In general, CR-VANETs will improve the performance of existing and emerging vehicular applications such as V2V communication, entertainment, and information systems, and public safety communication.

Therefore, CR could be the possible solution for the spectral congestion issue. The efficient utilization of the spectrum resource, self-adaptation, and dynamic spectrum sharing in a vehicular environment makes CR a primary candidate for vehicular communication. The significant rise in vehicular application in the urban environment with several vehicles leads to overcrowding of the band, hence degrading efficiency in vehicular communication. In vehicular communication, the CR allows opportunistic spectrum usage, along with the utilization of DSRC channels. In a vehicular network, CR is relatively a novel research technique since it requires considerable attention from the research community. Therefore, various researchers are working on CR-based vehicular communication. Based on the current literature, the research shows that CR networks could not be directly applied to vehicular communication. Hence, cooperative opportunities need to be taken while designing the spectrum management function for CR. Unlike static CR scenarios, CR in vehicular communication requires multiple cooperating vehicles, which can exchange spectrum information to get information on the available spectrum. This enables other vehicles to take proactive adaptive measurements according to the spectrum characteristics. Therefore, CR-based vehicular communication results in improved performance of various vehicular applications.

The primary objective of CR is highly reliable communication whenever and wherever needed for efficient utilization of resources. Some of the important functions of CR are spectrum sensing, spectrum management, spectrum mobility, and spectrum sharing. Spectrum sensing is vital because of its functionality, which determines which portion of the spectrum is available and detects the presence of bandwidth and acquires them temporarily until the PU occupies. The priority is to avoid interference with the PU. Thus, spectrum sensing is highly reliable. High mobility in vehicular communication could reduce the performance of the spectrum sensing. The majority of the work is focused on improving the performance of spectrum sensing in high mobility. In addition, a possible solution for high mobility issues could be in cooperative spectrum sensing. The vehicle with the spectrum sensing capability and frequently updated central spectrum database management, such as decision fusion controller (DFC) could be used for increasing the performance of spectrum sensing in vehicular communication. The delay and reliability of coordinated spectrum sensing in a vehicular environment is still under progress. An experiment suggests that sensing precision depends on vehicular speed and the location of the vehicle. There are various challenges in CR-based vehicular communication, in which one of the challenges is the hardware requirement for the vast infrastructure. In spectrum sensing, identifying the hidden PU is a major issue. In addition, identification of spread spectrum PU has limitations and also determining the sensing duration of the aforementioned problems, we, therefore, propose a system model for cooperative spectrum sensing on vehicular network.

5.1.1 VANET CHALLENGES

Here we describe the unique characteristics of VANETs and identify some major issues. Deploying a vehicular networking system requires addressing several challenges posed by the unique characteristics and requirements of vehicular communications.

5.1.1.1 Mobility and Dynamic Network Topology

High mobility (for instance, to 100 km/h) of vehicles makes the topology of VANETs very dynamic, resulting in short-lived vehicular communication links. Additionally, vehicular density keeps varying from sparse to dense, and high mobility in sparse areas may cause fragmentation problems for VANET, which, in turn, will result in network unreachability for some nodes. Further, high speeds can deteriorate the signal due to the Doppler effect and fast fading. These factors can degrade the performance of applications that have QoS requirements in terms of high reliability, low latency, and so forth.

5.1.1.2 Cognition Cycle

Here we first describe the two main features of the CR: cognitive capability and reconfigure ability. Then, we briefly discuss the concept of the cognition cycle of CR as well as some specifics related to CR-VANETs. A CR-enabled device adapts its operational parameters as a function of its environment. CR components are mainly radio, sensor, knowledge database, learning engine, optimization tools, and a reasoning engine. CR has cognitive as well as reconfigure capabilities. Cognitive capability allows CR to sense and gather information (e.g., different signals and their modulation types, noise, transmission power, etc.) from its environment and, for example, SUs can identify the best available spectrum.

The reconfigure ability features of CR allow it to optimally adapt the operational parameters as a function of the sensed information. CR systems involve PU and SU of the spectrum; PUs are license holders, while SUs seek to opportunistically use the spectrum through CR when the PUs are idle. The cognition cycle of CR consists of multiple phases: observe, analyze, reason, and act.

The goal is to detect the available spectrum, select the best spectrum, select the best operating parameters, coordinate the spectrum access with other users, reconfigure the operational parameters, and vacate the frequency when a PU appears. A spectrum hole refers to a portion of the spectrum not being used by the primary/licensed user at a particular place and time. It is detected through spectrum sensing and signal detection techniques. The SUs opportunistically access the spectrum, if the sensed portion of the spectrum is found empty. The SU can opportunistically use different spectrum bands by adaptively switching through spectrum hand-offs. However, the SU is responsible to detect the arrival of any PU. If a PU is detected, then it should vacate the licensed portion of the spectrum in order to prevent interference.

A possible cognition cycle for CR-VANETs is shown in Fig. 5.1, which illustrates the four stages—observe, analysis, reasoning, and act—with some customized functionalities for vehicular networks. The observe stage consists of sensing as well as the consideration of the location, policies, and application QoS needs. In the analysis and reasoning stages, the system performance and the radio environment are analyzed, similarities from the past are considered, and optimal parameters as well as optimal spectrum strategies are determined. The reconfiguration and optimal adaptation is finally done in the act stage.

The CR-VANETs cognition cycle has a lot of similarities with that of CR, but some differences are due to the nature of high-mobility vehicular environment. Most of the vehicles will be equipped with navigation systems, and hence location as well as mobility prediction based on the current direction of movement can be used for cognition. The use of knowledge database becomes more relevant as a vehicle may pass through the same location at approximately the same time of day. Thus, past experiences can be combined with the current location for optimizing the operational parameters. Finally, it should be noted that the requirements for CR-VANETs are stricter in terms of faster adaptability and faster running time of the cognitive cycle due to the dynamic nature of the vehicular environment.

5.1.1.3 Architecture

The network architecture of CR-VANETs consists of vehicles with on-board units (OBUs) and infrastructure units such as RSUs and base stations of network providers. Note that setting up roadside units everywhere may be costly; thus, V2V communication, including multihop, should be able to work without any infrastructure support.

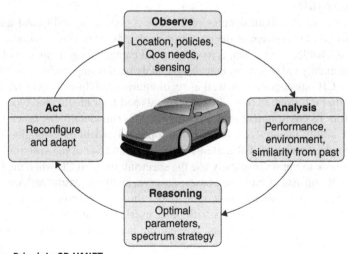

FIGURE 5.1 Working Principle CR-VANET

Several functionalities are needed for a CR-VANETs paradigm, and an initial architecture related to different functional blocks and protocols is discussed in detail in this section. The architecture proposed by its authors consists of several blocks related to policies such as those imposed by the FCC and local authorities and on-board sensors, including radio sensors and GPS. The architecture includes a knowledge database that consists of previously learned cases, rules, spectrum information, and road maps.

Further, the infrastructure consists of a cognitive engine (CE) that is the core of all functionalities. Additionally, there are software-defined radio or multiple radios, a performance measurement block for feedback, and finally a user interface to allow users to configure the system offline. Fig. 5.2 illustrates the architecture showing these different functional blocks for CR-VANETs. As illustrated in Fig. 5.2, the CE uses real-time data from onboard sensors and history and map information from the knowledge database to learn from the present as well as the past. It then controls the operation of software-defined radio through optimization of transmission parameters and decision making related to spectrum use and management. A taxonomy of machine learning approaches for CE is provided in Fig. 5.2. The classification is done in terms of supervised learning, decision making, and parameter tuning. Supervised learning can be used for prediction or classification, by learning the mapping between the given inputs and outputs. It is called supervised learning because the outputs for the given inputs are known beforehand. For example, in the case of signal identification, the target signal and the input signal features are known during the learning phase. Decision making is related to the problem of making optimal decisions. Some available tools for decision making use reinforcement learning, which can be used in unknown environments, or case-based reasoning based on history, and so forth. Parameter tuning is needed to set the parameters optimally. A system model is used, and some met heuristics can be used to find the optimal values of the system parameters for a given optimization objective.

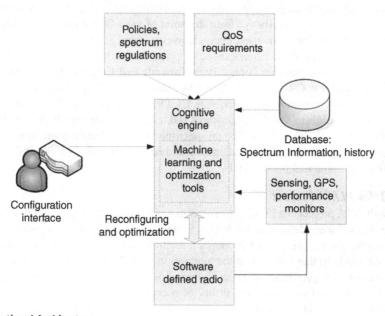

FIGURE 5.2 Functional Architecture

Multiple conflicting optimization objectives, such as maximization of bandwidth versus minimization of bit error rate, can be assigned with weights differently according to the desired mode of communication, ranging from bandwidth maximization mode to emergency mode for high resiliency, and so forth. Several machine-learning techniques have been studied in the literature to realize cognitive functionalities in the general context of CR. However, they need to be adapted for the CR-VANETs scenario. Some interesting ideas for applying machine learning to CR-VANETs are discussed.

We propose that case-based reasoning is interesting for CR-VANETs scenario because vehicles have a high chance of passing through the same locations at approximately the same time of day. This is especially the case, for example, for public transports such as buses and trains, but also for cars given that commuters travel every day from their homes to offices at approximately the same time. With case-based reasoning, the optimization process can be populated from the previously found optimal configurations, and then further searches for optimization can start from there. This can highly improve the convergence time of optimization algorithms such as genetic algorithms and simulated annealing, which in turn can be used for optimizing transmission parameters.

5.1.2 PROJECTS AND TEST BEDS

The research on CR-enabled vehicular networks is still in its preliminary stage, and there are not many related experimental platforms due to their complex setup and requirements. In this section, we describe some existing projects and test beds related to CR-enabled vehicular networks.

5.1.2.1 CORRIDOR

Cognitive Radio for Railway through Dynamic and Opportunistic Spectrum Reuse (CORRIDOR) is a French research project that targets opportunistic spectrum access for railways. Communication demands are increasing for modern railways from the point of view of railway operations as well as for providing Internet connectivity to the passengers. However, there is no single universal wireless technology that can answer the needs of heterogeneous services and railway applications. Modern railway applications and passengers' Internet connectivity demands call for more bandwidth and spectrum. One answer to such needs is CR. Thus, CORRIDOR plans to use CR technology to support multiple railway applications such as command and control, CCTV, maintenance, and Internet connectivity for passengers. The project aims to develop algorithms and technology for very high-speed environments that are typical of railways. The focus will be on spectrum access and management, exploiting TVWS, CE, cross-layer optimization, mobility management, and hand-over optimization. Different techniques will be validated with some real on-site trials.

5.1.2.2 PROTON-PLATA Project

The PROTON-PLATA project is a European project that aims at developing a reconfigurable prototype based on emerging software-defined technologies for telematics applications for cars-to-roadside and car-to-car communications. The project proposes a multitechnological, cooperative, advanced driver assistance system (ADAS) that is based on the integration of SDR devices in vehicles.

The first part of the project deals with developing a prototype, including SDR devices and driver assistance applications to demonstrate the utility of a cooperative ADAS for improving communication performance. This involves designing a multitechnological communication infrastructure and equipping OBUs with SDR devices that support different communication scenarios, that is, VV communications, VI communications, and broadcasting (infrastructure-to-vehicle) at the same time. The performance evaluation using network simulation tools forms the second part of the project.

5.1.2.3 Rail-CR Project

The Rail-CR project is a US project that is a part of the effort to implement the positive train control (PTC) technology to equip trains with wireless communication capabilities. This will allow trains to communicate with wayside wireless stations, while moving, and provide useful information related to their location, speed, direction, and so forth.

The project adapts Virginia Tech CR technology to improve safety and operations of the railways. The complex radio characteristics faced during train transportation such as continually changing position of the train as well as continually changing communications environment due to varying noise, multiple sources of interference, multiple users competing for scarce spectrum, and so forth, make wireless communication with trains very demanding. This has motivated the railway industry to use SDRs equipped with a reconfigurable platform for packet-data transmission. Though SDR provides interoperability and enables multiple configurations, it lacks the capability of integrating additional adaptation to all aviate crowded spectrum, intentional jamming, or learning from past experiences. In this context, the project developed a railroad-specific CR, namely Rail-CR, capable of fulfilling the requirements of future wireless communication systems for trains. The Rail-CR combines AI-based decision making and learning algorithms with SDR to address the specific need for adaptable communications in railway transportation.

The Rail-CR will enhance the performance of railway communications in terms of interoperability, robustness, reliability, and spectral efficiency, and will make it cost-effective to deploy and maintain. The Rail-CR system includes a CE that relies on the tunable radio parameters (knobs) and observable performance indicators (meters) of the SDR platform. Based on situational awareness from the radio in the form of observable parameters (meters), a CE uses software-based decision-making and learning algorithms to decide if the radio parameters (knobs) should be adapted depending on sets of predefined objectives. The Rail-CR was evaluated under different interference conditions, and results show that the CE can manage to overcome the interference by adapting configurable parameters, whereas a radio minus cognition capability was not able to overcome interference, resulting in high errors or a loss of connectivity. Furthermore, a case study, which demonstrates the use of META Cognition to improve wireless communication system for signaling and train control in railroads is illustrated in the article. In a metacognitive engine, a master monitors and adapts the cognition process (i.e., CE). Metacognition enhances the performance of a CR with better learning and decision-making capabilities.

The cognitive cars test bed research in VANETs has focused on simulation studies to evaluate the performance of communication protocols for VANETs. Testing and evaluation of VANETs communication protocols (e.g., VANETs-based multihop communication system) in real test bed scenarios, for example, on the road, has been considered a difficult task as there is virtually no highly dense vehicular test bed that exists.

Recently, a new cognitive approach to VANETs research was introduced that enables performing real vehicular experiments, which usually require several vehicles, using only a few vehicles equipped with wireless communication interfaces. This is done by setting up a virtual overlay network consisting of relaying and interfering vehicles on top of a group of only a few vehicles to conduct experiments. The communication packets travel over a random number of hops and experience interference from a random number of vehicle transmitters with varying transmission characteristics. The cognitive car test bed is based on the guidelines presented into conduct real experiments with VANET applications and communication protocols under constraints of vehicular environment and computing resources. The objective of the cognitive car test bed is to explore the possibility of using cognitive network technologies in an advanced vehicular test beds. It focuses on using CRs to study the impact of different frequency bands and different frequency switching delays on the performance of VANET communication protocols.

More specifically, a cognitive car test bed allows the evaluation of a communication protocol versus different variables, including number of hops, density of interfering neighbors, wireless channel conditions, transmission frequency, and switching delay at the node. In this context, it introduces the architectural guidelines for implementing a VANET test bed and, in addition, provides preliminary results of the experiments conducted on highways of a cognitive network based on the software radio (SORA) technology provided by Microsoft. Preliminary results show that cognitive interfaces can be used as an additional tunable dimension in an experiment platform where highly dense vehicular test beds can be set up with just a few real vehicular resources (e.g., a few cars and drivers). The cognitive interfaces enable testing novel techniques designed for addressing radio spectrum scarcity in a vehicular environment as well as performance of VANET communication protocols. The performance of the VANET communication protocol can be evaluated by tuning two additional variables: frequency band and switching time. The first variable is the frequency band used for transmitting and receiving communication packets and the second variable is the switching time needed to change from one frequency to another.

5.1.2.4 Virginia Tech CR Network Test Bed

Virginia Tech CR Network Test Bed (VT-CORNET) is an open-source CR network test bed developed by the US's Virginia Tech for the evaluation of CR wireless communication protocols and applications. The test bed consists of software-defined radio nodes (USRP-based nodes) deployed over the four floors of a building and equipped with a custom-made daughterboard covering the frequency range of MHz to GHz. The CORNET nodes are remotely accessible to the registered users. A unique feature of the test bed is that it uses the Software Communications Architecture (SCA) framework that assumes USRP nodes at the physical layer and provides support for generating and visualizing a range of radio configurations.

The test bed focuses on CE design, self-organizing networks, and topology research. VT-CORNET is a highly reconfigurable test bed that enables testing of independently developed CR engines, sensing techniques, applications, protocols, performance metrics, and algorithms. In addition to the static nodes deployed in the ceiling, low-power mobile nodes will also be available to support the vehicular environment. The rail-CR project has adapted the VR-CORNET CR technology for railways as described in the first part of this section. The CORNET test bed is openly available for conducting research on advanced CR networks. It provides a collection of resources to researchers lacking the ability to perform advanced experiments because of limited exposure to software-defined radio and CR platforms. Their sources are made available to researchers through flexible RF front ends, open-source software, and FCC experimental licenses.

5.1.2.5 ORBIT Test Bed

The ORBIT test bed is an open-access research test bed for next generation wireless networking that allows large-scale reproducible experimentation on next generation protocols and applications. It consists of an indoor radio grid emulator for large-scale reproducible experiments and an outdoor field trial system for supporting real-world experimentation and evaluations. A node radio grid emulator has been deployed at the WINLAB Tech Center building and is open for general use by the research community to conduct experiments.

The ORBIT test bed provides support for conducting a wide range of experiments including mobile ad hoc networks (MANET), dynamic spectrum coordination, network virtualization, wireless security, and vehicular networking. The radio grid test bed enables emulation of real-world network topologies via noise injection and packet filtering. The test bed has been recently upgraded to include programmable software-defined radios (GNU USRP/USRP) for flexible MAC/PHY experiments. The test bed users can access the radio grid through a web portal to specify their experiments and measurements. As mentioned previously, the test bed can be accessed worldwide for conducting experiments and evaluate protocols and applications related to ad hoc courting, PP, spectrum sensing, and DSA. Recently, the test bed has started providing support for vehicular mobility as well. The ORBIT management software has been extended to enable mobile vehicular (V2V networks) experiments, and the radio grid is now supplemented by a number of outdoor and vehicular nodes.

5.2 COOPERATIVE COGNITIVE RADIO NETWORKS

In the vehicular environment, spectrum sensing plays a very important role, and time consumption and spectral efficiency are major constraints on vehicular communication. In CR we have various types of spectrum sensing mechanisms in general, but cooperative sensing techniques are unique. The sensing reliability and the efficiency of cooperative spectrum sensing are more suitable for vehicular networks. The cooperative sensing in vehicular environment is a vehicle with CR share their sensing information with others and utilizes the sensing information shared by the other vehicles on a network for decision making. Vehicular users are considered as unlicensed/SUs and are capable of sensing, analyzing, and accessing the spectrum opportunities dynamically. Each CR communicates their decisions to the DFC) and the final decision is made for the occupancy of the spectral resources. The DFC is the centralized controller for channel assignment and scheduling the SU (i.e., CR user) in a vehicular environment. Fig. 5.3 shows the classification of spectrum sensing.

Cooperative spectrum sensing is used to enhance the reliability of detecting the PU in the vehicle environment. On using the cooperative spectrum sensing we can decrease the probabilities of misdetection and false alarm. The cooperative spectrum sensing solves two major issues: it solves the hidden PU problem and it decreases the spectrum sensing time. Due to fundamental characteristics of wireless channels, the performance of spectrum sensing is limited by noise uncertainty, multipath fading, and shadowing. If the PU signal experiences deep fading or is blocked by the obstacles, the power of the received spectrum at CR may be too weak to be detected, as illustrated in Fig. 5.4. If the CR user cannot detect the presence of the PU transmitter while the PU receiver is within the transmission range of the CR, the transmission of the PU will be interfered with. In order to address this issue, the cooperative sensing spectrum will be the feasible solution. With the cooperation of several CRs for spectrum sensing, the detection performance will be improved by taking advantage of independent fading channels and multiuser diversity. Based on the decision fusion techniques, cooperative spectrum sensing can be realized in either a centralized or a distributed manner.

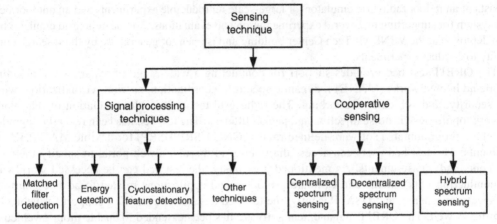

FIGURE 5.3 Classification of Spectrum Sensing

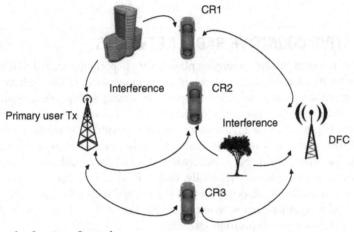

FIGURE 5.4 Cooperative Spectrum Scenario

There are two main classifications in cooperative spectrum sensing techniques:

1. centralized cooperative sensing and
2. distributed cooperative sensing.

5.2.1 CENTRALIZED COOPERATIVE SENSING

In centralized cooperative sensing DFC collects the information for decision making. In centralized cooperative sensing the CR user interchanges information about the existing status of spectrum availability to DFC in a vehicular environment. Then DFC makes the final decision. The CR user does not decide and just sends its observations to central unit or other CR users. The centralized cooperative spectrum sensing introduces an optimal linear cooperation for spectrum sensing in which to attain increasing in the probability of detecting the PU and to mitigate the fading effects. In centralized cooperative sensing the DFC coordinates three functions:

1. Initially DFC selects a spectrum band of interest for sensing and initiates all CR users to individually perform sensing.
2. CR user reports their sensing information through control channel.
3. Finally DFC combines the received sensing information determines the presence of PU and diffuses the decision back to CR user.

Fig. 5.5 illustrates the cooperative sensing methods.

5.2.2 DECISION FUSIONS TECHNIQUES

The DFC is responsible for decision making in centralized cooperative sensing in vehicular networks (Fig. 5.6). DFC uses linear fusion rules to obtain the cooperative decision. The frequently used fusion rules are AND, OR, and majority rules. In AND rules the entire system, that is, all the users in the CR network, should detect the presence of the spectrum availability. The AND rule works best when the number of CR users is small.

In real-time environments, the hidden node problem, fading and shadowing, and so forth, would diminish the spectrum sensing performance of CR users. To solve this problem, a cooperative sensing method is introduced. In the centralized cooperative spectrum sensing for decision fusion techniques we use a hard sensing mechanism (AND rule, OR rule) for spectrum prediction. In a real-time scenario using a hard, sensing mechanism we can considerably minimize the probability of detection and probability of false alarm. Comparatively, an OR decision fusion method is more efficient in a real-time environment.

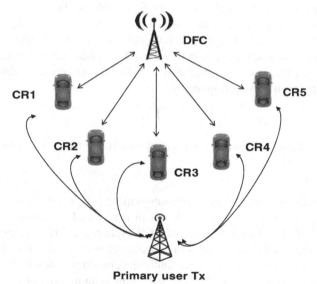

FIGURE 5.5 Centralized Cooperative Sensing

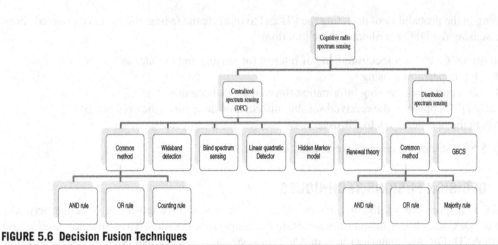

FIGURE 5.6 Decision Fusion Techniques

False alarm probability (C_{fa}) of cooperative spectrum sensing is given by:

$$C_{fa} = \prod_1^n P_{fa,i} \tag{5.1}$$

Detection probability (C_d) of cooperative spectrum sensing is given by:

$$C_d = \prod_1^n P_{d,i} \tag{5.2}$$

We can define n as the sensing diversity order of cooperative spectrum sensing since it characterizes the error exponent of detection probability (C_d). OR fusion rule predicts the presence of the primary signal if at least one of its received decisions from the users is positive (indicating presence). Whereas, in OR rule, if one CR user detects the spectrum hole, the entire system decides the availability of the spectrum. The OR rule works better when there are maximum numbers of CR users. $P_{d,i}$ and $P_{fa,i}$ are detection probability and the false alarm probability of the ith cognitive user. False alarm probability (C_{fa}) of cooperative spectrum sensing is given by:

$$C_{md} = 1 - \prod_1^n (1 - P_{d,i}) \tag{5.3}$$

The probability of missed detection in cooperative spectrum sensing is given by

$$C_{md} = \prod_1^n P_{d,i} \tag{5.4}$$

The detection probability of cooperative spectrum sensing is $C_d = 1 - C_{md}$.

Other than aforementioned rule, we use K out of n standard for decision fusion techniques. Under this rule, the DFC declares H_1 if K out of n CR users report "1." H_1 denotes the presence of a PU and is located near the SU; H_0 denotes the absence or is far away from the SU. The majority rule can be obtained from the K out of n state under the condition when $K \geq n/2$. Here, n denotes the number of SUs in the network, and K denotes the minimum number of SUs that must work for the K-out-of-n rule. Hence, determining the optimal value of K is important for minimizing the error detection. The K out n is also similar to voting rule or counting rule. These are some of the simple and commonly used decision fusion techniques. This method is also applicable for decision fusion techniques in a cooperative vehicular environment. The aforementioned techniques are not reliable or productive because in the case of AND rule the number of CR users, that is, vehicles—is limited. Therefore this scenario is impossible in the real-time environment. In addition, there are some advance fusion techniques that can be used to utilize the statistical knowledge of decision making.

5.2.2.1 Linear Quadratic Detector

The linear quadratic (LQ) fusion method is for correlation between CR users in a cooperative sensing environment in a network. The method provides a suboptimal solution to decision fusion problem by using the partial statistical knowledge which is illustrated in Eq. 5.5. Based on deflection criterion, the LQ detector compares an LQ function of the local decisions with a predetermined threshold and achieves better error probability with higher value of deflection. The deflection or the generalized SNR of a detection rule that compares a function $T(x)$ of observation x is given by:

$$D_T = \frac{[E(T(x)) - E_1(T(x))]^2}{Var0(T(x))}$$

(5.5)

Where the expected value of a random variable is intuitive to long-run average value of repetitions of the primary channel availability and its representation. We are dividing variable with expected value in order to determine the primary channel detection problem. Higher deflection is an indication of better error-probability performance. It is to be noted that the decisions contribute to the decision fusion hypothesis only through probabilities under two hypotheses.

5.2.3 WIDEBAND DETECTION

The wideband detection discusses about the detection of PU in a narrow fixed band. Wideband spectrum sensing would require many more resources, and as much as one CR user for sensing we need whole band which is impossible. The basic idea is to form a number of groups of CR and then each group decides towards detecting a particular band in the whole frequency spectrum. The CR users in a single group coordinate among themselves to make decisions for effective allocation of spectrum resources, for example, for DFC to decide whether the primary signal is available or not. While the optimal detector is hard to implement, as it requires the local parameter, the suboptimal detector works in two stages, the first stage is to detect the transmission using a detector and the second stage is to fuse the detected spectrum to predict the presence of the primary signal per Eq. 5.6. The fused decision is finally relayed on all the nodes.

$$L(ym) = \frac{f(ym/H_0)}{f(ym/H_1)}$$

(5.6)

The main challenge in wideband detection is the high data rate radio-front (RF) end requirement to sense the whole band, with the additional constraint that deployed CR user will be limited in data processing rates. To achieve reliable results, the sample rate should be above the Nyquist rate if conventional estimation methods are used. Hence, using wideband detection in cooperative vehicular communication is a challenging task.

5.2.4 BLIND SPECTRUM SENSING

The blind spectrum sensing assumes no information on the source signal. It uses Akaike Information Criterion (AIC) to detect the vacant subbands. The basic idea is that if we approximate an unknown pdf f by g, then the Kullback–Leibler discrepancy is an indication of how different they are from each other. The expectation in Eq. 5.7 can be estimated through the Akaike model

$$\text{AIC} = -E_0\left(\int f_x(x)\log g_0(x)\right)dx \tag{5.7}$$

The AIC is an approximate unbiased estimator of this expectation and is given by

$$AIC = -2\sum_{N=0}^{N-1}\log g_0(xn) + 2U \tag{5.8}$$

In this scenario the frequency band of the spectrum is scanned using sliding windows and Akaike weights are computed for the Gaussian distribution. In Eq. 5.8, n denotes the number of spectrum available, xn is sliding window value and U denotes the threshold. The maximum value of the Akaike weights corresponds to the vacant subbands and similar subbands are found with a reference subband. Finally, a threshold is set for the weights, based on which the prediction of the presence of primary signal is completed.

5.2.4.1 Hidden Markov Model

In the hidden Markov model (HMM) let us assume that the PU's status s_i ($i = 1, 2, \ldots$) is evolving according to the Markov chain and at each time based on the channel status s_i we have observation at the DFC, the observed data is a mixture model. The interference problem for HMM involves determining the input data and yielding output probability of distribution. The time consumption on processing those data is critical. Thus in such scenario HMM decision fusion techniques would be vulnerable for vehicular networks

5.2.5 THEORY OF RENEWAL PROCESSES IN CR

In proposing model, we consider CR user's influential behavior has renewal process and quantifying the average waiting time CR user in a particular PU transmitter through renewal theory. The application of the renewal process in order to determine the available spectrum holes is predominant. We consider primary channel ON–OFF state has renewal process. We assume the CR network with two PUs and n CR user's operation on two primary channels. Hence in CR network the PU can access the spectrum at any time, while the SU is occupying it. An SU is not aware when the PU will occupy the spectrum. In a CR network the CR user's final decision is determined by the DFC. In a CR network, the DFC is responsible for defining the PU behavior and deciding the availability of the primary channel. There is a control channel for exchanging the information between the DFC and CR user. The CR users should opportunistically access the primary channel to acquire more bandwidth for high data transmission.

Fig. 5.7 illustrates the operation of the proposed model. In a PU network we have PU Tx1 and PU Tx2, which has a spectrum hole currently available. CR user identifies the spectrum hole in the PU transmitter and occupies it. In the aforementioned scenario the available spectrum from PU Tx1 is occupied by CR1 and the available spectrum in PU Tx2 is occupied by CR3. CR1 and CR3 broadcast that information to CR DFC. The purpose of DFC in CR is deciding the availability of the PU; a new

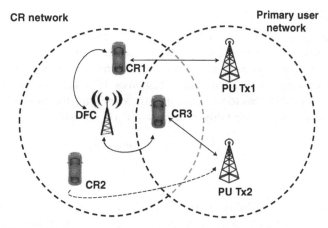

FIGURE 5.7 Proposed System Model

user CR2 is waiting for the service. We assume that the information broadcast by the CR1 and CR3 to DFC contains the available spectrum in the aforementioned scenario, it contains the information about availability of the vacant spectrum. The DFC can act as an intermediate node in order to the broadcast the available vacant spectrum for CR3. We assume that information processed by PU Tx is Poisson distribution, where we assume the common discipline is first come, first served (FCFS). Hence the CR user is severed according to FCFS discipline.

In our proposed model PU Tx is responsible for allocating the available spectrum resources to the CR user. In order to determine whether the PU is occupied or not, we alternately switch between 0s and 1s. If the spectrum is being occupied, it means the PU state is 1 and if the spectrum is available it means the PU state is 0. If the primary channel state is 0, then CR user can occupy the spectrum hole. We model the length of the state 1 and state 0 by two random variables: P_1 and P_2. The behavior of the PU is the combination of two Poisson processes, which is renewal process. The renewal interval is $P_T = P_1 + P_2$ and the distribution of T_P, is denoted by $F_P(T) = F_1(P) \times F_2(P)$ (Fig. 5.8).

The CR user in order to occupy the available spectrum resources has to send a request to PU transmitter (PU Tx1 or PU Tx2). Hence the PU serves the CR user request by FIFO queuing rule. During the whole process all the spectrum sensing and channel estimation work are done by DFC simultaneously with information provided by other CR user.

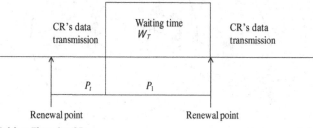

FIGURE 5.8 Average Waiting Time for CR

5.2.6 PROBABILITY OF DETECTION

The basic idea is to minimize the sensing time on cooperative environment. In order to determine the probability of detection, average primary channel power has to be examined. In addition to that channel energy detection, which is an important factor for detection performance. Henceforth it minimizes the duration of sensing for effective utilization of radio resources. In addition to that, threshold value and SNR (signal-to-noise ratio) value has to be determined for identifying the probability of detection in a renewal process. The equation of probability of detection (P_d) is given by:

$$P_d = Q\left(\left(\frac{\text{thres } x}{\delta_i} - s_n - \right)\frac{\sqrt{\text{sen } x}}{s_{n+}}\right) \tag{5.9}$$

Were P_s is the average primary channel power. Therefore, when doing energy detection on a channel, x, and for large sen x the probability of detection is P_d, where sen x is the sensing time, thres x is the threshold, and S_n is the signal-to-noise ratio. δ_i is the energy measured with the threshold. Hence the probability of detection would be efficient based on two major factors with less interference and primary channel transition state. These are two main factors for efficient probability of detection in vehicular networks. In addition to that, the fake SU issue is also a major concern. However, in cooperative spectrum sensing involvement, fake user in graduation is decreased due to a centralized approach.

5.2.7 DISTRIBUTED SPECTRUM SENSING

In distributed cooperative sensing each CR makes its own decision (Fig. 5.9). The vehicles in a distributed cooperative environment make their own decisions, also known as hard sensing. Each node decides on the presence or absence of the PU and sends its decision to the other nodes. One advantage of this method is that less bandwidth is required. On using distributed cooperative sensing we can minimize the network complexity and network overhead. Final decisions are shared among the user. Advantages In distributed sensing there is no need for a backbone infrastructure so it reduces cost.

In decentralized spectrum sensing approach there is no DFC. The CR users in the network will perform the local spectrum sensing individually. The information is shared among the collaborative users in the network to decide on the collective probability of the PU. Each CR user will decide between

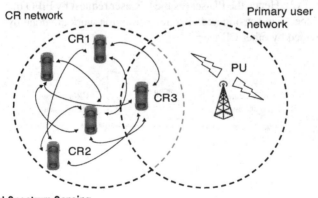

FIGURE 5.9 Distributed Spectrum Sensing

them with the collective information. For example, Fig. 5.9 has three CR users; the received collective information from three CR user corroborates the final decision made by the individual CR user. Similar fusion policies are used in the decentralized cooperative spectrum sensing approach in order to get the detection probability. In addition to that, we have gradient-based distributed cooperative spectrum sensing (GBCS) for decentralized spectrum sensing.

5.3 CONCLUDING COMMENTS

The recent advances and open research directions on applying CR in VANETs (CR-VANETs) focusing on architecture, machine learning, cooperation, reprogrammability, and spectrum management applications are analyzed. The primary objectives of the CR are highly reliable communication whenever and wherever needed for efficient utilization of the radio resources. Furthermore, several challenges and requirements have been identified A cognitive agent approach VANET is an example of a MANET, where mobile nodes are vehicles. Moving vehicles equipped with communication devices are an instance of long-envisioned MANETs. Data fusion methods are also employed for efficient data integration.

THEORY AND APPLICATION OF VEHICULAR NETWORKS

CHAPTER

6

6.1 AUTOMOTIVE CONTEXT-AWARE IN VEHICULAR NETWORK

The area of digital connectivity–based car-related applications is still rapidly evolving. Car communication is now a significant differentiator between car brands. Location-based services and navigation with dynamic traffic status are already well established, but numerous travel-related services are in the pipeline. These services are delivered via the automotive manufacturer or an intermediary acting as an automotive service provider ("Automotive") for this "captured customer base" of cars. First to be implemented is the already extensive range of MM (machine-to-machine) services, for example, car maintenance and remote diagnosis. Then, interactive services are launched, for example, roadside support, breakdown and emergency calling, plus local information, POI (point of interest), and so on. High bandwidth in-car entertainment services are now becoming available, with streaming music, audio books, or videos. More advanced car services include cashless transactions for petrol, tires, road tolls, and parking. Smarter dashboards enable much-improved user interaction, to support more than just MM for remote diagnosis. Car dashboards can now synchronize with personal phones to use built-in speakers, and also the opposite: that is, a smartphone can be used as an advanced user interface for services that operate via cars' connectivity. The advent of the Internet of Things (IoT) has already made great changes in the car industry, but now the era of full browsing and broadband content is arriving. While only the top models of cars had full connectivity before, now all cars are fitted with an embedded universal integrated circuit card (UICC) with mobile subscriber identity module (SIM).

Effectively, automotive manufacturers are becoming mobile virtual network operators (MVNO) when they comply with the EU directive to facilitate voice calls to emergency agencies. This requires the Automotive to behave like mobile service providers, managing cars as if they were mobile phones or tablets. For example, the Automotive needs to manage usage policies, for example, capping for a flat rate, and car roaming charges. Since developing these regulatory facilities is costly, the automotive industry now seeks further revenues that may be generated from the connectivity capabilities, with more profitable business as the next challenge. Once cars are treated as subscribers, the relationships of car owners with the Automotive are transformed, enabling ongoing direct contact. This allows the manufacturers to promote new car models to target an audience and to market different service packages under service level agreements (SLAs). It also allows mid-life upgrades and newly launched connectivity services, if the car's embedded software is incompatible. Direct contact with car drivers has not been possible before, as cars are sold through agents, and the Automotive is not informed when they change hands. Hence, car service subscriptions increase the addressable customer base and the potential for new revenue streams. Managing car subscriptions involve billing and policies. These facilities may be performed by the hosting mobile network operator (MNO), but most service providers prefer to control such tasks themselves, in order to differentiate their offerings.

The Automotive may also wish to select the best-fit network, best available access network, and roaming partners. Car sensors can indicate the status of fuel and car condition, which may be used in applications advising drivers of garages and fuel stations in the vicinity. Hence, context evaluation can support many revenue-earning and risk mitigation applications. The car's secure SIM is a great advantage. Car identity numbers are not published but used only in MM applications. The car SIM is well protected—it is safely embedded in a tamper-proof unit, which is welded to the car chassis. Yet, automotive manufacturers are still worried about stolen car identities and usage abuse. This is also because cars may be shipped to other countries that those intended when the SIM is sealed in at the factory. These cars are constantly roaming, and usage of their packaged flat rate needs to be curbed judiciously.

Enterprises' car fleets benefit from the greater versatility of car communications. General-purpose connectivity replaces the phones that replaced walkie-talkies. This reduces costs but requires different management rules and further security measures. With advanced user interface via synched terminals and touch dashboards, the car's Internet can be used by drivers for nonwork-related purposes as well as work, which could lead to abuse. Personal and business car usage is blurred, just as it is for mobile handsets when the enterprise embraces bring your own device (BYOD). Hence, enterprise policy is required to curb nonproductive usage of resources. Policies are even more important where the Enterprise provides for roadside expenses transactions, for example, fuel and parking.

6.1.1 DEFINABLE CAR CONTEXT

Car context, where the car is a subscriber, is somewhat different from the context for a smartphone user. The choice of applications is different, though cars' applications are not restricted to travel-related ones. Usage is likely to coincide with trips away from home/office, but could still occur while parked nearby. When only one driver uses the car, the context converges with a driver's context, but a single driver status cannot be assumed. Car context key factors (KF) share many of the logical KF of user context, as shown later, particularly those describing the destination, network, and media types, but some factors and their subordinate attributes are different, along with their sources and qualifiers. Some notable differences are in describing car situations and activities, for example, travel speed, which can automatically induce a preference for voice commands and text-to-speech options. Most of the differences come from inferences and interpretations, rather than the raw data. The following description shows examples of context-based car services and it illustrates the potential policy-based services, for example, predictive point-of-interest (by motion/speed/direction), indicating alternative access.

6.1.2 DESCRIPTION

S Space: tagged location, abroad
T Timing: work/leisure, scheduled
A Activity: Direction/speed/stationary, business trip, garaged
U Urgency: Accident/breakdown, away-from-home/office
C Charging: Bands for roaming, bands per car type
I Integrity: Apps risks, confidentiality, discrepancies
D Destination: Apps/website/PP, approved/entrusted, corporationapps
N Network type: wi-fi hotspots, Enterprise car-park, mobile G/G
M Media type: Video/voice/ text, duration/volume

6.1.3 **FROM FLAT RATE TO FLEET RATE**

The Automotive requires policy and charging facilities that are similar to those of a virtual operator. While previously, usage of networks was limited, now Enterprise fleet cars become heavy users, especially with streaming video content, so capping services are required to stay within budget. Value charging instead of "upfront lump sum" or flat rate is essential for fine-tuning of margins. Flat rate devalues the worth of the provided services while variable pricing reveals the real demand for different services and increases revenues in saturated markets. Therefore, the Automotive should evolve from flat rate to variable charging. The charges to the Enterprise fleet may be subject to a bulk discount, but some higher charges can be justified by selective security measures and by business prioritization, determined by the Enterprise's own preferences. The Automotive acts as an MVNO, that is, responsible for all communications for the car subscription while a sponsoring service provider is only handling specifically funded applications. The MVNO, like any carrier, must comply with the European directive (EC) of preventing "bill shock" by capping roaming data users and notifying them of higher charges. This requires an OCS (online charging system) that converts bandwidth consumption into spending amounts in the user's currency. Automotive's system that receives service requests and submits them to the proposed CAPS for context analysis. The results are forwarded to the OCS, which generates the charging rules, to provide context-based charging and capping, including avoid-bill-shock (ABS) and local transactions via car subscription, using car prepay service (PP). In addition, mobile-money (MM) financial services, such as money transfers and recharging prepay accounts, can deliver useful facilities while traveling. Enterprises can exercise context-based "selective funding," that is, pay for business usage but not for nonwork-related use, for example, entertainment apps. Similarly, enterprises can exercise policy rules on what is automatically covered as funded expenses, such as small roadside purchases. This direct funding of traveling expenses avoids costs of managing expenses claims. The Enterprise sets some charging rules that are based on car context, not only budgets, for example, what is acceptable when the car is used for a business trip (tagged location + trip schedule), the car is garaged for repair (calendar booking + tagged location), the car account pays for fuel on monthly quota (credit account + period), and more. The idea of car-pay service, which can be very useful for both business and personal users, needs several payment regimes (including vouchers for free trials and gifts), that benefit from car context analysis.

6.1.4 **SELECTING NETWORK BY CONTEXT**

Context-aware policy can be used to optimize the selection of the access network. Currently, the car SIM MNO is the Automotive's single point of contact for all types of services, in any country that the car may be. The Automotive cannot choose roaming partners or renegotiate roaming rates. Coverage is restricted by the territories in which the MNO has roaming agreements. Since the proposed MCIM standards have not been ratified, the Automotive cannot replace an MNO for cars in midlife. Constant roaming coupled with flat-rate browsing becomes intolerable as use begins to ramp up, and the revenues do not match consumption costs. To achieve global coverage at a reasonable cost, means of accessing alternative networks are required, as well as enabling the Automotive to renegotiate rates during the car lifetime. "Best-connected" network selection is becoming feasible due to the improved performance of WLAN standards (.ac was ratified last year) and availability of outdoor wi-fi boxes that can be mounted on lampposts. Access to wi-fi is not restricted by regulators and is not licensed to MNOs. Authentication procedures to wi-fi utilize the built-in SIM, but it is feasible for the Automotive to insert their own credentials and embed them in the same way as the SIM, in the tamper-proof unit. The WLAN may belong to alternative local MNOs, local hotspots, city wi-fi, "hospitality" establishments, home wi-fi or Enterprise premises. Enterprise car-park wi-fi is particularly useful when it is used for securely downloading work schedules and uploading travel visit reports to fleet cars. Option A shows the current situation of a single interface to roaming and network services. If multiple SIM cards are embedded to obtain wider coverage, Option B will is possible, always selecting the local MNO, but still only one MNO at a time. In Option C, a multi-MNO relationship is shown, with dual built-in SIM credentials, which could be activated by context. In addition, it shows a connection to multiple WLAN networks, whenever possible. This option can be described as the "always best connected" (ABC) feature that assists in selecting the optimal connection.

6.1.5 MITIGATING RISKS BY CONTEXT

The Automotive's risks in satisfying cars' connectivity requests are similar to those of an operator. The main issue is identifying valid subscriptions and preventing identity theft or abuse of paid services. Automotive service providers are concerned about the abusive behavior of flat-rate users as drivers get used to consuming "expensive" media. The car provides additional data quota, unrelated to users' smartphones, and this can be exploited if downloaded files are shared across other devices. However, occasional excessive usage could be allowed to keep good will, so historical usage context can help to make informed decisions to accept or reject service requests. The Enterprise requires further protection to defend their commercially sensitive data, but not all connected services qualify for the high level of security. Some cars are at the service of highly trusted personnel, but other vehicles are pooled between many drivers or staff members. Hence, risk policies depend on the context that includes the type of car, the user privileges, and the connected service and data. Such risk policies and filters must remain confidential, even from the Automotive. Therefore, the Enterprise should be able to produce its own context analysis and transmit only the results. This context can be integrated with the Automotive's own considerations, thus allowing the Enterprise to assert its policies and preferences.

6.1.6 EFFECTS OF POLICY-BASED SERVICES

A system that enables the range of persuasive selling features as described previously would have a considerable impact on the Automotive's car sales prospects. In particular, offering the Enterprise the ability to manage budgets and apply their own prioritization can win large corporate contracts for the automotive. Beyond car sales; there will also be growing service revenue streams throughout the car's life, instead of the one-off initial sales price. Since services are charged directly to users or enterprises, service margins can be higher than car sales margins, which are made through a network of agents. Another notable effect is the reduction of costs, where the Automotive applies selective capping and optimization of the carrying network, for example, utilizing citywide wi-fi. Avoiding abuse and detecting identity thefts early reduce operating costs significantly.

6.2 A NOVEL VEHICULAR INFORMATION NETWORK ARCHITECTURE BASED ON NAMED DATA NETWORKING

Vehicles are becoming increasingly intelligent and are being integrated with many information devices, for example, global positioning system (GPS), sensors, and mobile router (MR). Today, vehicles are eager to retrieve more information (e.g., traffic, road, and weather conditions) while on the road. In addition, vehicles are also providing information, which is being sensed around them. Intervehicle communication (IVC) enables the acquisition and processing of a large amount of data via intelligent vehicular-computing platforms. Consequently, drivers can acquire and deliver real-time information with minimum delay, and transportation authorities can get real-time information about road traffic and on vehicles' violations of traffic laws. In other words, various types of services can be supported through the IVC in a vehicular information network traditionally referred to as the intelligent transportation system (ITS). These services include road safety information exchange as well as other types of useful information for smart navigation, smart traffic management, smart parking, driver alerts about road congestions, accidents, weather conditions, offering information for tourists, targeted advertisement for local services, and promotional offers to drivers and passengers. To support the aforementioned services/applications and a large amount of information exchange in the vehicular information network, we need an efficient and scalable network architecture.

However, if the routing protocols and information identification schemes in the vehicular information network still follow the traditional TCP/IP protocol stack, the security, scalability, and efficiency shortcomings of the current Internet are all inherited. In particular, it has been observed recently that information (or content) data has become the heart of almost all communications and, in particular, over the Internet. This information-centric usage of the Internet raises various architectural challenges, many of which are not effectively handled by the current Internet architecture because the architecture is based on location-dependent communications using IP addresses. To address some of the security, scalability, and efficiency challenges, the information-centric networking (ICN) concept was proposed. ICN focuses on how to evolve the current Internet infrastructure so that it can support future network applications by introducing named data as an Internet principle. ICN targets the general infrastructure that provides in-network caching, name-based routing, and self-certification so that the information can be distributed in scalable, cost-efficient, and secure manner. In addition, ICN aims to achieve the reliable distribution of content by providing a general platform for communication services that are available only today in dedicated systems such as peer-to-peer (P2P) overlays and proprietary content distribution networks.

In the past few years, several research projects have been undertaken around the ICN concept and different solutions aimed at redesigning the Internet with the information-centric or content-centric perspective have been proposed. Some of the recent research projects include data-oriented network architecture (DONA), named data networking (NDN), publish-subscribe Internet technology (PURSUIT), and network of information (Netting). These solutions proposed content-naming (identification) techniques and routing schemes for an efficient and scalable Internet with a high number of devices and large-scale content. For example, the NDN concept performs content routing based on the content name rather than using location information (e.g., IP address in the TCP-/IP-based Internet). With a hierarchical content name and name-oriented routing, NDN aims to develop a novel network architecture that is better suited for efficiently accessing and distributing large-scale content.

6.2.1 REQUIREMENTS OF VEHICULAR INFORMATION NETWORK AND APPLICATION SCENARIOS

There will be over a billion vehicles in the world and more than a billion mobile devices globally by 2020. Besides, there will be billion "things" connected to the Internet, among which vehicles will constitute a major portion. As the vehicles and the devices carried by their passengers and drivers become increasingly Internet-connected and run more advanced applications, they will challenge the capacity of the underlying transportation and communication infrastructures and application design techniques. The vehicular information network is part of a growing ecosystem of human-centric sensing applications that use personal and community-scale participatory data collection. This kind of information ecosystem has been fueled by the proliferation of low-cost, high-performance sensing devices. These devices include billions of mobile phones in use and now expanding into active RF identification devices (RFIDs), smart residential wireless power meters, in-vehicle GPS devices, sensor-enhanced entertainment platforms (e.g., Wii-fit), and activity-monitoring sportswear (e.g., the Nike + iPod system) that have become accessible to the average consumers.

Nowadays, the information ecosystem of emerging applications processes and distils the various types of data generated by the plethora of devices into actionable information. For the vehicular information network case, the collected data typically include GPS trajectories to monitor traffic patterns, pollution traces to assess environmental impact, vehicular fuel efficiency measurements to find fuel-efficient routes, and healthcare data to monitor physical status of the driver or passenger. To collect such data, vehicles are being designed to enable seamless integration with more information devices (e.g., GPS, sensors, and MRs) and be capable of interacting with more of the aforementioned applications. Vehicles and drivers can make use of such information (e.g., traffic, road, weather, and health conditions) when they are on the road. Vehicles can also publish the information (such as photos and videos) sensed around them.

Route planning and turn-by-turn navigation, which incorporates traffic congestion detection, maximize road utilization while minimizing risk, incorporate high-precision travel estimation, avoid pollution hotspots, and/or provide time-varying road feature and hazard notification during critical events such as natural disasters as well as everyday driving. Predictive vehicle maintenance applications enable trillions of data points to be accessed privately by manufacturers on behalf of vehicles' owners. Data collected by in-vehicle sensors can be retrieved by the manufacturer to provide real-time maintenance support for the vehicle.

Local/microenvironment data sharing on air quality or cultural and civic events can be achieved. Emergency response applications can use vehicles' data to assist after accidents or during other critical events. Such applications can use medical information for monitoring passengers' conditions, provide tracking data to search for missing people at the time of a disaster, or detect potential accident risks and distribute relevant timely alert messages.

Considering these trends, we need to develop a novel vehicular information network architecture that can support high mobility of vehicles and manage a huge number of information objects in an efficient and scalable manner. A few typical future application scenarios of the vehicular information network are illustrated in Fig. 6.1. The vehicle is installed with GPS to get its current location and the time information, with sensors to collect the weather and temperature information, with MR to provide the Internet access, especially for passengers without Internet access ability. Vehicles can disseminate the sensed information or multimedia data through the network using push- or pull-based techniques, and vehicles can communicate with nearby vehicles in an ad hoc manner or via the communication infrastructure in order to receive or send traffic, road condition information, or multimedia data.

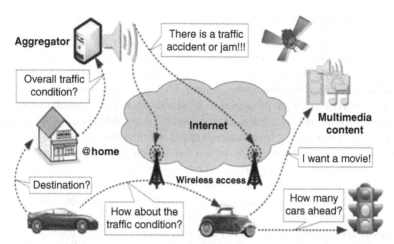

FIGURE 6.1 Vehicular Information Network Architecture Based on Named Data Networking (NDN)

An aggregator (such as a server) is used not only to collect and process data but also to provide processed information to other vehicles on demand. Based on the aforementioned communication requirements for the vehicular information network, the focus of this work is to develop a novel network architecture that enables high mobility, ad-hoc networking, and communication schemes to support the various application scenarios presented previously. In particular, we focus on how to enable a large number of devices to communicate the vehicular environment.

6.3 VEHICULAR CLOUD NETWORKING: ARCHITECTURE AND DESIGN PRINCIPLES

Over the past few decades, a lot of research efforts have been devoted to vehicular ad hoc networks (VANETs), ranging from physical layer communications to networking challenges in vehicle-to-vehicle (V2V) and vehicle-to-infrastructure (V2I) modes. With the technological advancement, VANETs provide drivers and passengers with safety and convenience and furthermore introduce new applications for entertainment and environment monitoring. The vehicular communication is about to evolve with emerging paradigms. The inherent properties of VANET contents and the way that VANET applications consume the contents are leading the evolution. More specifically:

- Vehicles produce and consume a great amount of content having the property of local relevance (time, space, and consumer).
- Vehicles simply seek contents regardless of their providers.
- Vehicles collaborate using their resources to create value-added services with minimum help from the Internet infrastructure. These characteristics, starting from applications, impact various aspects in VANETs. In particular, they will significantly change the computing (content generation-processing-consumption) and network (content distribution) models, which leads to a future vehicular networking system: vehicular cloud networking (VCN).

6.3.1 EMERGING APPLICATIONS ON WHEELS

Applications for in-vehicle communications have ranged from safety and convenience to entertainment and commercial services. This subsection discusses three noticeable characteristics observed in emerging VANET applications. Application content time-space validity vehicles produce a great amount of content while at the same time consuming the content. That is, they become rich data "presumptives." Such contents show several common properties of local relevance, local validity, explicit lifetime, and local interest. Local validity indicates that vehicle-generated content has its own spatial scope of utility to consumers. In safety applications, for instance, a speed-warning message near a sharp corner is valid only to vehicles approaching the corner, say within the explicit lifetime, reflects the fact that vehicle content has its own temporal scope of validity. This also implies that the content must be available during its entire lifetime. For instance, road congestion information may be valid for the minimum amount of time, while a roadwork warning is valid until the work is finished. Local interest indicates that nearby vehicles represent the bulk of potential content consumers. This concept is further extended so as to distinguish the scope of consumers. For instance, all the vehicles in the vicinity want to receive safety messages, while only a fraction of vehicles is interested in commercial advertisements.

6.3.2 CONTENT-CENTRIC DISTRIBUTION

Vehicle applications are mainly interested in the content itself, not its provenance. This memoryless property is characteristic of VANETs. In the fixed Internet, when one wants to check traffic congestion, one visits a favorite service site. That is, the explicit site's URL guarantees access to ample reliable information. In contrast, vehicle applications flood query messages to a local area, not to a specific vehicle, accepting responses regardless of the identity of the content providers. In fact, the response may come from vehicle in the vicinity that has, in turn, received such traffic information indirectly through neighboring vehicles. In this case, the vehicle does not care who started the broadcast. This characteristic is mainly due to the fact that the sources of information (vehicles) are mobile and geographically scattered.

6.3.3 VEHICLE COLLABORATION SHARING SENSORY DATA

Emerging vehicle applications consume a huge amount of sensor data in a collaborative manner. That is, multiple sensors installed on vehicles, record a myriad of physical phenomena. Vehicle applications collect such sensor records, even from neighboring vehicles, to produce value-added services. In Mob Eyes, for example, vehicles use few sensors (including a video camera) to record all surrounding events such as car accidents while driving. Thereafter, Internet agents and/or mobile agents (e.g., police) search the vehicular network for witnesses as part of their investigation. The Car Speak application enables a vehicle to access sensors on neighboring vehicles in the same manner in which it can access its own. The vehicle then runs an autonomous driving application using the sensor collection without knowing who produced what.

6.3.4 NETWORKING

The existing VANET networking model has been derived primarily from traditional wired networking protocols. However, due to the huge difference between the Internet and the infrastructure less ad hoc condition, the model shows several intrinsic limitations. First, the VANET protocol still assumes using IP address to represent a host. Assigning addresses to moving nodes is not trivial in ad-hoc environments. The assignment task often requires infrastructure support, such as a central dynamic host configuration protocol (DHCP) server, which directly conflicts against the philosophy of ad-hoc networks that operate in a self-organized manner without any infrastructure. Second, it is not easy to discover the IP address of the publisher of specific content in an ad network. Nodes join and leave the network frequently, and any node can become a new publisher of the content. Thus, the content of interest cannot be consistently bound to a unique address. Last, the VANET protocol simply performs IP-based end-to-end communications. During a routine procedure, a router simply relays and then deletes content. Although the content is so popular that many nodes also want it, the router cannot directly send it to them because the router does not save it.

6.3.5 VEHICULAR CLOUD COMPUTING

Vehicles and sensors within a local area generate vehicle contents. These contents are stored and searched in the vicinity, and processed and consumed within their lifetime period by neighbors. Recently, Gela introduced a new computing model, vehicular cloud computing (VCC), to account for these characteristics. VCC is a variant of mobile cloud computing (MCC), which begins from a conventional cloud computing model. To mobile nodes with limited resources, the Internet cloud offers network access for both using unlimited computing resources on the Internet and storing/downloading contents to/from the Internet. However, it is too costly to upload all content to the Internet cloud, and too time-consuming to search and download interesting content from the Internet cloud. Besides, most of the content picked up by vehicles has local relevance only and is best stored locally. In VCC, most queries from drivers are about the world surrounding us (i.e., local relevance), and vehicles are the best probes of this environment. VCC resolves the queries using a self-organized model of the local environment. That is, vehicles effectively form a cloud within which services are produced, maintained, and consumed. To realize the model, VCC leverages the increasing processing and storage capacity of vehicles: it constructs a cloud by using the collection of vehicles' computing resources, which primarily aim at extending the capability of interactions among vehicles.

6.3.6 INFORMATION-CENTRIC NETWORKING

ICN is initially conceptualized as a general form of communication architecture to achieve efficient content distribution on the Internet. ICN focuses on what (content) instead of where (host). This is to fulfill the primary demands of consumers, who are interested only in the content itself and not its provenance, and publishers, who strive to efficiently distribute contents to consumers. To this end, Incuses node or data attributes (e.g., content name, geo-location, or context) serve for routing rather than a specific node address (i.e., IP address). This decouples the content from the publishers. In this sense, content-based routing, geo-routing and context-based routing can be classified into types of ICN. Some of the recently proposed architecture forcing in the Internet context include data-oriented network architecture (DONA), named data networking (NDN), publish-subscribe Internet routing paradigm (PSIRP), and a network of information (Netting).

Of these architectures, NDN has recently been extended to VANET. NDN has two types of packets: interest, from consumers, and data (i.e., content), from publishers. A content name in these packets is used for routing. A consumer requests content by broadcasting an Interest with its name toward potential publishers. When a publisher receives the Interest and has data matching the interest, it replies with the data back to the consumer using the path of the interest in reverse. NDN allows routers on the path to cache the content so that they can reply with the cached content to consumers once they receive the matching interest. This way, NDN achieves an effective content distribution that critically requires supporting its content-oriented applications.

6.3.7 VEHICULAR CLOUD NETWORKING

Computing and networking models are two integral parts to support emerging VANET applications and services, which are efficiently supported by VCC and ICN, respectively. In this sense, integrating VCC and ICN would be an ideal choice, and we name the concept vehicular cloud networking (VCN). The subsequent section discusses VCN fundamentals, system operations, and service scenario.

6.3.8 VCN FUNDAMENTALS

The eventual goal of VCN is to create a vehicle cloud and encourage collaborations among cloud members to produce advanced vehicular services that an individual cannot make alone. Unlike the Internet cloud, which is created and maintained by a cloud provider, the vehicle cloud is temporarily created by interconnecting resources available in the vehicles and roadside units (RSUs). Such networked resources operate a common virtual platform on which the efficiency of collaboration is maximized. ICN together contributes to creating the cloud and running the virtual platform efficiently. Resources in the vehicle cloud are distinguished from the ones in the conventional cloud. Each vehicle has three categories of resources data storage, sensors, and computing. The data storage stores vehicle contents generated from applications and sensors as well as traditional multimedia files. It supports data sharing among cloud participants by accepting an external search query and replying with matched contents. The sensor is able to self-actuate as well as detect events in the physical world. With technological advancement, each sensor is directly connected so that external systems can read the sensor data and/or control the sensor. The computing resource is similar to that of the Internet cloud except that its capacity is limited because it is a collection of mobile resources. In VCN; the resources are internetworked via purely peer-to-peer connections. That is, each vehicle negotiates the level of resource sharing directly with each other. For efficiency, one vehicle in a cloud can be elected as a broker based on some selected metrics (e.g., connectivity to vehicles). Then it mediates the process of resource sharing as well as other cloud operations. An RSU that joins the cloud as a stationary member can be a good candidate for the negotiator role. We also envision the deployment of resource-constrained RSUs such as cameras. They may not have enough storage and computing power, but still have reliable connections to vehicles. If this is the case, they can store and manage data indexes for effective content discovery.

6.3.9 VCN SYSTEM OPERATIONS

Given the collection of resources from vehicles and RSUs and their potential interconnections, we illustrate how the VCN system operates to establish a virtual computing platform and enable cloud type collaboration in it.

6.3.9.1 Cloud Resource Discovery

When a vehicle runs an application, it becomes a cloud leader and recruits members (i.e., vehicles and RSUs in the vicinity) that can provide their resources to construct a vehicle cloud for the application.

The types and search range of necessary resources depend on applications. For instance, the search range can be a predefined distance, a road section, or an intersection. Having determined the set of necessary resource types, the cloud leader broadcasts a resource request message, RREQ, to nodes within the search range. Nodes willing to share their resources send a resource reply message, RREP, back to the leader with information on their resource capabilities.

6.3.9.2 Cloud Formation

Upon receiving RREPs, the cloud leader selects nodes (cloud members) with which it organizes a cloud. The selection mechanism may pursue minimizing total resource usage in the cloud while ensuring the correct operation of the application.

6.3.9.3 Task Assignment and Result Collection

The cloud leader splits the application into several tasks and distributes them to cloud members, considering the availability and accessibility of their resources. The leader also maintains a cloud table with members' IDs and their task assignment information. The cloud members return the results back to the leader after completing their tasks.

6.3.9.4 Content Publishing and Sharing

Once collecting all the task results from the members, the leader processes them to obtain output content be processed in a single node or the published contents cannot be stored in a single node, the leader organizes another vehicle cloud for the data processing or content storage. The published contents are shared over the entire network. That is, any vehicle can send a content request to search them. Upon receiving the request and having the matched contents in data storage, the cloud members, including the leader, can reply with the contents.

6.3.9.5 Cloud Maintenance

In a vehicle cloud, a member sends a cloud to leave a message to the leader on its leaving. Then, the leader selects a replacement among nodes that sent RREPs in their source discovery phase and have resources enough to complete the assigned task of the leaving member. The leader distributes the task to the new cloud member and updates the cloud table.

6.3.9.6 Cloud Release

When the leader no longer uses the cloud or moves out of the cloud, it releases the resources so that other clouds can reuse them. To this end, the leader sends a loud release message to all the members and removes the cloud member list.

6.4 TRUST-BASED INFORMATION DISSEMINATION FRAMEWORK FOR VEHICULAR NETWORKS

VANETs are the basis for different applications offered in ITS. These envisioned applications cover a large spectrum ranging from delay-sensitive safety-related applications such as accident notifications to delay-tolerant services such as file sharing. No matter what the application is, routing or in general, information dissemination in a vehicular network is challenging due to the highly dynamic and mobile nature of this network. Different applications in VANETs can be offered using either broadcasting the information, which is the case mainly in safety-related applications, or unicast/multicast, which happens mostly in no-safety applications. Over the past few years, researchers have proposed several broadcast and unicast routing protocols for VANETs that minimize the delivery delay or the communication interference. However, the missing key point in those methods is the security analysis. A node is assumed to be malicious when it manipulates or intentionally drops a message. Consider this simple example that explains the significance of the problem: suppose one vehicle has a message and it has two neighbors from which it chooses to forward its message. One of the neighbors is a trustworthy node that relays every message without any problem; however, routing from that node increases the delay.

The other neighbor, on the other hand, is on a fast route to the destination but it is malicious and drops the messages half the time. Now, based on a normal routing protocol that the only focus is on minimizing the delay, the malicious node will be selected to route the message faster. Hence, ignoring malicious nodes can avoid the whole algorithm efforts to minimize the delay.

This example clearly shows why there is a need for safe and reliable communication framework in VANETs. Note that our focus is on having a secure packet delivery in addition to a reliable one. Packet reliability and packet delivery ratio could be damaged by environment and network characteristics such as channel fading or collisions. Secure packet delivery, on the other hand, can be hurt because of attacks and intentional manipulations by malicious nodes. Trust is a human and psychological factor that is historically very well known in social interactions. Using artificial intelligence (AI) and bringing the concept of the trust to the information and communication technology (ICT) has been proposed and studied during the past decade. For instance, the trust of a relay node i can be defined as the number of packets that i has relayed without manipulating them, out of the total number of packets given to the i to be relayed. Then, the probability of i relaying a new packet is the trust value of i based on this simple rule: A node acts the same way that it has done so far. As the first contribution, the author leverages this concept to cover a range of application requirements such as security, privacy, delay, and reliability to name a few.

There is a trust value calculated for each of these parameters. Then, they developed a function of all these trust values to calculate the total trust for each path, which is our reference for choosing the best route. Mainly, trust in a VANET faces two main challenges: (1) the speed of vehicles, which changes the topology constantly and minimizes the contact times between the nodes; and (2) the lack of a centralized third party to evaluate and maintain the trust values. The majority of the trust models proposed for VANETs are entity-centric in which the focus is on verifying the vehicle credentials. Once the source is authenticated, the message can be trusted. There are a few data-centric approaches that focus on the correctness of the received message, instead. Both of these models suffer from scalability and the entity-centric models have the assumption that there is always a third-party certificate issuer in the vicinity that is often not valid in the context of VANETs. The survey presents state-of-the-art in trust models/systems and routing protocols in VANETs. Then, their next contribution, they proposed a novel two-layer framework for application-oriented context-aware trust-based communication (FACT) in VANETs, where nodes use only their most trusted neighbors to forward the message; otherwise, they carry the message by themselves. FACT consists of two modules: admission and dissemination. The key distinction of the FACT lies in its space-centric nature. It is a combination of entity-/data-centric methods in addition to its focus on location. Once a message is received, FACT first applies three safety checks in the admission module to make sure the message is secure: (1) it originated from a trusted region and traversed a trusted path, (2) it was not under attack on its path, and (3) it has a valid content.

Then, FACT admits the message and pushes it to the dissemination module to be forwarded through a trusted path. Each vehicle has a trust table where each road segment in the city has its own trust value and this value is constantly updated by the vehicle based on its experience in that segment. The intuition behind FACT is that some areas of every city are known to be safer, with better facilities. It is fair to assume that vehicles in those areas are more trusted, as well. Otherwise and when there are malicious vehicles in the area, that neighborhood's trust is reduced and it gets a bad reputation. They divided vehicular networks' applications into three main categories and then identify major requirements of each category. FACT is a general admission/communication framework that accommodates all requirements of each application while making sure the connection is trusted. It supports both broadcast and unicast/ multicast modes. After explaining the details of FACT, they evaluated their framework via simulation and showed that FACT outperforms other routing protocols when some areas of the city are not trusted. FACT gives network designers a full package, which delivers trustworthy messages through a safe path with high reliability and in a short amount of time. It is flexible enough, meaning the network admins can tune the parameters based on the network condition. Designers can incorporate their desired scheduling and routing schemes into FACT and still disseminate the messages safely. FACT is a framework that supports different applications with different requirements.

6.4.1 TRUST MODEL

In this section, we first described some of the definitions for the existing framework. Then, calculations regarding trust value and the total is given. The level of performing the expected service by a trustee is called satisfaction, from which is derived the level of trustworthiness. The four major parts of the trust system are initial trust, trust metric, operation, and trust management. Identifying the appropriate trust metric, which is relevant to the application, and a mechanism to measure the metric, for example, a binary or percentage unit, are part of a trust system. In addition, designing a system that manages the trust is needed, which can be centralized or distributed, or a combination of both.

Trust assessment can be direct or indirect. Indirect assessment, a trustor relies on its own experience about a trustee. For instance, in a wireless communication environment, if node S (trustor) sends a packet to node R (trustee), which is one hop away, to forward (service) the packet to node Q, which is two hops away, a scan overhears R, and observes if R is genuinely sending the packet. On the other hand and in indirect assessment, a trustor relies on other nodes' experiences in dealing with a trustee. FACT is based on carry-and-forward information dissemination. Therefore, if there is no vehicle in the vicinity, the vehicle carrying the message should continue carrying the message until it comes across another vehicle and then decide on forwarding the message.

The rest of this section is based on the assumption of having at least one vehicle in the transmission range. FACT is a general framework that allows messages of different categories of traffic to be securely delivered to their destinations based on their requirements. As shown in Fig. 6.2, all vehicles maintain a trusted map, which divides the city into several neighborhoods, and each neighborhood itself is divided into multiple segments. A segment is part of the road between two intersections. Their work is not limited to a specific sectoring method; it can be symmetrical or asymmetrical sectoring. Map division should be done in a way that meets the network administrator's resolution requirement without imposing excessive overhead.

In the trust map and for every segment, a trust value TR is recorded for each time of day in each specific day of the week. For simplicity, they considered only a rush hour and regular hour for one

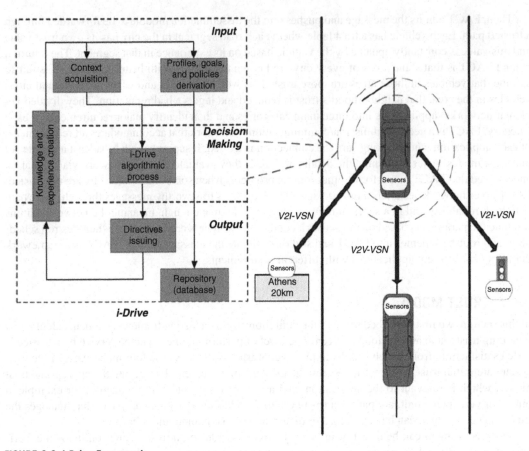

FIGURE 6.2 I-Drive Framework

day, that is, two entries per day and entries in total per week for each segment. It is possible to further simplify and differentiate only between weekdays and weekends, which lowers the number of entities for a segment to four. Every vehicle starts with an initial trust value of each neighborhood. Then, it gradually updates different entries of the trust map for that segment/neighborhood based on its experience. For example, if the vehicle experiences a trustworthy communication in that particular segment during rush hour in an weekdays, then it increases the corresponding trust value for those times and days. Whenever a vehicle is calculating the trust value of a road segment for the first time, it uses the neighborhood's trust value instead. Note that the key component of our trust framework is that instead of assigning a trust value to each node, which is not scalable and hard to maintain and even inefficient, they assign a trust value to a neighborhood and to each segment of that neighborhood. In other words, our main contribution is that FACT is space-centric, that is, it uses location information to evaluate the trustworthiness of messages.

There is a similar scenario in a real city where some neighborhoods are safer than the others. This is the intuition behind FACT. Furthermore, there are no predefined trust values for different neighborhoods because all cars start with the FACT by assigning the same value to all neighborhoods and then gradually update the database as they learn more about different areas. However, in different times of the day, cars from other parts of the city may travel to these areas and lower the actual trustworthiness of these areas. That is why FACT assigns different trust values to different times of the day and constantly modifies these values. The biggest advantage of FACT is its scalability, low complexity, and efficiency even for a metropolitan area. In this approach, where there is a trust value per node, resources are often wasted because they may never encounter a particular car again, but it is much more likely that they travel to the same area more than once.

6.5 KNOWLEDGE-BASED INTELLIGENT TRANSPORTATION SYSTEM

Information and Communication Technologies (ICT) have been long standing at the forefront of international research interest. This is reflected in efforts in international projects and standardization activities, which aim in principle at the provision of innovative services and applications, tailored to individualized user needs. The common denominator of the latest trends in networking technologies is the future Internet (FI), which will be connecting people, contents, and things, based on novel high throughput and low-latency network infrastructures and related technologies. The FI envisages mechanisms that promise easier overcoming of the structural limitations of telecommunication infrastructures and their management systems, so as to further facilitate the design, development, and integration of novel services and applications. An area of applications where ICT find prosperous grounding the FI era is transportation. The motivation for this is that many cities face a growing volume of traffic, which is associated with several unpleasant phenomena, such as time delays, high pollution, degradation of life quality, as well as accidents and emergencies. The aforementioned reveal important inefficiencies related to transportation, as identified by the research community of both public agencies and private industry. Those inefficiencies have established transportation management as a key service that should be offered by ICT.

In this respect, several innovative and cost-effective mobile services and applications for traffic networks are under investigation, emerging as the cornerstone of the so-called ITS. By enabling vehicles to communicate with each other via vehicle-to-vehicle (V2V) communication, as well as with roadside base stations via vehicle-to-infrastructure (V2I) communication, ITS can contribute to safer and more efficient roads. In light of the aforementioned, the author proposes a novel transportation management approach, namely "i-Drive," targeted at proactively managing vehicles and the surrounding transportation infrastructure quickly and efficiently, in a way that guarantees significant improvements in traffic/safety/emergency management. The particular contribution of the work mainly lies in the utilization of a knowledge-based decision-making algorithm, which can increase the overall levels of safety through recognizing potential emergencies as a priority, thus improving the total transportation quality. Moreover, it literally also addresses the integration of the advantages ovens in ITS through the description of a whole framework that can incorporate various services/applications that can improve the quality of transportation.

6.5.1 I-DRIVE DESCRIPTION

The whole framework in which i-Drive operates is shown in Fig. 6.2. It comprises wireless sensors placed on vehicles and on specific objects of the transportation infrastructure (traffic lights, road signs), as well as VSNs formed by neighboring vehicles and parts of the infrastructure. i-Drive utilizes the potential of

VSNs in ITS and validates this through an efficient heuristic. In general, the sensors are required to determine how to process in-vehicle data, which aggregated data are to be sent, how often, and so on. Sensor measurements are processed in a hierarchical manner with specialized reasoning techniques, which yield information about the vehicle–driver interactions at various abstraction levels. Moreover, the information exchanged is classified and the communication is enabled in a V2V–VSN (among neighboring vehicles), as well as in a V2I–VSN (between vehicles and infrastructure objects) manner, which results in information exchange that is transformed into collective intelligence. This intelligence is adopted by the i-Drive components, with the goal to decide upon issuing directives to the drivers and the overall transportation infrastructure. Moreover, communication in this respect is fast (VSNs impose only a few microseconds of delay), minimizing the associated time needed to reach a decision.

A detailed description of components is delineated in Fig. 6.2. i-Drive itself reflects an approach that disposes of certain inputs and outputs. The detailed description has been influenced by several related research attempts with regard to decision making.

6.5.1.1 Input: Context Acquisition
The input includes contextual information acquired from the vehicle's sensors and the VV–VSNs, regarding the status of the i-Drive vehicle, its velocity, direction, and neighboring vehicles' positions, directions, and velocities. Additionally, input information is acquired from the V2I–VSNs related to the condition of elements or segments of the transportation infrastructure (traffic lights, road signs, road conditions, congestion levels, and overall load in a telecommunications network). Let it be noted that sensor measurements provide i-Drive with input information very often (once per microseconds, as assumed herein), so as to cater to timely delivery of crucial information to the driver. Last, information transferred to i-Drive includes time-stamps for considering transmission delays, whereas, as mentioned previously, propagation delays are of minor importance to this work because of the presupposition of the reliable operation ovens. For the same reason, other aspects such as handling of errors are to be considered in future research attempts.

6.5.1.2 Profiles, Goals, and Policies Derivation
Last, the input includes information on the driver's profiles. To do so, a predefined driver status is inferred from interpreted driver monitoring data (this information is also retrieved from the vehicle sensors). In this respect, plan recognition techniques are explored to derive driver state and behavior. This means that sequences of interactions between the driver and the vehicle, the raw signals about a driver's physical condition (eye-blink frequency, eyelid opening, head movement, profile, operating the foot pedals, pressing buttons on the instrument panel, steering wheel activities), as well as vehicle state information, are all acquired in the form of facial driver recognition, which allows for the detection of differences between changing driving styles. Plan recognition techniques use an algorithmic process (defined in), in order to compare the driver profile parameters (mentioned subsequently) with the set of driver states and identifies the closest one.

Finally, driver's goals, priorities, and policies are also included. Goals and policies aim at maximizing the performance, safety, reliability, and stability of the decisions taken from an end-to-end perspective.

6.5.1.3 Output: Directives Issuing
The i-Drive algorithmic process results in issuing commands (directives) towards the driver, so as to adapt the vehicle's road behavior and tackle any emergency situations, through emergency braking or through vehicle direction correction (again based on perception and reasoning). Commands are issued

in the form of alert notifications of various levels of significance, as will be shown in the sequel. Moreover, congestion can be avoided through the reconsideration of the vehicle's advisable route, as well as through notifying the driver accordingly.

6.5.1.4 i-Drive Algorithmic Process

Several approaches can be envisaged for the decision-making process. In general, decision making should guarantee optimal safety, performance, reliability, and stability, from the end-to-end perspective. Moreover, cost factors can also be addressed, this being left for future reference. As will be described in the subsequent sections, i-Drive utilizes a heuristic that can exploit the inputting terms of optimizing an objective function (OF), which includes several aspects of the vehicle's behavior (overall delay, mean velocity, etc.).

6.5.1.5 Knowledge and Experience Creation

The information acquired is processed and appropriately interpreted, so as to infer knowledge and experience. To do so, all combinations of input parameters and related decisions are kept in an appropriately structured database. The knowledge model captures the following aspects: (1) it keeps track of certain contextual situations (recurrent or emergencies) and the way they have been confronted is retained, so as to serve for future decisions; (2) it tries to estimate what constitutes a dangerous situation, in terms of improving the specification of certain values of parameters that would be more "subjective" than others, such as the road condition and the congestion level; and (3) it tries to estimate the importance of each parameter, judging from previous situations encountered and decisions taken, so as to gradually learn and improve the specification of parameters' weights.

Several context matching and reasoning techniques can be envisaged for this part of i-Drive, whereas the algorithm proposed in is utilized herein. In particular, whenever the specific contextual situation is encountered, i-Drive performs an initial search in the appropriate part of the (classified) database, so as to check whether a similar situation has been encountered also in the past and how it has been tackled (through an optimal or suboptimal solution). In affirmative, the algorithm proposed herein does not need to run and the previous decision is applied again. Otherwise, the i-Drive algorithm needs to run and reach a decision, through the process described in the following. Since sensor measurements provide i-Drive with input information continuously, through the exploitation of knowledge and experience, the algorithm needs to run only when something changes (when the present contextual information has not been addressed before). In this respect, valuable time is saved and the overall complexity is reduced.

6.6 HYBRID SENSOR AND VEHICULAR NETWORKS

Vehicular networks are a typical IoT application. An IoT application is commonly based on WSN (wireless sensor networks) to get awareness and connectivity. Due to vehicular movement properties, vehicles from self-organizing VANETs (vehicular ad hoc networks) dynamically, and they also connect to a WSN that has the node in the road or parking lot. Combined with the two characters, a new network named a hybrid sensor and vehicular network (HSVN) has been developed. In VANET and HSVN, the connections between vehicles and network infrastructure are nonstatic and are different from the typical network, so the traditional information service architecture is not suited to this environment. Among the WEB services, representational state transfer (REST) architecture focuses on avoiding application state in the server and has an important concept that a service scenario can be represented as URI-identified resources. All interactions between client and server can contain all the service state information that is necessary and the server does not have to keep resource session state with the client, Compared with SOAP-based web-service, REST aggressively improves the scalability, versatility, and components' independence of web services. There is no doubt that it is suitable for wireless vehicle networks that need to handle vast amounts of different information types. After analysis typical scenario about HSVN information services, this work introduces a method for vehicular sensor information services based on REST. The framework is an uneconomical way to meet the demand for vehicular sensor information services. The road terminals erected on the edge of the road and with parking terminals make up a static WSN that connects to the backbone (such as the Internet) in a cable way. And the vehicle's own sensor services, added to the static WSN, form a dynamic network.

The driving vehicles from self-organizing VANETs link with each other while they are in WSN. And VANETs together can share traffic information and perform rapid data interchange. In VANETs, vehicles spontaneously join from the network and the communication status among them is not continuous but peer to peer under the potential condition, especially in a case with two vehicles that are close to each other. On one hand vehicles can collect their own state information; on the other hand, they can store road information and upload their respective information to update the WSN's database as they pass through the network. There are three types of interactive scenes to be considered in Fig. 6.3: (1) interaction between WSN and vehicles in a VANET, (2) interaction between vehicle and vehicle that are moving in the same direction, and (3) vehicular interaction based on vehicle group moving in the opposite direction.

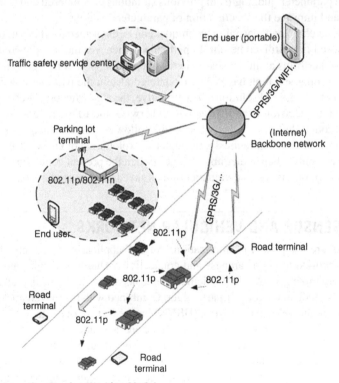

FIGURE 6.3 HSVN Information Service Working Model

6.6.1 HSVNS SERVICE MODEL

By analyzing the typical service scenario, three interactive objects can be abstracted in HSVN: (1) vehicular terminal users (VTU), (2) base station of transport services (BSTS), and (3) traffic safety service center (TSSC). One purpose of HSVNs is to protect traffic safety and provide users with "safe travel" service. As the core of the whole service system, TSSC maintains the independence and security of services. Generally, it has a dedicated database system to interconnect with the traffic system (TS), geographic information system (GIS), and other systems. Working together with road traffic sensor networks in HSVNs, TS can store the data collected from each node, plan data classification, and do administrative controlling on classified services effectively. Typical services include:

- Vehicular warning (speed, safety valve, etc.)
- Alert driver of dangerous conditions, like running off the road
- Road information (traffic flow, reports of accident, etc.)
- Warning of road anomaly
- Meteorological service (temperature, precipitation, etc.)
- Weather information coming from base station
- Geographic service (longitude and latitude, electronic map, etc.)
- Vehicular location, path planning, and so forth

The BSTS shown in Fig. 6.3, consisting of a series of road terminals and parking terminals and so on, is one kind of sensor network. According to the design of traffic safety, these base stations (terminals) can be designed as a simple access point for network or can be a smart unit that comes with its own system. To satisfy the demand for sensing safety, BSTS will be designed as a small computer system with a small database that is capable of monitoring the traffic information and can be regarded as one data access point. For the BSTS, which has its own rules of resource control, it can receive and store data from any vehicular node and provide information services for vehicles. Limited to the capacity of the base station's sensor, different BSTS have different coverage.

BSTS offers sophisticated communication among vehicular terminals. Vehicles obtain services from BSTS such as road terminals and parking lot terminals. These services are identified by road segments because the relationship between vehicles and road terminals is dynamic. BSTS interact with TSSC regularly to update information, act as an interface between wired networks and wireless networks, and gather service information respectively. In Fig. 6.3, scene service structure is presented. Every vehicular node has an independent display system and traces its driving routes to collect service data. It cannot only accept services from BSTS and TSSC but also share in self-data. In VANETs, every vehicular node will exchange information mutually. For the area without the BSTS coverage, vehicular terminals have the ability to communicate with backbone via mobile networks (G/G network).

6.6.2 CHARACTERISTICS OF HSVN INFORMATION SERVICE

According to the aforementioned analysis and the mobile features of vehicular terminals in HSVNs, we can get the features of HSVNs information services as follows. Information dissemination is multichannel and multirouting. Vehicular terminals can obtain services from TSSC directly or through the BSTS. A node (vehicular terminal, road terminal) in the entire network can be a client (for services), and also can be a server (provide information services). Information can be divided into two major categories of emergency and nonemergency. To the emergency, real-time communication is necessary.

Generally, the emergency information can be designed to short frame format for convenient delivery while nonemergency information, such as real-time traffic video information of the road, is transmitted by greater bandwidth. Concise service information is good for transmission. Because in the process of moving the connection between road terminal and the vehicle will often switch, so it will be better if that one service can be handled completely within the coverage of one road terminal.

6.7 INTRAVEHICLE NETWORKS

Recent advances in computer hardware and processing power have led to many innovations in the automotive environment. In-vehicle electronic systems are rapidly advancing in complexity and diversity. A multitude of sensors and processors are used in different parts of the vehicle for various functions. Antilock braking system (ABS) and electronic stability control are examples of systems that monitor a vehicles' internal performance and dynamics; whereas camera, radar, and ultrasonic sensors are being used to sense the environment around the vehicle and provide drivers with more information about their surroundings. The wireless interconnection of sensors and other devices within the vehicle, such as radio frequency in the case of tire pressure monitoring systems (TPMSs), ultra-wideband, or IEEE. x–based solutions, is currently being investigated. While wireless solutions offer advantages over wired systems in that they alleviate cabling requirements in-vehicle, they still require connection to the electrical power source in the vehicle, which mitigates this advantage. Some researchers have raised concerns about security in wireless networks, demonstrating that eavesdropping can occur on a TPMS network, and even reverse engineering and injecting false data is possible in a moving vehicle. Due to the absolute need for reliability and security in safety-critical systems, wired solutions are expected to dominate for the foreseeable future. Historically, each new electronic sensor or application in the vehicle has been implemented by adding a new standalone electronic control unit (ECU) device and subsystem.

This has led to in-vehicle networks growing in both size and complexity in an organic fashion. This often leads to many complex and boxed heterogeneous systems in a single vehicle. This is undesirable because there can be a number of different network protocols in use, which inhibits communication between systems. It also increases the cost to the manufacturer in terms of hardware costs, development costs, and support costs. To overcome these problems, communication links were established between relevant ECUs, allowing ECUs to share data with one another and enabling more advanced functionality. For example, the ABS subsystem may communicate with a seat-belt pretensions system to activate it in the event of a collision. This approach is very inefficient as, with point-to-point links, the number of connections required exponentially increases with the number of ECUs installed in the vehicle. To overcome this problem, multiple ECUs are connected to one another using bus-based networks such as controller area network (CAN) or Flex Ray. The use of bus-based networks is an improvement on the point-to-point link system; however, it presents its own problems since, as the number of ECUs connected to a bus increases over time, the bandwidth consumed significantly increases. The question of bandwidth does not generally manifest as a significant issue in control applications within the vehicle due to the limited bandwidth requirements of the sensors involved. However, the bandwidth issue has been brought into sharp focus through the introduction of infotainment and camera-based advanced driver assistance systems (ADAS). These applications significantly require more bandwidth than traditional control applications, and as such, the technologies and techniques used on current networks are insufficient for the needs of a next generation in-vehicle network architecture.

Recently, there has been a general desire within the automotive industry to streamline the development of these systems through standardization of technologies between manufacturers, leading to greater reuse and interoperability between original equipment manufacturers and manufacturers. Most major automotive companies are members of one or more special interest groups and bodies centered on this goal. These bodies include the One Pair Ethernet Special Interest Group (OPEN-SIG), the AVnu alliance, and the Japanese Automotive Software Platform and Architecture (JasPar) group. This work aims to comprehensively describe the most recent developments in the field of in-vehicle networking at all levels of the network stack, from the underlying physical layer connection and the data link layer to the operating systems on which next-generation advanced driver assistance systems will run. Each level of the automotive software stack illustrated in Fig. 6.4, and the most recent trends and developments will be discussed. This work includes more in-depth exploration of physical layer technologies for next-generation ethernet networks, as well as of important middleware technologies in use in the automotive industry. We also provide high-level discussion on the overall future direction of each of the explored areas based on trends identified from published research in this area. We aim to identify the key requirements for a highly standardized interoperable next generation automotive network and outline approaches taken in the literature to achieve this goal. A vehicular network organizes and connects vehicles with each other, and with mobile and fixed locations resources.

An automobile in an in-vehicle network adopts four vehicle bus protocols: CAN, LIN (Local Interconnect Network), MOST (Media Oriented Systems Transport) and Flex Ray. However, these

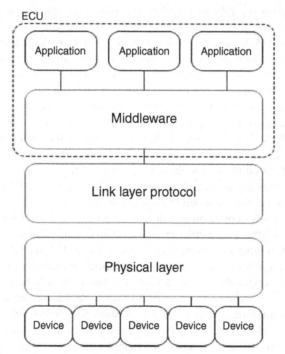

FIGURE 6.4 Advance Driving Assistance Working Protocol

protocols cannot intercommunicate with each other. Therefore, the OSEK operating system is designed as standard software architecture for the various ECUs. In the out-vehicle network, the on board unit (OBU) in the automobile can communicate with the infrastructure via the Internet. The authors discuss next-generation vehicular network architecture, the modern in-vehicle networks, onboard computers and the Internet, mobile telecommunications, and telemetric applications in the ground vehicles, and finally, we introduce future desired features. This chapter discusses the architectures in a vehicular network environment. The first section introduces the overview of in-vehicle and out-vehicle network architectures. The next section describes in-vehicle network architecture for disaster communication network by combining various automotive bus protocols. The third section describes the out-vehicle network architecture for disaster communication network by combining various wireless LANs. The last section discusses next-generation vehicular network architecture, the modern in-vehicle networks, onboard computers and the Internet, mobile telecommunications and telemetric applications in the ground vehicles, and introduces future desired features.

A vehicular network organizes and connects vehicles with each other, and with mobile and fixed locations resources. Many telemetric architectures, including navigation services architecture, traffic information architecture, location-based services architecture, entertainment services architecture, emergency and safety services architecture have been provided. In these architectures, traffic information and navigation services are generally provided by central TSPs (telemetric service providers). Emergency and safety services are supplied by an onboard platform, which is likely to be installed by the individual car manufacturers.

In contrast to these conventionally adopted architectures, telemetric architectures are rarely applied in public local hotspots such as public parking lots, hotels, restaurants, airports, and shopping centers. In local hot-spot architecture, a vehicle is considered as an alternative mobile computing platform (logically equivalent to a PDA, laptop, or a cellular phone) with short-range localized WLAN (wireless LAN) devices such as Bluetooth and wi-fi. This local (hot-spot) architecture allows the car driver to interact with many local services. Telemetric architectures will be useful for telemetric services only for vehicles providing traditional services such as traffic information, navigation services provided by the central TSP, and local services provided by distributed third-party service providers that can supply the appropriate contextual data. For instance, consider a driver wishing to drive a car to a convention center. The driver initially finds routes to the center using a navigator, then selects a route free from a traffic jam based on traffic information from a TSP. The car automatically discovers the resources of the convention center, obtains directions to the designated parking lot, and makes associated payments using the WLAN communication, as it enters the premises. The driver can obtain various local services provided by the convention center even before stepping out of the car.

Current telemetric systems depend on mobile infrastructures to deliver telemetric services to service users. Therefore, deploying a telemetric service between mobile networks is a very expensive task. System developers need to have strong knowledge about the underlying mobile network. Additionally, a telemetric terminal cannot be applied for the telemetric service from another telemetric service provider, since telemetric service developers devise their own protocols between telemetric terminals and a service provider. Fig. 6.5 shows an overview of in-vehicle network architecture and out-vehicle network architecture. An automobile in an in-vehicle network adopts four vehicle bus protocols, CAN, LIN, MOST, and Flex Ray. However, these protocols cannot intercommunicate with each other. Therefore, the OSEK operating system was designed as standard software architecture for the various ECUs. In the out-vehicle network, the OBU in the automobile can communicate with the infrastructure via the

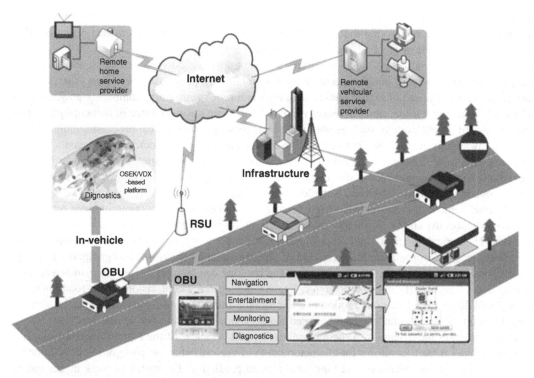

FIGURE 6.5 In-Vehicle and Out-Vehicle Network Architecture

Internet. The remote home service and remote vehicular service providers provide particular services to an automotive user. The in-vehicle and out-vehicle network architectures are discussed in detail in the next two sections.

6.7.1 IN-VEHICLE NETWORK ARCHITECTURE

This section introduces an in-vehicle network architecture for disaster communication network that combines different automotive bus protocols, namely CAN, LIN, and the recently developed Flex Ray protocol standard. Moreover, the OSEK/VDX operating system, a joint project of the automotive industry, manipulates automotive messages between different bus protocols to support efficient usage of resources for automotive control unit application software.

6.8 VISION-BASED VEHICLE BEHAVIOR ANALYSIS

In the United States, tens of thousands of drivers and passengers die on the roads each year, with most fatal crashes involving more than one vehicle. Research and development efforts in advanced sensing, environmental perception, and intelligent driver assistance systems seek to save lives and reduce the number of on-road fatalities. Over the past decade, there has been significant research effort dedicated to the development of intelligent driver assistance systems and autonomous vehicles, which is intended to enhance safety by monitoring the on-road environment. In particular, the on-road detection of vehicles has been a topic of great interest to researchers over the past decade.

A variety of sensing modalities has become available for on-road vehicle detection, including radar, and computer vision. Imaging technology has immensely progressed in recent years. Cameras are cheaper, smaller, and of higher quality than ever before. Concurrently, computing power has dramatically increased. Furthermore, in recent years, we have seen the emergence of computing platforms geared toward parallelization, such as multicourse processing and graphical processing units (GPUs). Such hardware advances allow computer vision approaches for vehicle detection to pursue real-time implementation. With advances in camera sensing and computational technologies, advances in vehicle detection using monocular vision, stereo vision, and sensor fusion with vision have been an extremely active research area in the intelligent vehicles community.

On-road vehicle tracking has also been extensively studied. It is now commonplace for research studies to report the ability to reliably detect and track on-road vehicles in real time, over extended periods. Theoretical, practical, and algorithmic advances have opened up research opportunities that seek a higher level of semantic interpretation of on-road vehicle behavior. The aggregate of this spatiotemporal information from vehicle detection and tracking can be used to identify maneuvers and to learn, model, and classify on-road behavior. Fig. 6.6 depicts the use of vision for on-road interpretation. At the lowest level, various motion and appearance cues are used for on-road vehicle detection. One level up, detected vehicles are associated across frames, allowing for vehicle tracking. Vehicle tracking measures the dynamics of the motion of detected vehicles. At the highest level, an aggregate of spatiotemporal features allows for characterization of vehicle behavior, recognition of specific maneuvers, behavior classification, and long-term motion prediction. Examples of work in this nascent area include prediction of turning behavior, prediction of lane changes, and modeling typical on-road behavior. In this paper, authors have provided a review of vision-based vehicle detection, tracking, and on-road behavior analysis. They concentrated their efforts on works published since, referring the reader to earlier works. They have placed vision-based vehicle detection in the context of on-road environmental perception, briefly detailing complimentary modalities that are commonly used for vehicle detection, namely, radar and lidar. Afterward, we reviewed vision-based vehicle detection, commenting on monocular vision, stereo vision, monocular–stereo combination, and sensor-fusion approaches to vision-based vehicle detection. We also discussed vehicle tracking using vision, detailing image-plane and D techniques for modeling, measuring, and filtering vehicle dynamics on the road. We then discuss the emerging body of literature geared toward analysis of vehicle behavior using spatiotemporal cues, including modeling, learning, classification, and prediction of vehicle maneuvers and goals. Finally, we have provided insights and perspectives on future research directions in vision-based vehicle detection, tracking, and behavior analysis.

6.8.1 ON-ROAD ENVIRONMENTAL PERCEPTION

While the focus of this work lies in vision-based vehicle detection, it is pertinent to include a brief treatment of complimentary modalities currently used in on-road vehicle detection. In this technique, they discussed general sensor-based vehicle detection to place vision-based vehicle detection in the overall context of on-road environmental perception. They took this occasion to discuss conceptual similarities and differences that the various sensing modalities bring to vehicle detection and discuss

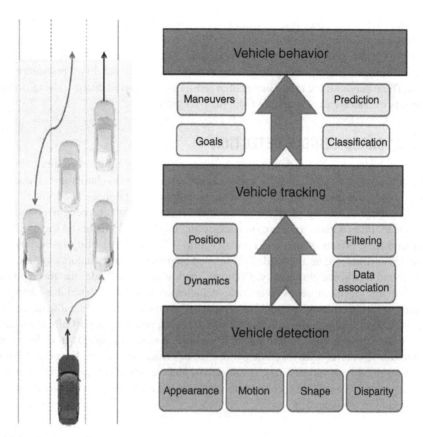

FIGURE 6.6 Vision-Based Vehicle Behavior Analysis

the emerging avenues for data fusion and systems integration. In particular, they briefly discussed the use of millimeter-wave radar and foliar, alongside computer vision, for on-road vehicle detection. Millimeter-wave radar is widely used for detecting vehicles on the road. Radar technology has made its way into production mode vehicles, for applications including adaptive cruise control (ACC) and side warning assist. Typically, a frequency-modulated continuous waveform signal is emitted. Its reflections are received and demodulated, and frequency content is analyzed. The frequency shift in the received signals is used to measure the distance to the detected object. Detected objects are then tracked and filtered based on motion characteristics to identify vehicles and other obstacles. The radar sensing used for ACC generally features a narrow angular field of view, well suited to detecting objects in the ego vehicle's lane. Fig. 6.6 depicts the operation of radar for on-road vehicle detection.

Radar sensing works quite well for narrow field-of-view applications, detecting and tracking preceding vehicles in the ego lane. Radar vehicle tracking works fairly consistently in different weather and illumination conditions. However, vehicle-mounted radar sensors cannot provide wide field-of-view vehicle detection, struggling with tracking cross-traffic at intersections. Furthermore, measurements are quite noisy, requiring extensive filtering and cleaning. Radar-based vehicle tracking does not strictly detect vehicles; rather it detects and tracks objects, classifying them as vehicles based on relative motion. Lidar for on-road vehicle detection has increased in popularity in recent years due to improved costs of lasers, sensor arrays, and computation. Lidar has been extensively used for obstacle detection in autonomous vehicles and is beginning to make their way into driver assistance applications such as ACC. The receiver of the range finder then senses backscattered energy. Using occupancy grid methods, objects of interest are segmented from the background.

6.8.2 VISION-BASED VEHICLE DETECTION

The lowest level depicted in Fig. 6.6 involves detecting vehicles using one or more cameras. From a computer vision standpoint, on-road vehicle detection presents myriad challenges. The on-road environment is semi-structured, allowing for only weak assumptions to be made about the scene structure. Object detection from a moving platform requires the system to detect, recognize, and localize the object in the video, often without reliance on background modeling. Vehicles on the road are typically in motion, introducing effects of ego and relative motion. There is variability in the size, shape, and color of vehicles encountered on the road. The on-road environment also features variations in illumination, background, and scene complexity. Complex shadowing, man-made structures, and ubiquitous visual clutter can introduce erroneous detections. Vehicles are also encountered in a variety of orientations, including preceding, oncoming, and cross traffic. The on-road environment features frequent and extensive scene clutter, limiting the full visibility of vehicles, resulting in partially occluded vehicles. Furthermore, a vehicle detection system needs to operate at real-time speeds in order to provide the human or autonomous driver with an advanced notice of critical situations. Here, we review on-road vehicle detection along with various cues, assumptions, and classification approaches that are taken by researchers in the field. We split this section into studies using monocular vision and those using stereo vision for on-road vehicle detection.

6.9 NETWORKED VEHICLE SURVEILLANCE IN ITS

With the rapid development of urbanization, traffic congestion, incidents, and violations pose great challenges for traffic management systems in most large and medium-sized cities. Consequently, research on active traffic surveillance, which aims to monitor and manage traffic flow, has attracted much attention. With the progress in computer vision, the video camera has become a promising and low-cost sensor for traffic surveillance. Over the last years, video-based surveillance systems have been a key part of ITS. These systems capture vehicles' visual appearance and extract more information about them through vehicle detection, tracking, recognition, behavior analysis, and so forth. Generally, existing surveillance systems collect traffic flow information that mainly includes traffic parameters and traffic incident detection. Traffic incident detection is more challenging and has much research potential. Although great progress has been made on video-based traffic surveillance, researchers are still facing various difficulties and challenges for practical ITS applications. A summary of the existing challenges for video-based surveillance systems is as follows:

- All-day surveillance: The lighting conditions changes at different time of a day, particularly between daytime and nighttime. Supplemental lighting equipment can be used for nighttime operation; however, their visual ranges are usually limited.

- Vehicle occlusion: In busy traffic scenarios, vehicles are easily occluded by other vehicles or no-vehicle objects, such as pedestrians, bicycles, trees, and buildings.
- Pose variation: Vehicle pose can vary greatly when they are turning or changing lanes.
- Different types of vehicles: There are various vehicles with different shapes, sizes, and colors.
- Different resolutions: When a vehicle drives through the camera's field of view (FOV), its image size in pixels changes. This leads to the loss of some detailed visual information and challenges the robustness of detection models.
- Vehicle behavior understanding on the road network: Tracking a vehicle traveling through the road network requires the cameras to coordinate with each other in order to understand the full traffic status through global behavior analysis. Based on the analysis of existing surveillance systems, we present a general system architecture of hierarchical and networked vehicle surveillance (HNVS) in ITS (see Fig. 6.7) with the aim of vehicle attribute extraction and behavior understanding. The HNVS hierarchy is constructed from four layers, which are defined as follows:

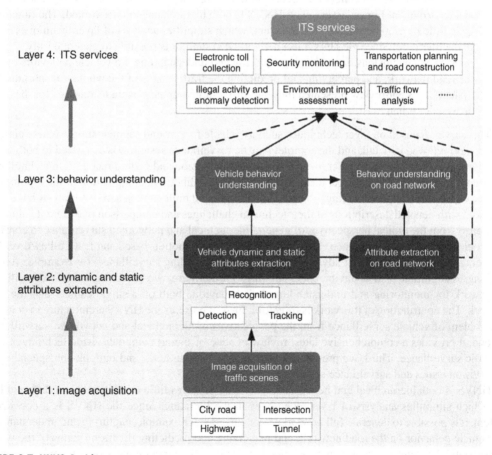

FIGURE 6.7 HNVS Architecture

- Layer Image Acquisition: The function of this layer is to sense traffic scenes and obtain images using visual sensors.
- Layer Extraction of Dynamic and Static Attributes: Based on the obtained images, this layer is used to extract the vehicle's dynamic and static attributes. The dynamic attributes refer to the attributes with respect to vehicle motion characteristics, including velocity, the direction of movement, vehicle trajectories on a single camera and on the road network, and so forth. The static attributes represent the features of vehicle appearance description, which consist of license plate number, type, color, logo, and so forth.
- Layer Behavior Understanding: This layer aims to analyze the vehicle's dynamic and static attributes, understand vehicle behaviors, and finally perceive traffic status of the transportation system. Vehicle behaviors are analyzed both from a single camera and over the road network in order to obtain and predict the traffic status of the whole transportation system.
- Layer ITS Services: Based on the outputs of the previous layers, this layer provides ITS services for efficient transportation management and control. For example, ITS services include electronic toll collection, security monitoring, illegal activity and anomaly detection, and environment impact assessment. HNVS is both hierarchical and networked. The functions have little overlap between different layers, which simplifies analysis of layer techniques in the literature. Since the HNVS is a networked system, it is possible to generate fully networked conclusions, for example, capturing and understanding the vehicle behaviors on the road network, and perceiving and predicting the traffic status of the whole transportation system. A recent review presented the state-of-the-art computer vision techniques for the analysis of urban traffic.

This survey focused on layer techniques such as vehicle foreground segmentation, vehicle classification was reviewed in detail, and the complete traffic surveillance system was discussed in both urban and highway environments. Further, the five key computer vision and pattern recognition technologies required for large area surveillance, including multicamera calibration, computation of the topology of camera views, multicamera tracking, object identification, and multicamera activity analysis have been reviewed with detailed descriptions of their technical challenges and comparison of different solutions. We depart from the typical perspectives of general hierarchical and networked surveillance to consider the problem of vehicle surveillance explicitly. We survey both motion-based and feature-based vehicle detection methods and the latest advances in other fields regarding surveillance, for example, vehicle tracking, recognition, and behavior understanding. Furthermore, we present a vehicle surveillance framework for monitoring and understanding their behaviors, both on a single camera and the road network. The contribution of this work is threefold. First, it presents the HNVS architecture to consider the problem of vehicle surveillance from the perspectives of hierarchical and networked surveillance. Second, it provides a comprehensive latest review of state-of-the-art computer vision techniques used in traffic surveillance. Third, we present detailed analysis, discussions, and outlooks on special computer vision issues and surveillance systems as shown in Fig. 6.7.

HNVS is both hierarchical and networked. The function saves little overlap between different layers, which simplifies analysis of layer techniques in the literature. Since the HNVS is a networked system, it is possible to generate full networked conclusions, for example, capturing and understanding the vehicle behavior on the road network, and perceiving and predicting the traffic status of the whole transportation system. A recent review presented the state-of-the-art computer vision techniques for the analysis of urban traffic. This survey focused on layer techniques, such as vehicle foreground segmentation and vehicle classification, which were reviewed in detail, and the complete traffic surveillance system was discussed in both urban and highway environment. Further, the five key computer vision and pattern recognition technologies required for large area surveillance, including multicamera calibration, computation of the topology of camera views, multicamera tracking, object identification, and multicamera activity analysis, have been reviewed with detailed descriptions of their technical challenges and comparison of different solutions. Hence, we depart from the typical perspectives of general hierarchical and networked surveillance to consider the problem of vehicle surveillance explicitly.

6.10 CONCLUSIONS

In this chapter, we discussed various aspects of theories and applications of vehicular networks. First, we described context aware application in the vehicular network, in which various techniques for selecting a network and avoiding risks are mentioned. In addition, the concept of a vehicular named data network is broadly discussed and various requirements as well as application scenarios are described. Communication among vehicles can be achieved by using cloud resources, in which sensory information is shared using cloud resources. In the given scenario, there are various aspects of cloud operating systems that are mentioned. For instance, cloud resource discovery, cloud formation, results aggregation, cloud maintains, and so on. Another important factor in the vehicular network is the trust-based communication, in which the trusted pair is selected by exploiting algorithms. Moreover, ITS and hybrid sensor and vehicular network model is extensively studied and presented by providing various characteristics. For such scenarios, intravehicular communication as well as intervehicular communication play a vital role in ITS, where middleware as well as link layer protocols can assist the network by providing preferable channel requirements. Similarly, a vision-based vehicular network also provides a use remedy for communicating with neighboring vehicles.

VEHICULAR NETWORK AS BUSINESS MODEL IN BIG DATA

7

7.1 BIG DATA TECHNOLOGY IN VEHICULAR NETWORKS

The exponential growth in terms of complexity and capacity of data in the past few years has led to notable research in the field of Big Data technology. The terminology of Big Data is becoming ubiquitous nowadays. Big Data technologies are still in the nascent stage of development. Big Data today is at the point where the World Wide Web was in 1993. The data on the Web is growing and the Web might get bigger and bigger, but very few of us completely understand what "Big" may mean. Today, we believe that we aren't even scratching the surface of the Big Data opportunity. Big Data is the hottest catchphrase in a current computing environment. International Data Corporation (IDC) defines Big Data as: "Big Data technologies describe a new generation of technologies and architectures designed to economically extract value from very large volumes of a wide variety of data, by enabling high-velocity capture, discovery, and/or analysis." Communication systems in Big Data technology are realized by collecting and integrating data from heterogeneous services. In a heterogeneous networking environment, further investigations are needed to make technology more user-centric.

Research in this area includes data warehouse products with large-scale distributed data processing platforms such as Hadoop, and data analytic technologies, such as machine learning and data mining. Big Data is an emergent technology for both practitioners and researchers, which raise significant challenges for academia, industry, and other organizations. There is a need for novel techniques to manage and analyze Big Data to create value that increases the accuracy of predictions, improves management and security, and enables informed decision making. Earlier definitions of Big Data focused on only the structured data, but now researchers have realized that most of the information resides in semistructured or even in unstructured format (also known as multistructured), mainly in the form of multimedia, sensor data, XML documents, and social networking data, to name a few. Vehicular ad hoc network (VANET), a special form of the mobile ad hoc network (MANET), is a technology which has its roots in traffic engineering and has received enormous attention in recent years. VANET exploits vehicles as nodes in a network and involves vehicle-to-vehicle (V2V) and vehicle-to-roadside infrastructure (V2I) wireless communication. Each partaking vehicle is turned into a router or wireless node that can connect and become a part of the network in the range of 100–300 m approximately. Network is dropped when vehicles fall out of the range. Any vehicle can join the network, if it comes within the range to form a VANET. "Fixed infrastructure belongs to the government or private network operators or service providers." Advancing trends in ad hoc networks are envisaged to instigate a collection of wireless technologies as a type of Wi-Fi, satellite, cellular, dedicated short-range communication (DSRC), and WiMAX. VANET can be perceived as a component of ITS.

The main goal of VANET is providing safety and comfort for people and goods. Motorists are given the time to react to life-endangering events. For this, special electronic equipment is placed inside each vehicle to provide ad hoc network connectivity. VANET has its roots in traffic engineering, which is concerned with traffic signal timing, traffic volume and flow counts, and other studies that determine the need for a certain roadway and safety design. In VANETs, data is collected through various vehicles and roadside units through GPS that can gain useful insight from a huge amount of operational data, to improve traffic management processes, such as planning, engineering, and operations. The complexity of data is increased by applying these Big Data technologies to VANETs.

7.1.1 VANETS AS A BIG DATA PROBLEM

With companies now generating digital representations of existing data and acquiring the latest technology and software, data growth rates over the last few years have been very high. In fact, these days nearly all the sectors have started adopting digital representations of data, resulting in huge data volume. Some of the sectors that have contributed to the growth in Big Data are networking, engineering, healthcare, transportation, retail, telecommunications, government, entertainment media, video surveillance, and more. Big Data can help businesses to target their potential customers and recommend the services that they are craving. Big Data has come across many issues and associated challenges like storage, scalability, processing, timeliness, privacy, and security.

Big Data has been expanding very swiftly into the transportation arena, that is, VANETs. Most of the concerns regarding VANETs are in the same as encountered for MANETs, but the minutiae varies (although marching forward in a haphazard manner, vehicles tend to progress in a predetermined way). The effects of Big Data can be more clearly seen on roadside units. Vehicles are delimited in their scope of motion, constrained to follow a paved path. In the literature, VANETs access large amounts of data in real time for planning and management of safe and efficient traffic flow in transportation systems.

"Big Data" was characterized initially in 2011 by Doug Laney, a META Group and now Gartner analyst, as the three Vs: volume, variety, and velocity. In 2012 IBM finished research on two more Vs—value and veracity—thus finalizing the list of the five Vs of Big Data: volume, variety, velocity, value, and veracity. Similarly, researchers have tried to map some VANET characteristics to attributes of Big Data to rationalize why VANET problems can be treated as Big Data problems and can be solved using the same techniques. Various VANET characteristics have been mapped as real-time data issues: VANET's data is in real time and is automatically updated at regular intervals and stored in databases, resulting in large tables needed for routing decisions. This maps to the "volume" attribute of Big Data, which refers to the amount of data being generated by different data sources contributing to Big Data in real time.

With millions of miles of road, millions of vehicles, and millions of drivers providing data collected over years, the sheer number of data points is astounding. It is only now, through modem Big Data technology, that this much data can be analyzed in a reasonable amount of time for it to be useful. From this enormous choice of data, one needs to build adaptive models to help transportation companies decide on the best routes to optimize time to delivery, safety, cost, and fuel consumption. By quantifying traffic behavior in bad weather, logistics companies can figure out alternative routes that allow delivery on schedule. The need is to develop predictive models of border crossing delays, a key problem for goods shipped between various states or countries.

There is an even greater need for developing models that may predict whether accidents are likely to occur due to road conditions and driver behavior—eventually leading to more secure roads. This work is not pie-in-the-sky dreams about how everything will change because of some nebulous Big

Data trends. This research has revealed benefits in ensuring greater safety, lower transportation costs, more ecologically friendly infrastructure, and predictable material delivery for manufacturing, which is especially important for modern just-in-time systems.

A single application can be generating/collecting many types of data. Data is generated fast and needs to be processed fast. These data contain useful information and can be mined for getting this useful information. Traditional relational databases cannot process such large volumes of data. Therefore, new techniques are needed. For example, Hadoop is an open source platform that processes a large amount of data.

When a company needs to store a huge amount of data they can adopt two options: either procure a big machine with extra CPU, RAM, disk space, and so on, or contract with a database vendor. The two options have their own problems. There are practical limits on procuring a big machine. Furthermore, scaling is a challenging task. The second option infers that scaling will occur horizontally. The solution provided by this option is not cheap and requires significant investment and specialized skills. Today, "the data is being generated not only by the users and various applications and/or devices but is also machine generated and such data is exponentially leading the change in the Big Data space. Dealing with big datasets in the order of terabytes or even petabytes is very challenging." In the modern computing environment, a widespread data processing engine used for Big Data is Hadoop, an implementation of the MapReduce framework. Hadoop provides reliable, shared, and distributional storage through Hadoop Distributed File System (HDFS) and distributed computing capabilities through MapReduce, a programming model.

7.1.2 HADOOP

Hadoop is an open-source framework that processes a very large amount of data for developing and executing various distributed applications. It specifies the methodology that distributes across a swarm of machines in a cluster and that thrusts analysis code to nodes closest to the data being analyzed. Hadoop provides distributed storage called Hadoop Distributed File System (HDFS) and distributed computing through a programming model called MapReduce.

Hadoop is not an alternative for databases and data warehouses. It provides a framework for Big Data processing. The processing of structured data is much easier in relational databases. In addition, Hadoop is one of the Big Data processing platform that is developed by Apache Software Foundation in Java to support data-intensive distributed applications. Moreover, Hadoop provides distributed computing and distributed storage. It also enables the applications to work with millions of nodes and yottabytes of data. Google File System and Google's MapReduce papers store work with Hadoop. Hadoop is used widely by many business platforms such as Search Yahoo, which is its biggest contributor. The two main components of Hadoop are HDFS and MapReduce.

7.1.3 HADOOP DISTRIBUTED FILE SYSTEM

The HDFS cluster is working in a master–worker pattern with two types of node, that is, a NameNode (the master) and a number of DataNodes (workers). File-system namespace is managed by the NameNode. It also asserts the file-system tree and the metadata of all the files and directories in the tree. The workhorses of the file system are DataNodes. The HDFS collects and recover blocks when they are conveyed by clients or the NameNode and they convey back to the NameNode periodically with lists of blocks that they are collecting. The replication of data blocks is decided by NameNode.

The default block size is 64 MB in a typical HDFS with a replication factor of three (local rack holds a second copy and remote rack holds a third copy). The replication factor can be changed according to the user's wishes. HDFS have default replication policy such that each DataNode contains at most one replica of any block and each rack contains at most two replicas of the same block, as long as there are sufficient racks on the cluster. The NameNode ensures that each block has a sufficient number of replicas. It will continuously check whether the block is overreplicated or underreplicated. If it is overreplicated, NameNode will select a replica to remove. Similarly, if it is underreplicated, NameNode will create another replica in any node or in the same node. The replica removal or replica creation is done based on the replication policy.

To read a file from the HDFS, the client first contacts the NameNode and gets the information where blocks of the needed file and replicas of each node reside. Then, the client reads the block from a node that is closer to the client. In order to write a file again, the client needs to contact the NameNode and get permission for a write. Then the client writes the data into any one of the nodes and passes the block content into another node or the same node in order to provide replication. During each operation, the DataNode sends a heartbeat message to the NameNode indicating that the DataNode is still alive and the block replicas are available. If the NameNode doesn't get any message from a DataNode within a particular span of time, then that DataNode is considered to be out of service and the replicas residing on that DataNode are copied into another node.

7.1.4 MAPREDUCE

MapReduce is a linearly scalable programming model introduced by Google that makes it easy to process in parallel massively large data on a large number of computers. MapReduce works mainly through two functions: Map function, and Reduce function. Map function takes a set of key/value input and maps it into zero or more sets of key/value. The reduce function then takes each unique key and groups its associated values into a unique key/value set. MapReduce provides ease-of-use, scalability, and failover properties.

- Map function: The map function is summarized as follows. "Map, written by the user, takes an input pair and produces a set of intermediate key/value pairs. The MapReduce library groups together all intermediate values associated with the same intermediate key (I) and passes them to the reduce function." We can further state that the input keys and values have different domains compared to the domains to which the intermediate keys and values belong.
- Reduce function: "The reduce function, also written by the user, accepts an intermediate key (I) and a set of values for that key. It merges together these values to form a possibly smaller set of values. Typically just zero or one output value is produced per reduce invocation. The intermediate values are supplied to the user's reduce function via an iterator. This allows us to handle lists of values that are too large to fit in memory." We can further say, in Reduce part, the intermediate keys and values have the same domain as the output keys and values. But the original input keys and values have different keys and values as compared to the final output keys and values.

The MapReduce library first splits the input files of the user program into M pieces of normally 16–64 MB per piece. Then, many copies of the program on a cluster of machines are initiated. All the functions are controlled by the master. The rest of the nodes that are assigned work by the master are workers. There are M map tasks and R reduce tasks to assign.

The idle workers are picked by the master and each one is assigned a map task or a reduce task. The contents of the corresponding input file are read by a worker that is assigned a map task. It parses key/value pairs out of the input data and passes each pair to the user-defined map function. The map function generates the intermediate key/value pairs and buffers them in memory. Sporadically, these buffered pairs are noted to local disk. The partitioning function then partitioned them into R regions. The output of the Map is stored in the local disk temporally, which is removed as soon as the Reduce function is completed. This temporary storage of Map output helps in fault tolerance and recovery. That is why, when a Reduce function fails, the system need not start the Map process again. The Map output is then passed back to the master on the local disk. The master is liable for redirecting these locations to the reduce workers.

After getting a notification about these locations from the master, the reduce worker invokes remote procedure calls to read the buffered data from the local disks of the map workers. Reduce worker reads the intermediate data for its partition and sorts it by the intermediate keys so all existences of the same key are assembled concurrently. The sorting is necessary as normally various different keys map to the same reduce task. If the volume of intermediate data is excessively large to fit in memory, an external sort is needed. The reduce worker recapitulated over the sorted intermediate data. Then the user's reduce function is given the key and corresponding set of intermediate values. In the case of a system failure, completed reduce tasks do not need to be reexecuted since their output is stored in a global system. For this reduce partition, the output of the reduce function is added to a final output file. The master stimulates the user program after the completion of all map and reduce tasks.

7.2 DATA VALIDATION IN BIG DATA

The term "Big Data" is a widely used buzzword to describe the vast changing scenario of large storage computation embracing the emerging Big Data platforms. According to an IBM survey, users create quintillion bytes of data every day. This data comes from everywhere: sensors used to gather climate information, posts to social media sites, digital pictures and videos, purchase transaction records, and cell phone GPS signals, and so on. This huge set of information is only possible with the trend toward Big Data. A survey of the US National Security Agency predicts that petabytes of data are being processed per day on the Internet. The digital data have proliferated 9 times in volume in just 5 years and researchers are suggesting that the volume will increase at a rapid rate and will amount to almost a trillion gigabytes. This explosive trend offers ample opportunities and considerable transformation in various sectors, such as enterprises, healthcare industrial manufacturing, and transportation.

Big Data employs a novel technique of probability to collect, manage, and analyze the vast quantities of data, which can indeed be extended to support smart cars and intelligent transportation. The emerging Big Data exemplar, owing to its broader impact and wider application, will augment transportation efficiency and concurrently minimize infrastructure costs. Road traffic management is an imperative aspect of the intelligent transportation system. Companies like Toyota, Intel, and Ford are working on a Big Data platform to proffer efficient modes of transportation in a vehicular environment, as shown in Fig. 7.1.

Real-time data analysis in the vehicular environment is predominant because vehicles need instant data or information for intelligent navigation. Nowadays the data storage capability is easier; however, transforming these raw data into meaningful information in real time is a challenging task. In general,

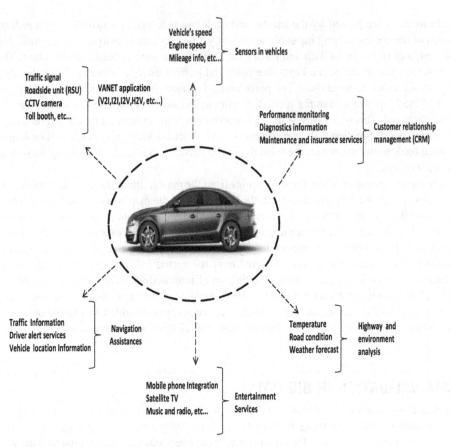

FIGURE 7.1 Possible Applications for Big Data in Vehicular Networks

real-time data processing connotes processing data at that moment instead of storing the data. The raw data will be structured and unstructured information, and a decision will be quickly made about the validity of the data. Another important factor about the near real-time analysis is that after attaining validity, the information aggregated should be analyzed in the near real-time scenario. The appropriate decision should be made with respect to the set of valid information already obtained, or pattern matching can be done with historical information, or information from the previous analysis. Thus, it is obvious that data validation and data analysis plays a vital role in near real-time Big Data analysis in vehicular networks.

There are various challenges for empowering Big Data in vehicular networks, such as the need to enable centralized access to image and video traffic data stored in the data centers of different divisions. In addition, the sole purpose of Big Data is to optimize utilization of a massive data storage vehicle, monitoring data for as long as possible to give information for intelligent transportation of vehicles. By using that specific set of data, we can deal with emergency situations such as traffic mishaps or accidents. Furthermore, security and data reliability is a major cause of concern for Big Data on vehicles. This scenario calls for immediate steps to propose a detailed framework focusing on near real-time customized bid data solutions.

7.2.1 PROPOSED SYSTEM MODEL

In VANET multiple sources information is involved to provide a feasible intelligent transportation systems (ITS) environment, such as a vehicle, RSU (roadside unit), base station (BS), traffic infrastructure (traffic lights, CCTV camera), GPS data, and so forth. The aforementioned sources are deployed with a huge number of sensors and a processor that produces enormous data. In addition, data are being generated through various sources such as mobile devices interacting with VANET and so forth. The amount of data that has been generated is of invaluable information and could be used for various applications, and those data contain lots of benefits, both from a corporate perspective, as well as yielding revolutionary data management mechanisms in line with the nature of the environment. Likewise, the data achieved through VANET will enable us to make better decisions in an ITS portfolio.

In an era of ITS the volume data will thrive at an extraordinary rate. These humongous data exceed the processing capability of conventional database systems. Statistics shows that with the inclusion of hybrid vehicles and connected cars, the amount of data produced would be around 10 TB (Terabytes) per hour approximately. The traditional architecture could not cope with the rapid development of data from these sources. Thus, this endeavor aims to foster an alternative and effective way in concurrent processing capability, real-time data presentation for the massive information processing. Big Data would be the possible powerful system-level solution for ITS.

The term "Big data" is designated to mean large, diverse, and complex datasets that are generated from various data sources in vehicular networks, including sensors, GPS, and other available source information for effective use on VANET applications. Normally, these raw datasets are associated with different levels of expertise. The focus is on GPS datasets and various sensors deployed on the vehicles, for which values are relatively easy to understand. Nevertheless, there are overwhelming technical challenges in collecting, processing, and analyzing these datasets, which demand new solutions in the vehicular network. In the proposed architecture, unstructured or raw data that are collected should be analyzed first through a filtration process as shown in Fig. 7.2.

For data acquisition, the information from various vehicles and its sources are subdivided into data preprocessing and data postprocessing. First, because data may come from a diverse set of sources, various sensors are deployed in the vehicles and GPS datasets. In general, data collection refers to a tool that obtains raw data from a specific data production environment. Similarly in the proposed model, raw data is obtained from the vehicle and its sources. In addition, after accumulating the raw data, there is a need for a high-speed transmission mechanism to transfer the data into the appropriate data-storage system for further analyses. The vehicular environment requires special assistance for high-speed transmission.

The collected raw datasets might contain many meaningless data; redundancy is common in most datasets collected from sensors deployed to monitor vehicles and various data compression technologies can be used to address this issue. The data acquisition technique is a preprocessing mechanism where collected datasets are filtered, as depicted in Fig. 7.2. The data obtained are classified and further data validation takes place. Thus, it is conceived that pattern matching, data prediction, and data detection on comparing with historical data provides data validation in vehicular networks.

A data storage system can be divided into two parts: distributed data storage and centralized data storage. Distributed data storage contains a pool of datasets that is for real-time analysis. The data through data acquisition process, is validated in order to distinguish between the real-time data and batch data. Batch data are for centralized data storage, which is processed later for various applications. In the proposed model shown in Fig. 7.2, a vehicular cloud server is the backup or restores the necessary

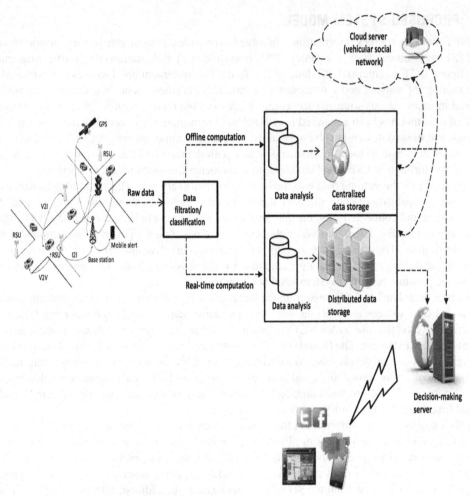

FIGURE 7.2 Architecture for Big Data on Vehicular Network

valid information. This vehicular cloud will be used in terms of real-time analysis and processing. Additionally, to analyze or interact with the stored data, storage systems must provide a platform for several interface functions, fast querying, and other programming models for further efficiency.

7.3 REAL-TIME ANALYSIS OF DATA IN VANET

In a real-time data analysis, everything occurs in fractions of a second. For vehicular networks, we have to model a system that is applicable for real-time data analysis, update the model accordingly to the user requirement, and storage aspects of the data in real time must be considered. The system should be appropriate for faster response to new changes. Huge amount of data are coming per second from various sources in VANET. Second, it is essential to handle the distributed processing of this data as and when it is being collected, since a distributed environment is suitable for the real-time

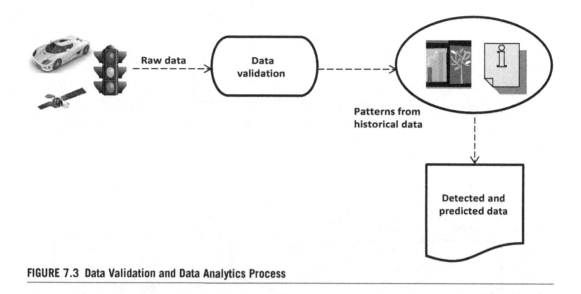

FIGURE 7.3 Data Validation and Data Analytics Process

vehicular application. Finally, it should extract the meaningful information from this moving stream. The aforementioned steps should be undertaken without any fault and in a distributed manner, as shown in Fig. 7.2. In addition, the system should be a low latency system so that the computation can happen very fast with near real-time response capabilities. Fig. 7.3 depicts the near real-time Big Data analysis of vehicular networks. Furthermore, data validation and data analytics are the two important methodologies that have to be examined.

7.3.1 DATA VALIDATION
In a real-time environment, a platform is needed that is capable of collecting information from various sources in a vehicular environment, that is, the data from the vehicle, GPS, and traffic infrastructure, and so forth, as shown in Fig. 7.3. Real-time information should be captured and, therefore, there should be an authorized data validation mechanism, with the appropriate fault-tolerant mechanism. In a vehicular environment fault, the tolerant mechanism is vital because of its vulnerability. The system should be scalable. The data received in a real-time scenario should be continuous. These are some of the major restrictions in the real-time environment.

7.3.2 DATA ANALYTICS SYSTEM
For pattern matching and historical data, there is a need for a Big Data analytical system that is capable of performing parallel processing. Since in the vehicular network, there will be enormous data with the different set of information. The Analytics system should be reliable because of the type of data it receives. And the system should be feasible for data replication. Data analysis can be classified into two types, descriptive analytics and predictive analytics. In descriptive analytics, it exploits historical data to describe what has occurred in the scenario using those data, and can analyze or predict the behavior of vehicles. In the predictive analysis, the focus is made on predicting the future trends and occurrence; the data mining algorithm extracts various patterns to provide insight and forecast the vehicular networks.

The workflow diagram in Fig. 7.4 illustrates the working of the proposed architecture. The data generated through VANETs is unstructured raw data, and data acquisition is done before data validation.

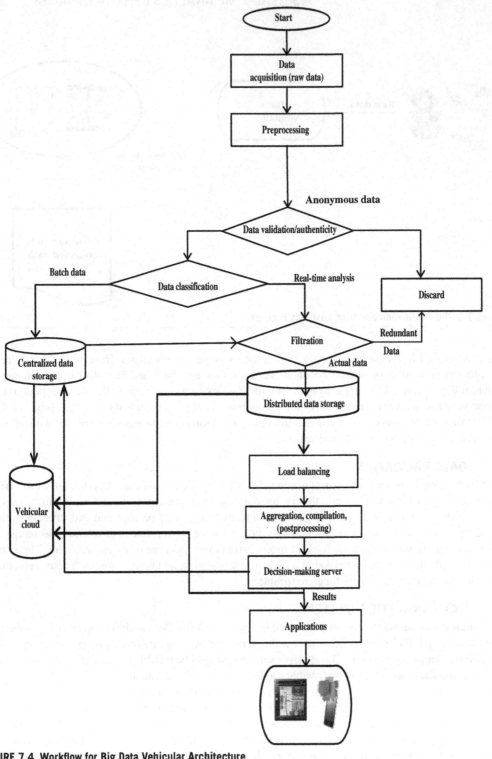

FIGURE 7.4 Workflow for Big Data Vehicular Architecture

After data is collected, the authentication of data is done, in which the dataset is validated and the anonymous data will be discarded. Furthermore, data classification is carried out, in which the real-time data and batch data are separated. Offline data are sent to centralized data storage and streaming data are sent to distributed data storage. In order to remove the redundant data, the filtration process is carried out. The actual data are distributed for the postprocessing mechanism where the data load balancing and data aggregation process are done. Decision-making servers process the information for appropriate results. Furthermore, the vehicular cloud is used as a backup or to restore the necessary valid information from the centralized and distributed data storage. That information can be used for a historic pattern-matching algorithm.

7.4 VEHICULAR DENSITY ANALYSIS USING BIG DATA

The basic idea behind vehicle density analysis is to organize the traffic flow in a specific location. In addition, by using the historical data, we can predict the vehicle flow and determine the traffic pattern for minimizing the traffic flow and reducing vehicular density in a particular locality. The Navigation information or Latitude and Longitude (LAT & LONG) information from the onboard unit (OBU) in the vehicle is sent to the data acquisition server. The general purpose of the data acquisition server is to organize and analyze the vehicle flow in a particular location or place. On using the data acquisition server, we can effectively utilize the massive data sets provided by the great number of vehicles on roads. In order to provide the feasible application for vehicular density analysis, an algorithm has been designed.

7.4.1 ALGORITHM DESCRIPTION

In order to ensure the process on effective utilization of vehicle location information, a system is developed that is capable of analyzing the data sets. Two algorithms are available in the literature that facilitate the vehicular density analysis on Big Data. The algorithm deals with data validation in order to differentiate the offline data with real-time data in vehicular networks. The algorithm deals with organization and analysis of vehicle flow in a particular location or place according to specific location information.

ALGORITHM:

Step : Input - unstructured raw data from vehicular environment for pre-processing
(The data set can be defined as u_s, u_s, $u_{s,\ldots\ldots\ldots} u_{s\,n}$)
Step : Pre-Processing - data validation, data verification data authenticity of unstructured data.
// After data validation, the dataset contains separate header information to differentiate the offline data and the real-time data and anonymous data is discarded
Step : Data classification of pre- processed data (data has to be classified for offline computation or for real-time computation based on header information. Which can be defined as B_i for offline computation and S_i for real-time computation)
Step : if the dataset contains S_i info then move the specific data set for real-time computation for D_S or send to C_S.
Step : While (D_S = true)
{
// In distributed storage the dataset should separate according to specific event, type for near real-time computation if the data related to location information its should process separately if the data is related to traffic information its should process separately.
Step : If (D_S = Event type)
//Eis allocated for processing the location information

Step : then move_dataset (D_S, E)
Step : else if (D_S = E_n event type)
Step : Then move_dataset(D_S, E_n)
}
// Goto step for next periodic analysis

ALGORITHM:

To organize and analysis the vehicle flow in a particular location or place according to specific location information

Step : Input if (D_S = E)
Step : L, L, L, L, L location data
// L, L, L, L, L is the specific location information for a particular area. Lcontains specific LAT & LONG value.
{
Step : If (U_{Sn} = L, location)
Step : Else if (U_{Sn} = L, location)
Step : Then move _datasets (U_{Sn} = L);
Step : Else if (U_{Sn} = L, location)
Step : Then move _datasets (U_{Sn} = L);
Step : Else if (U_{Sn} = L, location)
Step : Then move _datasets (U_{Sn} = L);
Step : Else if (U_{Sn} = L, location)
Step : move _datasets (U_{Sn} = L);
Step : Else
Step: move_datasets (U_{Sn} = L_n);
// If the data validation process is completed, the iteration is repeated for the another specific set of data in order to organise the vehicle flow in specific locations.

7.5 VEHICULAR CARRIERS FOR BIG DATA

Cost-effective scalability, large companies, organizations, universities, and governmental agencies constantly move their data and applications within and between data centers to balance workloads, handle replication, and consolidate resources. As a result, the demand for bandwidth-intensive services such as cloud computing, multimedia transfers, data migration, disaster recovery, and online backups has strained the Internet infrastructure to its limits. Despite the ever-growing demand for bulk transfers, the price of bandwidth remains prohibitively high, especially at the network core. As a result, many edge providers are rate limiting or even blocking the use of bandwidth-intensive applications. While bulk traffic can be seen as expensive when considering the high bandwidth consumption incurred, data intensive applications are also less demanding when it comes to the requirements in terms of delay. Compared to most interactive applications that are highly delay-sensitive, the average throughput is the main criterion to evaluate the performance of bulk transfers and also to improve the user experience.

Current methods for transferring data include adaptations to standard file transfer methods or the use of hard drives and DVDs together with a courier service. These solutions, although simple, can be either time consuming, or costly, or both. Recent alternatives propose to schedule data traffic during off-peak hours or using transit storage nodes. Nevertheless, as long as the legacy Internet is used, the underlying technology stays the same and the ISPs are still handling all the traffic. The bandwidth consumption requirements are at a steady rise and are mostly dictated by demands at peak hours. We argue that disruptive solutions should be considered when it comes to moving huge amounts of data between geographically distributed sites. In this work, the author exploited the delay-tolerant nature of bulk transfers to deliver data over the existing road infrastructures. Their work is motivated by the increasing number of vehicles driven and miles traveled around the world. The vehicle fleet in operation worldwide surpassed the 1 billion mark in 2010 and is expected to double in the next two decades.

The number of vehicles is forecast to grow to up to 4 billion by mid-century. By leveraging the communication and storage capabilities in vehicles will soon enhance the vehicular performance. They advocate the use of conventional vehicles as the communication medium for Big Data migration in an opportunistic manner. Given the flow of vehicles daily traveling roads, our system design built on top of the road network can effectively offload the legacy Internet infrastructure for massive delay-tolerant data transfers. To evaluate their system, a comparison is made with a state-of-the-art bulk data transfer scheme and they demonstrated that a vehicular-based solution may lead to significant improvements in terms of bandwidth. In summary, the contributions of the proposed work are as follows:

- Offloading scheme. They describe a novel vehicular-based opportunistic bulk data transfer system, designed to offload the Internet from delay-tolerant content.
- Capacity improvement. They show that the system has the potential of moving massive amounts of data in short time periods compared to today's traditional techniques.

7.5.1 OFFLOADING ONTO CONVENTIONAL VEHICLES

In this section, we argue that by taking advantage of the characteristics of future smart vehicles, such as data storage capabilities, these can be used to transport massive quantities of data between two geographical locations. To improve the services offered to users, data needs to be moved closer to the consumer along the provision-based infrastructure. It can also require data restoration functions in a disaster scenario, keeping services running while problems are being solved or a distribution scheme that requires multiple geographic locations to work efficiently. In the literature, authors find that provisioning high levels of bandwidth with today's existing techniques has a determinant impact on the development and maintenance budget of a company.

Though bulk data transfers are on the basis of some popular services such as high-definition multimedia content delivery, many ISPs are using scheduling, traffic shaping, and queue management techniques to limit the rate of bandwidth intensive applications. An example of service affected by the ISPs policies is Netflix, which is responsible for about 29% of North America's fixed Internet access bandwidth utilization. Initially launched as a DVD rent-by-mail company, Netflix began streaming movies online in 2007 in an attempt to avoid the postal costs incurred by delivering DVDs by mail. To address the ISPs rate-limiting policies and the costs of serving content, recommendation algorithms are expected to be used in combination with peer-to-peer networking by Big Data service providers.

To address the shortcomings faced by bulk data applications, a system is proposed called NetStitcher, which exploits diurnal patterns of network traffic to schedule bulk transfers at times of low

link utilization, depending on the time zone. Although this technique allows a good return on investments for dedicated lines, the physical medium is still limited due to the high cost and limited capacity
of today's Internet infrastructure. Furthermore, efficient scheduling decisions require real-time information regarding the network load and a transport layer needs to be designed so as to be able to send
all delay-tolerant traffic when spare bandwidth is made available.

A work that is similar to ours, in essence, is the idea of exploiting airplane passengers boarding air-
line flights to bridge remote airports. Messages to be delivered are loaded onto the passengers' mobile
devices at the airport depending on their destination while they are waiting for their flight. Another
work suggested the combined use of the Internet together with the postal system to send a part of the
data using hard drives. Even though this system offloads some of the data onto a carrier other than the
Internet, it still relies on a methodology that requires detailed scheduling, and can only be used for
data able to tolerate delays of up to several days. Furthermore, data on physical media such as tapes or
removable disk drives have the downside of requiring manual handling at arrival.

7.5.2 SYSTEM OPERATION

In order to overcome the limitations in terms of capacity and design of the Internet, vehicles are
equipped with one or more removable memory storage devices, such as magnetic disks or other non-
volatile solid-state storage devices. The term "vehicle" refers to both passenger and commercial vehicles; in the latter case, it may be part of a fleet vehicle owned or leased by a business or governmental
agency. An assumption is made, that is, vehicles are also embedded with one or more communication
network interfaces and a positioning system. The system mentioned later includes vehicles in operation
and their users, a service provider, and content providers.

Memory devices can be owned by a party other than the user of the vehicle. Typically, a service
provider may own the memory devices and owners of the vehicles can be compensated based on the
amount of data transferred. A content provider distributes the data to be piggybacked onto the vehicles
through a wide-area data network such as the Internet. The service provider charges the content provider for the amount of data to be transferred along the road infrastructure. A network of offloading spots
provides the data to be piggybacked on the memory of vehicles. We use the term "offloading spots" to
refer to locations that provide the data to be transferred to the memory devices of the vehicles or where
on-board memory devices can be exchanged for preloaded memory devices that match the destination
of the vehicle. The offloading spots can be placed at locations where vehicles may be parked. For example, an offloading spot can be located in a shopping center parking lot, a street parking spot, or at the
users' homes. At a higher level, a collection of offloading spots is from an entry/exit point to the system.

The service provider selects the offloading spots from the group consisting of the loading stations
that transfer the data to the already in-place memory of the vehicle and the memory swap stations that
replace the onboard memory of the vehicle. Vehicle memories can be loaded with data while parking at the offloading spot or exchanged for ready-to-ship memory devices so that users can continue
their travels without waiting for the data to be loaded. The selection of the offloading spots is based
in part on the geographic location of the vehicle and if available, it's planned destination. The service
provider also monitors the status of the offloading spots, which include the available parking space, the
memory exchange bays that are free, the destination of the data made already available for shipment.
The service provider also periodically queries the vehicles over the data network to determine the current geographic location and destination of the vehicles. The positioning system of the vehicle includes

a navigation system that generates routes and guidance between a geographic location and a destination. The historical locations and addresses are stored in a geographic location database managed at the service provider's control center. The service provider also keeps a record of the status of the offloading spots in a specific database. The service provider matches the destination of the vehicles to a group of offloading spots selected based on park space availability. If preloaded memory devices are ready to be shipped, the service provider checks for free exchange bays at the offloading spots or contacts the content provider in order to transfer the data to be loaded on the memory devices.

Let us first denote the frequency of vehicles passing an entry point and traveling toward the same exit point (destination) as f. This value will be important to compute the maximum achievable capacity of the system. In practice, an assumption is made, that is, not all vehicles will have enough incentives to take part in the system. They call P the penetration ration of the technology, that is, the probability that a vehicle accepts to carry data. We set this value to 20%, which corresponds to the approximate market share value of some of the major car producers in France. They assumed that the content provider takes all necessary security precautions to preserve the confidentiality of its own data. The service provider ensures that no physical harm can come to the data storage devices and that data integrity and confidentiality is preserved by limiting the access of the driver to the storage device. The entire set of data-handling operations taking place at the offloading spots is automated, requiring no human intervention during normal functioning conditions.

They also assumed that all the vehicles that enter the highway at entry point A reach exit point B. Therefore, the value of $f \times P$ for vehicles leaving A is identical for vehicles reaching B. This allows us to calculate the vehicular system performance unhindered by routing errors and data loss. We denote the total amount of data to be transferred between A and B as D. This amount is chunked and divided among the participating vehicles. For this computation, we denote as S the storage capacity of each vehicle. Finally, we call d the travel distance between A and B and s the average speed of the highway.

With these in view, vehicular carriers-performance analyses were made by the French researcher, to see the density of vehicles on the highway as well as their average transfer traffic delay.

An assumption is made on a particular approach where data is loaded using batteries and swap stations. In this approach, data is preloaded to batteries before cars enter the station. The loading time is then reduced to the time required to swap batteries (in the order of a minute). In the literature, researches did not consider the impact of the vehicles that exit the highway prematurely, leading to data loss. As dataset does not allow tracking an individual vehicle, hence there is a need to develop probabilistic models based on information from the traffic domain. Nevertheless, throughout the evaluation of our architecture, they have used quite a conservative value regarding the flow of vehicles on the highway segments in hope of reducing the impact of data losses due to vehicles leaving the highway prematurely. We would like to stress again that the main purpose of this work is to present and demonstrate the potential of performing vehicular-based bulk data transfers in an opportunistic way and therefore we do not discuss data loss and routing related issues. We invite the reader to refer to Chapter 4 for some discussion regarding this subject.

The goal of this section is to point out several research topics that could contribute to the development of the Internet-based bulk data transfer system.

7.5.2.1 Routing and Data Delivery

One of the most pressing issues that require attention is data delivery over longer distances. In the case of a highway linking three consecutive cities, it is not reasonable to make the assumption that all vehicles leaving the first city will reach the third city. This motivates the development of specialized routing protocols that limit data loss and ensure efficiency when drivers stop at intermediary points. The limited battery capacity would force the driver to stop, for example, at recharge stations or at battery swap stations. Such "points of interest" could act as routers where data could be swapped from one vehicle to another, heading in the right direction.

7.5.2.2 Scheduling and Transfer Planning

Vehicular traffic has observable diurnal patterns with dramatic increases in vehicular frequency during rush hours contrasting with much smaller values during nighttime, when most of the traffic is represented by commercial freighters. This pattern of movement is dictated by constraints that characterize the driver's behavior (like working hours or driving preference) and it can be anticipated to a certain extent. In order to use efficiently the opportunistic vehicular-based system, data transfers must be properly scheduled and thus appropriate methods should be developed.

7.5.2.3 Data Loading

Today's technology is advancing and is offering new alternatives to loading data onto vehicles. If battery swap stations are deployed on a large scale, vehicles could be "fed" with data when they get a newly charged battery, and this could occur in a very short period of time (about 1 min). Another option would be to use state-of-the-art microchips that allow wireless transmission speeds up to 1000 times faster than current technology.

7.5.2.4 Incentives and Business Plans

Vehicles participating in the system would be private property and as such, they cannot be used to transfer data without the consent of the owner. A mutually beneficial business plan needs to be developed to motivate car owners to participate while a partnership between multiple companies could potentially reduce the servicing costs of such a system.

BIG DATA COLLISION ANALYSIS FRAMEWORK

8

Nowadays, we live in a more and more interconnected world that generates a great volume of information every day, from the logging files of the users of social networks, search engines, and email clients, to machine-generated data and the real-time monitoring of sensor networks for dams or bridges and various vehicles such as airplanes, cars, and ships. Big Data requires exceptional technologies to efficiently process large quantities of data within tolerable elapsed times. Technologies being applied to Big Data include massively parallel processing databases, data mining grids, distributed file systems, distributed databases, cloud computing platforms, and scalable storage systems. The real- or near real-time information delivery is one of the defining characteristics of Big Data analytics. Latency is therefore avoided whenever and wherever possible. A wide variety of techniques and technologies has been developed and adapted to aggregate, manipulate, analyze, and visualize Big Data. These techniques and technologies draw from several fields including statistics, computer science, applied mathematics, and economics. This means that an organization that intends to derive value from Big Data has to adopt a flexible, multidisciplinary approach. Thus, the authors applied Hadoop and HBase, which can store and analyze real-time collision data in a distributed processing framework. This framework is designed as a flexible and scalable framework using distributed CEP that process massive real-time traffic data and ESB that integrates other services.

In this work, we processed road traffic data. In particular, traffic collision data was analyzed as a significant and growing problem that affects the entire nation's population. Also, traffic congestion is a dynamic problem in which sporadic traffic incidences affect travel time delay and spatiotemporal environmental factors affect traffic behavior in the region and for the duration of the event.

8.1 ROAD TRAFFIC DATA

California Freeway Performance Measurement System (PeMS) operated by the California Department of Transportation is providing useful traffic data from loop detectors. The data contains speed, flow and occupancy of traffic flow at each detector location. The data from Traffic Accident Surveillance and Analysis System (TASAS) were used for collision analysis. The TASAS data contains the information of all collision cases including the collision time, severity, type of collision, and number of involved vehicles. By integrating PeMS and TASAS data, we obtained the collision probability. The chosen research site was north of the I-880 freeway section. The route starts from San Jose and ends near the Bay Bridge. The total length of the route in this research was about 45 miles, and the traffic data were gathered from 74 detectors. The average interval between detectors is about 0.6 mile. The traffic and collision data from 2001 to 2011 were collected and information from each detector, such as postmile, time, and the 5-min data including speed, flow, and occupancy, were used for the analysis.

8.2 COLLISION RATE MODEL

The traffic flow variables and the number of collisions are assigned to each section and time period. The collision rate is defined by the ratio of the number of the collision and the exposure to traffic situation during a given interval. The collision potential affects the entire traffic moving in a certain section of the freeway. The vehicle miles traveled (VMT) for a given time period were used as the measure of exposure to the traffic situation.

8.3 DESIGN OF ROAD TRAFFIC BIG DATA COLLISION ANALYSIS PROCESSING FRAMEWORK

In this section, we describe architecture of the road traffic Big Data collision analysis processing framework. The framework architecture is composed of traffic event cloud, traffic event elastic load balancer, distributed CEP, event service integration, traffic Big Data storage, and traffic Big Data processing part. Traffic Event Cloud enables users to search for traffic events and patterns of events within a repository for historical events. Traffic event cloud processes events, thereby creating an index for events and correlations between events in order to enable an effective event search. Traffic Event Elastic Load Balancer automatically distributes incoming road traffic event across multiple distributed CEP. It enables us to achieve even greater fault tolerance in our applications, seamlessly providing the amount of load balancing capacity needed in response to an incoming road traffic event.

Complex event processing (CEP) refers to technology that processes and analyzes in real time complicated and massive event that is constantly generated in real world operations. However, massive events can't process the one CEP instance.

The distributed CEP dynamically distributes event-processing load in road traffic event cloud environments to ensure an ability to operate in real time without stopping service. Also, the proposed ESB is a highly distributed, event-driven, enterprise SOA that is geared toward integration. It is a standard-based integration platform that combines messaging, Web services, data transformation, and intelligent routing to reliably connect and coordinate the interaction of significant numbers of diverse applications across extended enterprises with transactional integrity. The ESB can provide a kind of mechanism that makes it easier to add new applications or services. Every application is connected to the ESB, all services communicate with each other via ESB.

8.4 VEHICLE XML DEVICE COLLABORATION WITH BIG DATA

Every day, time is wasted in traffic congestion. This problem is suffered by millions of people. Traffic congestion can cause the waste of millions in a nation's currency. Every country's government proposes a budget every year to solve traffic mobbing, the escalation of traffic volume. On the basis of this need, new dynamic travel time systems with traffic intensity information should be developed. Big Data is considered to increase many oversight aspects of municipalities and countries. For example, it allows municipalities to adjust road traffic movements based on real-time traffic flow information. Several cities are currently conducting Big Data analytics with the aim of turning themselves into Keen Cities, where the transportation infrastructure and utility routes are all combined.

Further, analysis of Big Data turns road traffic data into valuable resources. It can increase efficiencies and a country's competitive advantage. For this reason, data science will help us to produce valuable information from raw data. The term "Big Data" refers to traditional enterprise data, machine-generated or sensor data, social data, and so forth. In this proposal, machine-generated data will be included. The system manipulates these machine-generated data and uses the observations per road segment and estimates a travel time based on the average speed.

8.4.1 BIG DATA PLATFORM

Nowadays, IT infrastructure is developing in such a way that produces unique requirements considering Big Data platform components. To develop the paper proposal, the system should go through some Big Data requirements:

- Big Data acquisition
- Big Data organizing process
- Big Data Analysis
- Solution prediction

There are several surveys underway to find out the parameters in the concept of Big Data. In a simple way, an assumption is made where the volume of data (road traffic data) is one of the parameters. In fact, it is not only the parameters that control Big Data terms: in addition, volume, velocity, variety, and value are considered. Each year, the amount of data is mounting by 40%, as reported by McKinsey Global Institute researchers, and larger quantities of data are produced by machine-generated data. In Big Data terms, traditional data and nontraditional data formats are in contrasting positions. Among these concepts, we face the challenge regarding which data are valuable, and that valuable data should be used for analysis of road traffic data to ensure traffic efficiency and can potentially help to improve traffic situations in large cities.

The continual growth of road traffic increases the need for solutions, and allowing monitoring and controlling of traffic helps to increase road safety, improve traffic flow, and to protect the environment. Consequently, a system that provides traffic management solutions allowing road authorities and operators to manage, monitor, and maintain their roadways while giving road users intelligent information to ensure convenient and safe trips. For ensuring an effective road traffic network system, we should determine the proper ways to monitor and control traffic. Data acquisition is the method of evaluating an electrical or somatic phenomenon such as current, voltage, pressure, temperature, and sound with a computer. A Data Acquisition system consists of devices, hardware, and a computer with programmable software.

Compared to traditional measurement systems, PC-based data acquisition systems abuse the processing power control, productivity, demonstration, and connectivity capabilities of industry-standard computers, providing a more authoritative, stretchy, and cost-effective measurement clarification. All data from the devices as well as manual actions of the operating staff are considered. Traffic management systems enable the automated generation of traffic information. Raw traffic data and environmental data are processed so that customers can access the information via a broad spectrum of telecommunication technologies such as web services. Assembling, evaluating, and processing the entire data from various devices on the roads enables us to understand and monitor in real time the prevailing traffic conditions. This analysis is the last step in providing correct information to the user.

The government of a country may have a large budget for organizing the traffic system. Billions of dollars can be lost. People waste their time in traffic congestion. To ensure traffic efficiency, we can survey road traffic data. But how are the road traffic data is collected? In which way can we provide the users with the traffic information? Does the Big Data concept applied here offer any possibility of providing road traffic data? Data acquisition is presently a challenge for us. In the past, some ways were proposed to provide this type of service. To acquire road traffic data, we have to collect data using a point-based approach. For a short time, a control server was proposed. The data obtained from control server is processed through a centralised storage unit. Hence Time consumption is very high in this method. Furthermore, how much bandwidth and transfer rate will be needed are some of the issues. To solve the aforementioned problem, we have to use less data information but not whole. We can use an XML format to display information on a user's device.

8.4.2 TRAFFIC FLOW PREDICTION WITH BIG DATA

Accurate and timely traffic flow information is currently strongly needed for individual travelers, business sectors, and government agencies. It has the potential to help road users make better travel decisions, alleviate traffic congestion, reduce carbon emissions, and improve traffic operation efficiency. The objective of traffic flow prediction is to provide such traffic flow information. Traffic flow prediction has gained more and more attention with the rapid development and deployment of intelligent transportation systems (ITSs). It is regarded as a critical element for the successful deployment of ITS subsystems, particularly advanced traveler information systems, advanced traffic management systems, advanced public transportation systems, and commercial vehicle operations. Traffic flow prediction heavily depends on historical and real-time traffic data collected from various sensor sources, including inductive loops, radars, cameras, mobile Global Positioning System, crowdsourcing, social media, and so forth. With the widespread traditional traffic sensors and new emerging traffic sensor technologies, traffic data are exploding, and we have entered the era of Big Data transportation. Transportation management and control is now becoming more data driven.

Although there have been already many traffic flow prediction systems and models, most of them use shallow traffic models and are still somewhat unsatisfying. This inspires us to rethink the traffic flow prediction problem based on deep architecture models with such rich amount of traffic data. Recently, deep learning, which is a type of machine learning method, has drawn a lot of academic and industrial interest. It has been applied with success in classification tasks, natural language processing, dimensionality reduction, object detection, motion modeling, and so on.

Deep-learning algorithms use multiple-layer architectures or deep architectures to extract inherent features in data from the lowest level to the highest level, and they can discover huge amounts of structure in the data. As a traffic flow process is complicated in nature, deep-learning algorithms can represent traffic features without prior knowledge, which has good performance for traffic-flow prediction. A mechanism is given in the literature about the deep learning–based traffic-flow prediction method. Herein, a stacked auto-encoder (SAE) model is used to learn generic traffic flow features, and is trained in a layer-wise greedy fashion. To the best of our knowledge, it is the first time that the SAE approach is used to represent traffic-flow features for prediction. The spatial and temporal correlations are inherently considered in the modeling. In addition, it demonstrates that the proposed method for traffic flow prediction has superior performance.

As early as the 1970s, the autoregressive integrated moving average (ARIMA) model was used to predict short-term freeway traffic flow. Since then, an extensive variety of models for traffic-flow prediction has been proposed by researchers from different areas, such as transportation engineering, statistics, machine learning, control engineering, and economics. Previous prediction approaches can be grouped into three categories, that is, parametric techniques, nonparametric methods, and simulations. Parametric models include time-series models, Kalman filtering models, and others. Nonparametric models include k-nearest neighbor (k-NN) methods, artificial neural networks (ANNs), and others. Simulation approaches use traffic simulation tools to predict traffic flow.

Due to the stochastic and nonlinear nature of traffic flow, researchers have paid much attention to nonparametric methods in the traffic-flow forecasting field. Davis and Nihan used the k-NN method for short-term freeway traffic forecasting and argued that the k-NN method performed comparably with but not better than the linear time-series approach. A technique is given based on a dynamic multiinterval traffic volume prediction model based on the k-NN nonparametric regression. Also, a system is developed, that is, a kernel smoother for the autoregression function to do short-term traffic-flow prediction, in which functional estimation techniques were applied. Similarly, a method that is used is a local linear regression model for short-term traffic forecasting. A Bayesian network approach was proposed for traffic-flow forecasting. An online learning weighted support vector regression (SVR) for short-term traffic flow predictions. Various ANN models were developed for predicting traffic flow.

To obtain adaptive models, some works explore hybrid methods, in which they combine several techniques. A system is proposed based on aggregation approach for traffic flow prediction based on the moving average (MA), exponential smoothing (ES), ARIMA, and neural network (NN) models. The MA, ES, and ARIMA models were used to obtain three relevant time series, which were the basis of the NN in the aggregation stage. Moreover, a system is developed based on different linear genetic programming, multilayer perceptron (MLP), and fuzzy logic (FL) models for estimating 5- and 30-min traffic flow rates. An adaptive hybrid fuzzy rule-based system approach was proposed for modeling and predicting urban traffic flow.

In addition to the methods aforementioned, the Kalman filtering method, stochastic differential equations, the online change-point–based model, the type-2 FL approach, the variation infinite mixture model, simulations, and dynamic traffic assignment were also applied in predicting short-term traffic flow. Comparison studies of traffic flow prediction models have been reported in the literature. The linear regression, the historical average, the ARIMA, and the SARIMA were assessed in, in which it was concluded that these algorithms perform reasonably well during normal operating conditions, but do not respond well to external system changes. The SARIMA models and the nonparametric regression forecasting methods are evaluated. It was found that the proposed heuristic forecast generation methods improved the performance of nonparametric regression, but they did not equal the performance of the SARIMA models. The multivariate state-space models and the ARIMA models are compared, and the results show that the performance of the multivariate state-space models is better than that of the ARIMA models.

In the literature, a comparison is made between SVR models and SARIMA models, and they concluded that the proposed seasonal support vector regressor is highly competitive when performing forecasts during the most congested periods. It also reported the performance results for the ARMA, ARIMA, SARIMA, SVR, Bayesian network, ANN, k-NN, Naïve I, and Naïve II models at different aggregation time scales, which were set at 3, 5, 10, and 15 min, respectively. A series of research is dedicated to the comparison of NNs and other techniques such as the historical average, the ARIMA models, and the SARIMA models. Interestingly, it could be found that nonparametric techniques obviously outperform simple statistical techniques such as the historical average and smoothing techniques, but there are contradicting results on whether nonparametric methods can yield better or comparable results compared with the advanced forms of statistical approaches such as the SARIMA. In summary, a large number of traffic flow prediction algorithms have been developed due to the growing need for real-time traffic flow information in ITS, and they involve various techniques in different disciplines.

However, it is difficult to say that one method is clearly superior over other methods in any situation. One reason for this is that the proposed models are developed with a small amount of separate specific traffic data, and the accuracy of traffic flow prediction methods is dependent on the traffic flow features embedded in the collected spatiotemporal traffic data. Moreover, in general, the literature shows promising results when using NNs, which have good prediction power and robustness. Although the deep architecture of NNs can learn more powerful models than shallow networks. The existing NN-based methods for traffic flow prediction usually have only one hidden layer. It is hard to train a deep-layered hierarchical NN with a gradient-based training algorithm.

8.5 BIG DATA TECHNOLOGIES IN SUPPORT OF REAL-TIME CAPTURING AND UNDERSTANDING OF ELECTRIC VEHICLES

Over the years, energy overconsumption and greenhouse gas emission have been well recognized as the main culprit accelerating air pollution and global warming. As dependence on fossil fuel–based vehicles in daily life around the world is largely considered as one of the main factors making the environmental crisis worsen year after year, electric vehicles (EVs) have recently been promoted by governments as a viable and promising alternative transportation means for consumers. Indeed, the adoption of EVs is a growing trend in the global auto market. The successful stories of EV introduction to and/or penetration into auto marketplaces are very encouraging, including the presentation of EV transportation in the 2008 Beijing Olympics and, recently, the astonishingly robust sales of Tesla EVs.

However, there is a variety of issues impeding EVs from the fast adoption in the global auto market, such as cost, battery range, governmental promotion and subsidy policy, charging infrastructure, reliability, and safety. As the issues bear different priorities that surely vary with marketplaces locally and internationally, it is essential for the auto industry and policymakers to capture and understand the acceptance and behavior of EV consumers from the customer perspective.

Hence, appropriate measures and/or policies can be strategically and tactically defined and accordingly executed to speed up the adoption of EVs, meeting both the business objectives and the environmental protection goals that are laid out by different stakeholders and governments. Technological breakthroughs have significantly improved the lifespan and quality of batteries used in EVs. The reliability and quality of EVs are the same as conventional vehicles, if not better. EVs are still new and disruptive technologies to most customers. Scholars and practitioners around the world have conducted numerous studies, aimed at looking into the insights of customer experience, attitudes, and perception of adopting EVs from marketplace to marketplace. The survey-based and cross-section empirical research has been a dominant approach in both academia and industry. We understand that it becomes essential for EV makers and governments to capture and understand the dynamics of EV consumers in real time. Decision-makers can make informed decisions if the acceptance and behavior of EV customers from the marketplace to marketplace can be well deciphered at the point of need. This paper explores how the emerging Big Data technologies can be applied to meet such a need.

8.5.1 CURRENT STATUS OF THE EV MARKET

EVs and other alternative fuel vehicles have attracted much attention over the past decade or so as they are well recognized as a viable and promising solution to sustain transportation mobility for the world's populations in the long run. Although the number of EVs currently in use is considerably small compared to the number of conventional vehicles, global leaders hope to have about 20 million EVs on the roads around the world by 2020. To help the world achieve the goal, the EV City Casebook provides the best practices from 16 cities across 9 countries.

To promote and further the use of EVs, many of the profiled 16 cities have leveraged their purchasing power by adding EVs to municipal fleets and public transport systems, installing charging stations across cities, and offering EV owners discounted electricity rates. In great detail, the Casebook reports the basket of financial and nonfinancial incentives that have been implemented to boost demand for EVs and charging stations. "Rebates or tax credits on vehicles (often augmented by subsidies from the national government), exemptions from vehicles' registration taxes or license fees, discounted tolls and parking fares, and discounts for recharging equipment and installation" are examples of financial incentives, while "preferential parking, access to restricted highway lanes, and expedited permitting and installation of EV supply equipment" are examples of nonfinancial incentives.

For example, the Chinese government uses the term new energy vehicles (NEVs) to designate plug-in electric vehicles, and only pure electric vehicles and plug-in hybrid electric vehicles are subject to purchase incentives. On Jun. 1, 2010, the Chinese government announced a trial program in five Chinese cities including Beijing to provide money incentives up to 60,000 Yuan (about US $10,000) for a citizen who purchases an NEV. More specifically, Beijing has recognized that over 500 million cars on the roads adversely impact its air quality. Thus, Beijing has been focusing on putting EVs in use in support of its public transportation. Beijing plans to have 50,000 NEVs on the streets by 2015: 30,000 NEVs will be owned privately, 8,000 electric or hybrid buses will replace a third of the total number of public buses that are now in use, and 10,000 EVs will be used in Beijing's taxi fleets.

EVs are noted for their high performance in the transformation of power from the battery into mechanical energy while lithium batteries are widely used in EVs. Truly, lithium batteries have become more energy efficient than ever before. However, the average driving range of a current EV with lithium batteries is around 150 km. According to, the major issues for EVs are battery and battery management, charging facilities, and cost from the customer perspective. Indeed, the Casebook acknowledges that the world must overcome many significant hurdles to reach the 2020 target mentioned earlier. Evidently, the Casebook reports that many profiled cities leverage "their convening power to bring together city planners, automakers, utilities, infrastructure suppliers, academic and research institutions, and city and national officials to identify and address technical, economic, and regulatory barriers to EV adoption and integration." In the Beijing's example mentioned previously, Beijing has also finished the world's largest EV charging station, which can charge up to 400 electric sanitation vehicles per day. According to, China's most efficient EV charging and battery swapping station have been put into operation in Beijing. The station can charge eight EVs simultaneously and it takes less than 6 min to swap a battery for an EV. Hopefully, an EV charging and battery-swapping network consisting of six large-scale concentrated charging stations, 250 charging and battery-swapping stations, and 210 small delivery stations would be in operation by the end of 2015.

As discussed earlier, main issues for the fast adoption of EVs generally include battery driving range, battery management, charging facilities and networks, cost, governmental promotion and subsidy policies, reliability, and safety. Because there is an array of issues hindering EVs from fast adoption in the global auto market and different priorities that surely vary with marketplaces, it becomes essential for EV makers and governments to capture and understand the needs, perceptions, and attitudes of their respective EV consumers in real time rather than in conventionally empirical studies, resulting in making timely, informed, and effective decisions and/or policies at the customer's point of need. Therefore, to support survey-based and cross-section empirical research, a new approach to address this new challenge is needed.

The convergence of the recent advances in science and technology has made possible the design and development of the needed methods and tools, allowing us to capture and understand customers' dynamics in real time. This offers an overview of an approach to implementing Big Data–based EV marketing campaigns in support of promoting consumption of EVs. We focus on customers' dynamics (or simply customers' experience, perceptions, and attitudes), in order to meet both their utilitarian and sociopsychological needs. For instance, what are the top three priority issues in the Beijing EV marketplace from the viewpoint of EV customers?

We explore how the emerging Big Data technologies can be applied to facilitate the process of deciphering the acceptance and behavior of EV customers from marketplace to marketplace. A Java-based software program was written, which crawls a list of designated websites for a given marketplace. The pages collected from these websites are saved as files that are preprocessed by running data retrieval and mining algorithms. The results are saved as files that are managed and processed by an IBM Big Insights platform as Hadoop files. Although data can be collected using surveys and interviews, this paper discusses web-based real-time retrieving and mining supports. IBM Big Insights platform technologies, including Hadoop, Streams, SPSS modeler, and text analytics, are utilized for looking into the insights of collected data. In this prototype project, they did not utilize the support of streams computing yet. Therefore, data collected from websites are mainly stored in two files, named as customers and comments. The customers' file contains profiles of registered EV customers while the comments file stores all the comments from registered or nonregistered EV customers.

8.6 CONCLUSIONS

In this chapter, we describe Big Data technologies, and address various issues and challenges in VANETs using Big Data. Such challenges include variable network density, dynamic topology, and anonymous addressee. Moreover, to analyze these data sets in VANETs, various tools are presented, such as Hadoop, HDFS, and MapReduce. Moreover, various architectures are described that relate to various applications in VANETs. These architectures are capable of analyzing real-time data. In addition, offloading and capacity improvement schemes are presented for massive amounts of data in short time periods compared to today's traditional techniques. Apart from architectures, we have also provided a detailed description about the Big Data frameworks that are used for data acquisition, data organization and processing, data analysis, and their prediction. In order to understand the real-time capturing and understanding electric vehicles, which give the current applications of the EV. For this purpose, we have considered several case studies, which enable electric vehicle markets and their application in various fields.

FUTURE TRENDS AND CHALLENGES IN ITS

9

9.1 NEXT GENERATION VEHICULAR NETWORKS

Nowadays, the field of intelligent transportation systems (ITS) is a challenging research area due to the potential of new vehicular applications. Research efforts in vehicular ad hoc networks (VANETs) are in fact split between industrial consortia and the academic community. Unfortunately, there is no general consensus with respect to fundamental service models and the universal platform architecture. The first generation of vehicular platforms is a result of international projects and standardization activities: IEEE 802.11p (WAVE), the Vehicle Safety Consortium (VSC), and Car-to-Car Communication Consortium (C2C-CC), ETSI ITS, Advanced Safety Vehicle Program (ASV) and Vehicle Infrastructure Integration Program (VII). Many recent projects, like CarTALK2000, Fleet Net, Now, CVIS, SAFESPOT, COOPERS, Genet, and GST are focusing on the usage of the existing communications technologies like Wi-Fi, DSRC, or UMTS. Among the existing problems related to VANETs, two are the most challenging. The first one is related to communications reliability in a highly dynamic environment while the second one deals with the definition of services.

In order to cope with these issues, current contributions focus on disruption-tolerant forwarding mechanisms for intermittent communications, adaptations of the existing TCP/IP stacks, new routing protocols, and many others. In spite of the several proposals for solving VANET's specific problems, there is no open architecture able to deal with incremental improvements or upgrades of the existing mechanisms while keeping the overall design intact. In the literature, a new structure for a generic framework for next-generation vehicular networks (NGVNs) is proposed that supports concepts like context-awareness and disruption-tolerant communications, in order to obtain reliable, adaptive, and scalable architecture. This framework supports interoperability across heterogeneous networks, which tolerate long delays. Mobility patterns play an important role in the communication scheme, as vital contextual information used for the improvement of the overall network performance and content delivery.

Core VANET research topics include nodes clustering, specific routing schemes, disruption-tolerant forwarding mechanisms, and context-awareness. The clustering algorithms deal with the highly dynamic network topology, which depends on the mobility of nodes. These algorithms perform node grouping into stable clusters, to reduce the network size and provide reliable communication and routing among cluster members. However, due to various mobility patterns of the nodes, many of them are stand-alone nodes and the continuous connectivity cannot always be ensured for them. There have been many papers focusing on new routing protocols or data dissemination schemes specific to VANET, for example, GeoDTN + Nav, OPERA, VADD, and many more, in order to achieve increased communications reliability in some mobility scenarios (e.g., highway or urban areas) or particular applications. Unfortunately, these approaches still remain purely theoretical; they are not deployed in any commercial network.

The diversity of the proposed solutions calls for a single, unified communications and service platform that can be used for all possible scenarios. A reliable communication has to deal with the intermittent connectivity of VANET nodes. Adapting disruption-tolerant networking (DTN) to VANET provides a way to cope with temporary disconnections. The combination of DTN with node mobility information can be used for advanced content dissemination (the store–carry–forward paradigm). In the existing approaches, disruption-tolerant forwarding is a part of a convergence layer that enables dynamic address binding and data rate adaptation. Until now, there have been several, mostly theoretical approaches to context-awareness, which deal with context at the service level in next-generation networks. In the MIDAS project, the approach was to develop a secure middleware platform for context-aware MANET services, which includes a context engine implementing mechanisms to retrieve, model, synthesize, and distribute the context information in a mobile distributed environment. It is also worth noting an attempt to use the existing infrastructure of a telecom operator for the creation of V2V services—a practical approach that combines advanced concepts of ITS with the IP Multimedia Subsystem (IMS).

Although IMS integration is an advantage, the local context is ignored and the scalability can be an issue. Despite the significant research efforts in VANET, most of the proposed contributions are assuming "closed architectures," which are not mutually compatible. In order to deal with this issue, a framework is developed that is able to integrate the existing concepts related to communications protocols and service definitions. One possible usage of this framework combines VANETs with disruption-tolerant networking and context-awareness, in a unique approach that ensures the flexibility of the system, able to adapt to the changing context information.

9.2 FRAMEWORK DEFINITION

This section focuses on the definition of a framework for NGVNs, driven by the context data exchange and decisions based on it. In the proposed framework, there is an internal separation into three functional layers (Fig. 9.1), namely, the Mobility Layer (ML), the Connectivity Layer (CL), and the Application Layer (AL), representing basic functionality related to mobility, connectivity, and application. Each layer is described by a set of key parameters, which can be represented as context information. This information can be exchanged between layers to optimize their internal behavior (e.g., the selection of a routing/forwarding mechanism that is the best matched to a certain mobility context), but not by direct transfer between them. The context is not only referring to a set of external constraints on the system for a given instance. However, in this case it relates to any piece of information regarding the network and the services it can include internal or external control data or can be instance related. The advantage of using important parameters as contexts is the possibility to identify the most significant data related to the intralayer mechanisms, which can be described in a unified way and to use the context information to enable the crosslayer transversal interaction. There is no direct context transfer between layers in the framework. The context information is exchanged bidirectionally only after applying the crosslayer adaptation mechanisms for it.

This also assures functional separation between the layers. The NGVN framework is based on the importance of mobility context information and the relations between neighboring nodes. The mobility context refers to GPS position, node velocity (both instantaneous and average), direction, and neighbor movement data. This information is analyzed inside the ML according to an algorithm (e.g., nodes

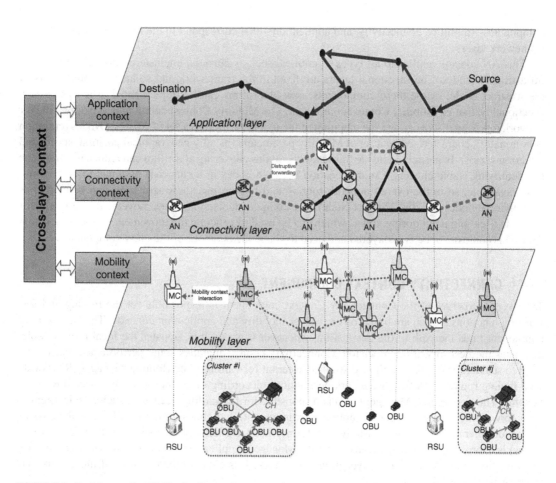

FIGURE 9.1 Next Generation Vehicular Network

OBU, on-board unit; *RSU*, roadside unit; *MC*, mobility context; *CH*, cluster head; *AN*, abstract node.

clustering) and as a result, the stable node structures are identified, together with some nodes, which are potential candidates to be assigned to such structures. Some important mobility information can be passed in a crosslayer manner to the CL or the AL. Inside the CL, the network topology is built and the most appropriate routing and forwarding schemes are applied (including DTN). The definition of the framework and the exchange of the crosslayer information in a unified format enables possible improvements and extensions in order to integrate many of the existing VANET algorithms. These improvements especially concern the specific intralayer mechanisms and algorithms (e.g., a new clustering algorithm, a new routing or forwarding scheme, a new information dissemination mechanism, etc.). However, the framework does not allow changes in the internal structure. Based on the interactions and dependencies between the nodes in the network at each of the three layers of the framework, a node internal architecture can be defined on the idea of context transfer in a component-based approach. This generic architecture is defined for Abstract Nodes (AN). It emphasizes the three key components—mobility, connectivity, and application—that correspond to the three previously defined framework layers.

This AN concept applies to all types of entities, such as clusters, unclustered nodes and roadside infrastructure nodes. The functional layers are fixed in the framework and so are the components of the Abstract Node. Inside these components, new algorithms can be implemented to introduce new functionality, that is, Mobility Context component. The Mobility Context component is responsible for network topology discovery and the mapping of the real network into a set of Abstract Nodes (common denominator), characterized by a set of Mobility parameters (usually geographical position, speed, and direction vector). In particular, inside this layer, the nodes clustering algorithm can reduce network size by identifying stable clusters. Communication between nodes in a cluster is assumed to be continuously available, so in the overall network routing and forwarding, these structures can be treated as single virtual nodes (i.e., the Abstract Node). The component also maintains movement information of the node itself and neighboring nodes, which can be used to generate the movement prediction context data. This context can be crosslayered and used to shape the behavior of the other components.

9.2.1 CONNECTIVITY CONTEXT COMPONENT

The overall structure of the Connectivity Context component is responsible for the routing and forwarding functions, which are based on crosslayer mobility and application contexts. The connectivity component finds the path to the destination, whenever it is possible, updates the local routing table, and takes the best forwarding decision. Connectivity context includes some performance metrics related to standard routing, as well as disruption-tolerant forwarding. The Routing Manager (RM) deals with finding routes to particular network destinations, according to an appropriately selected Routing Scheme. The Forwarding Manager (FM) is responsible for forwarding decisions, such as selecting the right forwarding scheme (either disruption-tolerant or not) and choosing the next hop. In the case of disruption-tolerant forwarding, custody transfer mechanism (delivery responsibility transfer between nodes) is coordinated by the dedicated Custody Manager. Application Context component has similar functionality to the Application Layer in the OSI stack. It is close to the end user of the system and interacts with some applications.

It can also be involved in the creation of new context-based services. At the Application Context component, a key issue to be resolved is related to addressing of nodes and services, especially if there is the requirement of enabling disruption-tolerant communication between nodes. In the case of highly dynamic vehicular networks, most applications require some type of controlled broadcast of information and there is not much need for unicast. Therefore, assigning a constant address to the node is irrelevant. Since the destination is constantly on the move the address of the destination is unclear hence, the destination address is guaranteed by the source. Much more important is the context information related to the destination group, location, and neighborhood.

The Cross-Layer Context component has a crucial role in our design, as it implements a set of key functions: F1 gathers important contexts related to mobility, connectivity, and application and stores it in a local repository. F2 performs context analysis in order to make intelligent decisions related to the distribution of context to other layers. F3 schedules DTN bundle events. F4 provides the necessary support for interworking with multiple communication stacks. F5 handles security functions related to data validation and user authorization the core functionality (F1 and F2) are provided by a Cross-Context Manager (CCM). Scheduling (F3) is performed by the Scheduling Manager, which is responsible for selecting a particular Scheduling Scheme (e.g., Deficit Weighted Round Robin), which will be applied in the case of bundle events (send or receive). By using crosslayering operations on the contexts, the system is capable of behaving differently according to the given context, and learns from previous experience, in order to adapt to the topology changes and service requirements.

9.3 SUPPORTING AUGMENTED FLOATING CAR DATA THROUGH SMARTPHONE-BASED CROWD-SENSING

A wide range of ITS services, including safety applications, traffic efficiency, predictive maintenance, infotainment, smart green mobility, and pervasive sensing, can be provided by letting vehicles exchange data with each other and with the road infrastructure. The following "day-one" vehicular applications have been selected for deployment by the leading European ITS stakeholders starting in 2015: in-vehicle signage, floating car data (FCD), intersection safety/green wave, road works warning, traffic information, strategic routing, hazardous location warning. Among them, especially FCD-related services have the potential to support many practical applications for safety, vehicle diagnostics, and road traffic monitoring. FCD refers to the position and kinematics data of a collection of vehicles (e.g., speed, direction of travel) to get traffic information for ITS applications. Furthermore, thanks to the advancements in vehicle telematics, FCD can also include reports about the status of microprocessor-based electronic control units networked within the vehicle through the Controller Area Network (CAN) bus. Environmental sensors (like pollution detectors) can be easily brought into the picture to augment the scope of FCD-enabled applications toward urban sensing operations so that vehicles can be integrated in the future smart-city infrastructure. Henceforth, the resulting set of collected data is referred to as "augmented" FCD. These augmented data can be processed by remote control centers for multiple purposes, for example, to monitor road traffic conditions and prevent congestion to inform fleets of vehicles cooperatively driving, to detect possible in-vehicle malfunctions, to collect traffic statistics, to get car maintenance tips and service information.

Depending on the purpose of the FCD collection, data may have different time validity (a time interval during which the information is relevant for the service) and accuracy demand. For example, if extracted traffic-related data are used for traffic signs adaptation, then a few seconds validity is reasonable, whereas long-term road traffic statistics may tolerate longer validity times, up to some minutes, and a lower number of samples; finally, data pertaining to long-term car maintenance can be stored for days on the vehicle before transmission. Despite the wide range of services potentially enabled by augmented FCD and the surging interest within standardization bodies, such as 3GPP (Third Generation Partnership Project), ETSI (European Telecommunications Standards Institute), and SAE (Society of Automotive Engineers) International, the deployment of standard communication technologies and protocols for the remote transfer of FCD is still underway. Stakeholders worldwide are struggling to finalize standards to allow specialized wireless on-board units (OBUs) to directly interact with the CAN bus and to communicate with other OBUs and with roadside units, under any propagation condition, intermittent connectivity, and traffic density. Nonetheless, both technical (harsh vehicle environment) and economic barriers slow down the large-scale deployment and market penetration of VANETs and OBU equipped cars.

Such factors challenge the capability of the automotive industry and standardization process to be fast enough in developing and pushing the new technology before the current consumer electronics and network technologies available in the market offer valuable alternative solutions. It is the authors' conviction that the current need for augmented FCD could be satisfied by using mass-market users' devices, such as smartphones, and available technologies, such as cellular and Wi-Fi networks. This conviction is shared with the scientific community and many running initiatives are pushing toward enabling users' portable devices, such as tablets and phones, to access in-vehicle telematics and to monitor in-vehicle services through low-cost devices and open-source software. In addition, several solutions have been proposed that leverage smartphones in the automotive context, for example, for safety and traffic management purposes or to collect driving habits. Finally, the Open Automotive Alliance (OAA), a group of leading automotive manufacturers and technology companies, also argue for a close alignment of consumer and automotive technologies and pushes toward bringing the Android platform to the car, to make in-car technology safer and more intuitive for everyone. Although the use of smartphones is a timely solution to offer automotive services with a short time-to-market, some issues need to be addressed when considering FCD-based services.

Specifically, the amount of uploaded data from a large number of contributing vehicles with a frequency of seconds risks burdening the cellular network and drain the smartphone's battery. Consequently, either traditional cellular traffic (e.g., voice) could be penalized or FCD applications could achieve poor performance, being unable to meet timely delivery and integrity requirements. Solutions in the literature, targeted to solve such an issue and alleviate the cellular network load, either leverage the upcoming IEEE 802.11p technology to collect data to be aggregated and remotely delivered, or probabilistically selects a subset of cars to take part in the process by assuring only partially accurate data retrieval. This work addresses the support of FCD services in a more comprehensive way, with the design and demonstration of a solution encompassing smartphones for (1) efficient data collection from a wide set of heterogeneous (in-vehicle and external) sensors to effectively provide augmented FCD services, and (2) opportunistic data delivery through a simple cellular traffic offloading technique designed to exploit on-the-road Wi-Fi connectivity by leveraging the built-in smartphone's Wi-Fi network interface card. Cellular network offloading may significantly reduce costs for cellular operators to tackle increasing traffic demands, by avoiding the deployment of additional base stations or the upgrading of the existing ones.

Unlike previous literature on offloading techniques, typically focusing on downlink data transfers in low-mobility scenarios, our work addresses uplink data packets offload in vehicular environments. Indeed, in vehicular Wi-Fi offloading is preliminarily debated as a promising research direction, provided that some issues uniquely arising in the vehicular environment (i.e., short and intermittent connectivity, fast fluctuating wireless channels) are properly overstepped. Some of those concerns may hinder the effectiveness of offloading in the presence of bulky contents, but are deadened in the case of small packets. An early version of the smartcard (smartphone-based floating CAR data collection) design and its preliminary demonstrator are extended in this paper with further functionalities to specific target augmented FCD applications. The prototype deployed on board the vehicle leverages low-cost off-the-shelf hardware and open source software (e.g., Arduino platform and Android), which give the designed solution the potential and has been an effective mobile crowd-sensing tool.

9.3.1 THE CENTRAL ROLE OF THE SMARTPHONE

The smartphone plays a central role in our proposed solution and implements most of the required tasks, ranging from data collection and preprocessing to remote delivery. A functional scheme of our Smartcard platform is reported in Fig. 9.2.

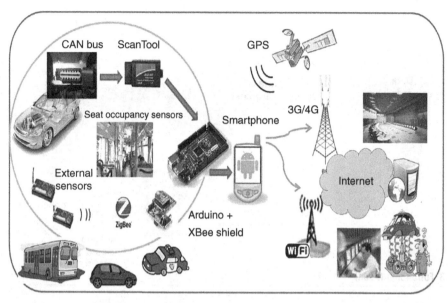

FIGURE 9.2 Architecture for Smartphone Vehicular Platform

The smartphone simultaneously collects information provided by multiple heterogeneous sources:

- The embedded GPS receiver: FCD should at least include timing and position coordinates of the vehicle; this information is directly taken from the smartphone, which is endowed with self-positioning capability.
- The in-vehicle CAN bus: In addition to kinematics-related data, information concerning the specific vehicle status (e.g., engine status) is also retrieved from the CAN bus.
- Seat-occupancy sensors: This feature is an add-on with respect to the platform described. Detecting and remotely transmitting the seat occupancy status can serve several purposes, for example, facilitating the planning of rescue operations from remote centers. As a matter of fact, ETSI hazard notification messages also carry this information. Moreover, such an information may provide statistics about passengers in public vehicles (like taxi, bus, minibus) for ticketing and service planning, hence of particular interest for fleet management applications.
- Environmental sensors: The traditional FCD retrieved from the in-vehicle telematics, air quality mean-sacraments gathered through cheap sensors mounted on the vehicle to avoid the deployment of sophisticated sensors or pollution-monitoring stations on the roads.

The smartphone is also responsible for delivering the retrieved data to remote processing centers, through its built-in cellular or Wi-Fi radio interfaces. In order to offload the cellular network, the smartphone is augmented with a software module (Data Store & Transfer) that chooses the interface to transmit the collected data, as detailed in the following section.

9.3.1.1 The Smartcard Architecture and Functional Modules

The smart car prototype: (1) collects in-vehicle FCD and environmental sensing information from out-side, and (2) opportunistically transfers them to meet their delivery constraints and offload the cellular

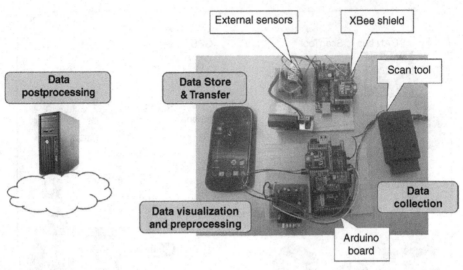

FIGURE 9.3 Functional Model

network. The platform includes the following functional modules running over the main smartcard components as shown in Fig. 9.3.

- Data collection module: It is responsible for collecting, merging, and temporarily storing data. It is implemented in a dedicated USB-enabled microcontroller board receiving data inputs from a variety of sensors, on board the vehicle and in its close surroundings. The open-source, low-cost, flexible hardware/software Arduino platform is used for this purpose. It can be configured to offer a variety of wired and wireless communication interfaces. The customized homemade microprocessor could also replace Arduino.
- Data visualization and preprocessing module: It is implemented in the smartphone. It is independent of the kind of collecting data, the type of sensors, and the CAN bus network. It hides from the end-users details about implementation and sensing devices. The smartphone application retrieves data from the Arduino board and shows them after processing on a graphical user interface (GUI).
- Data store and transfer module: It is implemented in the smartphone, remotely transmits collected augmented FCD according to the data validity, the available network coverage, and radio interfaces. It implements the offloading strategy.
- Data postprocessing module: It is implemented in the remote server to track vehicles and store the augmented data sent from the smartphone. Mobile alphas have been implemented that runs on the smartphone using the Android open source operating system. The software includes the following main functions (1) retrieving data from the Arduino board, (2) tagging data, (3) showing data to the end-user through a GUI, and (4) remotely transfers them. Functions (1)–(3) are performed by the Data Visualization and Preprocessing module; function (4) is performed by the Data Store and Transfer module.

9.3.2 THE DATA COLLECTION MODULE

9.3.2.1 In-Vehicle Telematics

Data supplied from the vehicle's CAN bus can be read through the Onboard Diagnostics (OBD)-II interface. OBD-II is the standard that specifies the type of diagnostic connector and its pinout, the electrical signaling protocols, and the messaging format. Specifically, it provides both real-time vehicle data and a standard-sized series of Diagnostic Trouble Codes (DTCs), allowing to quickly detect and solve malfunctions in the vehicle. The OBD-II interface is not available on a smartphone, rather it can be provided with an OBD connector. An ELM327-chipped scan tool has been used for this purpose; it includes a controller, a CAN transceiver, and an OBD male connector; it is compliant with the OBD-II specifications. Several ready-to-use OBD connectors are available on the market, either endowed with USB interface or providing Bluetooth and Wi-Fi connectivity to directly interact with smartphones.

In this prototype, an Arduino board is included between the OBD connector and the smartphone, instead of enabling direct communications over the radio interface. In particular, the ELM327 acts as a bridge between the OBD ports and a standard RS232 interface. Through the latter one, it is connected to the Arduino board over which AT commands are sent. The designed module can potentially retrieve the full spectrum of standardized in-vehicle data. A software module, loaded into the Arduino platform, filters data from the CAN bus to avoid polling a high number of in-vehicle sensors, which would increase the contention on the CAN bus and reduce the data sampling rate. The sampling rate can be set according to the application requirements.

OBD-II parameter identifiers (PIDs) are used to request a specific vehicle parameter from the CAN bus. The scan tool, triggered by Arduino, sends a PID to the vehicle's bus. The device responsible for that PID reports the corresponding value to the bus; then the scan tool reads the response and replies to Arduino. Some PIDs like the vehicle speed are closely related to traffic management purposes, while others give information about the vehicle status and enable the car diagnosis from a remote site, to detect possible malfunctions and to collect vehicle statistics. The Arduino is interfaced with an Android smartphone. Such an interface is deployed through the Accessory Development Kit (ADK), a standard powered by Google to enable communication between Android devices and external hardware (in this case, the Arduino microcontroller board). In particular, an Arduino Mega ADK microcontroller has been used and equipped with a Secure Digital (SD) memory card to temporarily store data. It has a USB host interface to connect with Android-based phones. Smartphones with new Android releases natively support ADK.

9.3.3 ADD-ON SENSORS

Currently, in addition to the CAN-bus, our prototype foresees the interaction with

1. The homemade, low-cost, seat-mounted proximity sensors located in the vehicle to monitor the passenger load,
2. Environmental sensors located outside the vehicle for monitoring purposes.

The seat occupancy sensors are based on capacitive effects. The set-up scheme is relevant to seat occupancy. An electrode is placed on the seat to be monitored. This electrode is built up from a thin circular metal plate. In its cheapest realization, it could be obtained from aluminium foil. The electrode is covered by a piece of nonconducting material, which can be the seat upholstery itself or a paper covering. The electrode constitutes one plate of a capacitor and the chassis of the vehicle constitutes the second plate of this capacitor. When a human body occupies the seat, the electrical properties of the sensor electrode and the ground change and the total capacitance of the system above.

The environmental sensors transfer measured data to the Arduino board, which has been augmented with XBee modules to support ZigBee communication. The Arduino board can retrieve environment-related parameters at the same or at a different frequency from the one used to get data from the CAN bus. Further sensors can be easily integrated, by adding proper shields to the Arduino board (e.g., biometric data can be collected from drivers and passengers to give more information to rescue teams in case of car accidents). The augmented FCD information collected from the mentioned set of heterogeneous sensors is packed together and passed to the smartphone.

9.3.4 THE DATA VISUALIZATION AND PREPROCESSING MODULE

The information retrieved from Arduino is complemented with information gathered by the mobile phone itself, that is, GPS information, time and position coordinates. Although the type of collecting data depends on the remote application, the user is allowed to select the parameters to be directly visualized on her smartphone. The parameters of the selected sensors are then shown in the main window of the GUI and periodically refreshed to give the user feedback about the car performance.

A sample snapshot of the application visualizing some of the in-vehicle monitored parameters is represented in the GUI. The data store and transfer module collected data, tagged by the Visualization and Preprocessing module, are separately queued, based on the priority and lifetime set by the application, and then transmitted to a remote server. Cellular and Wi-Fi interfaces are alternatively used for this purpose. In a smart car, available connectivity options are monitored in the device by leveraging off-the-shelf Android utilities. Our solution avoids the energy consumption related to continuous scanning for nearby APs since the smartphone is powered by the vehicle's battery. The decision on the network interface to be used for the remote delivery is based on opportunistic offloading principles. Similar to the solution in the previous model, data are always exchanged (uploaded in our case) via Wi-Fi whenever an access point (AP) is detected. Otherwise, when the cellular connection is the only one available, the decision whether to transmit data or not is taken according to the data lifetime associated with each packet (time-to-live [TTL]).

In particular, three data types are identified, that is, high priority, medium priority, and low-priority delay-tolerant data. High-priority data, reporting information about a sudden vehicle fault, typically have a lifetime on the order of milliseconds and are immediately transmitted over the most reliable and lowest-latency radio interface; the message could be enriched with information about the number of passengers detected by the seat occupancy sensors. The lifetime for medium priority data may vary according to the application processing them. For instance, it can range from a few seconds if extracted traffic-related data are used for traffic sign adaptation, to some minutes for long-term road traffic statistics. Moreover, the TTL can vary according to the time of the day and the vehicle speed. For instance, during rush hours, the TTL should be short in order to provide up-to-date information on the traffic situation; on the other hand, data received at night can be considered valid for longer as it is unlikely that the traffic situation will abruptly change. Delay-tolerant data, such as the diagnostic trouble codes concerning the specific vehicle status, to be sent to car manufacturers and workshops for monitoring and diagnosis purposes, can be stored in the smartphone until the vehicle falls under the coverage of a Wi-Fi network or the user owning the device reaches her home/office network. Overall, medium and low priority packets can be stored in the smartphone until their lifetime expires.

Each packet of size is labeled at the smartphone with a timestamp representing its generation time (Tgen); the packet expiry time is fixed to (Tgen + TTL). Tlast is set as the last time instant that the smartphone can wait before transmitting the packet on the cellular network. If a Wi-Fi hotspot is detected before Tlast, then the packet is transmitted to the AP; otherwise, the packet is transmitted through the cellular network. Tlast is computed as the difference between the packet expiry time and the end-to-end packet transfer time transfer. The latter parameter includes the delay across the cellular network (both radio access and core network segments) and across the Internet to the remote server. The data postprocessing module data delivered to the remote server can be stored, processed, and analyzed by different applications. Anonymous information is collected about the vehicle and the driver is not transferred to prevent privacy violation. The anonymization method can be used for this purpose. Data collected by smart car–equipped vehicles over a large scale can be used to feed providers' servers that monitor the actual traffic situation in real-time (e.g., speeds, volumes) and offer accurate and reliable information both to drivers and road authorities. How such procedures are managed is outside the scope of the present work.

9.4 ENABLING VEHICULAR MOBILITY IN CITYWIDE IEEE 802.11 NETWORKS THROUGH PREDICTIVE HANDOVERS

In recent years, the number of mobile users connected through 802.11 networks has significantly increased. At the same time, the increasing number of wireless network deployments opens the way toward ubiquitous network connectivity. However, under vehicular mobility, the selection of the AP in providing the most sustainable network connectivity is a challenging task. In this context, the standard IEEE 802.11 handover comprises three phases—scanning, authentication and association—and are inefficient in ensuring a seamless transition to the best AP. It is well known that the scanning process in which the Mobile Station (MS) probes nearby APs on each channel and waits for probe responses, is the major bottleneck. This inefficiency is mainly caused by two factors, that is, (1) by the long delay in the handover and (2) by the lack of indication of short-term changing in the nearby APs' Received Signal Strengths (RSS). The first implies long disconnection periods while the second leads to potentially inconsistent AP selection. Many solutions have been proposed to mitigate these issues with some success, mostly by reducing the disconnection period during the handover. The future emergence of IEEE 802.11p/WAVE networks, which have been specifically designed for vehicular communications, opens the way toward seamless handovers.

One of the major modifications proposed in this standard is the suppression of the authentication and association phase, and the transmission of Wireless Access in Vehicular Environments (WAVE) beacons containing the service transmission characteristics over a dedicated channel. However, this standard still provides no guidance as to how AP selection may be optimized. As a result, in current and future 802.11 deployments, the inconsistency of the AP selection remains an open issue. Currently, the majority of the proposed handover optimization relies only on the instantaneous sensing of the RSS. However, this metric provides only a snapshot of the current state of the network and does not provide any trend for its evolution, which is critical in the context of vehicular communications. Gustafson and Jonson distinguish session continuity as one of the mobility management enhancements that is necessary to achieve the always best connected (ABC) paradigm. The MS needs to augment its knowledge of nearby networks and vehicle's mobility such that it can anticipate their evolution. This anticipation allows the MS to avoid abrupt connection disruption due to inappropriate AP selection and to provide a seamless connection to the AP. In this article, a context-aware predictive handover technique conceived with the aim of optimizing vehicular communications through a metropolitan IEEE 802.11 hotspot network is discussed. The AP selection process of COOPERS uses a prediction of MS connectivity over the near future, such that the roaming decision is performed at the most appropriate location. In this case, a prior knowledge of the route taken by the vehicle would allow computing optimal handover locations. However, most of the time, people drive on previously known routes, and thus do not need to be assisted by any embedded system. As a result, there is no way to know the destination, nor the route the driver plans to take in advance. In fact, this information is not reliable since the driver may change the route on impulse. Consequently, COOPERS includes a direction detection module that provides a short-term prediction of the direction of the vehicle. In order to perform the direction detection and the AP selection, COOPERS uses the knowledge of the road topology, the APs' locations and their modeled RSS, all stored in a context database (CDB).

During vehicular mobility, an MS connected through 802.11 networks faces frequent handovers and must select the next AP and associate within the shortest delay. Prior studies on the standard IEEE 802.11 handover mechanism identified the scanning phase as the most costly in time. Indeed, during scanning, the MS probes nearby APs and waits for responses on all available channels. Scanning implies a disconnection period because the MS cannot exchange frames with the current AP while listening on other channels. Several approaches have been proposed to reduce or even eliminate the impact of the scanning phase during handover. Montavont et al. proposed an optimization to this process by performing short interleaved scanning phases with ongoing data communication. In Sync Scan, Armani and Savage investigated a modification of the infrastructure where the APs synchronously broadcast beacon frames on the same channel so that the MS just needs to switch the channel and wait for a short period to retrieve the available APs. Another solution consists in relocating the scanning to a second interface.

The experiments in the literature show that such a solution can provide a significant gain in terms of the time that the MS is associated. In the prior work, the researcher evaluated the impact of adding a second radio and showed that the MS can reach up to 98% of layer 2 connection time. Even though the impact of scanning on handover duration can be significantly reduced, it still suffers from providing inaccurate results. Indeed, scanning is an instantaneous sensing of the network that does not always reflect reality. Because of beacon loss, scanning can miss an available AP, especially in dense deployments. To overcome this issue, a solution is to use repeated multiple scans, split into short interleaved scanning. However, this approach is not applicable to vehicular communications, as the sensed values become rapidly obsolete because of the relatively high velocity. In order to provide a dynamic knowledge of nearby APs, a scheme is proposed that performs RSS predictions based on smoothed RSS trends. Nevertheless, this kind of prediction can only be performed over a very short period, since it does not consider any information regarding the vehicle's motion.

For instance, the MS will not be able to predict a sudden signal decrease when the vehicle leaves the line of sight of the AP. In the literature, multiple 802.11p network architectures for vehicle-to-infrastructure (V2I) communications have been proposed, including multiple handover mechanisms. The network architecture described in consists of IEEE 802.11f Inter Access Point Protocol (IAPP) compatible Roadside Units (RSU) interconnected by a set of layer 2 switches connected to a gateway router. This makes the network appear as a single distribution system and mobility management is handled at the layer 2, avoiding the use of Internet Protocol (IP) mobility protocol such as Mobile IPv6 (MIPv6) or Proxy Mobile IPv6 (PMIPv6). The handover is triggered when the on-board unit (OBU) sends an IEEE 802.11 disassociation message to the current RSU. The RSU, then, communicates the OBU address to the next RSU by forwarding the packets addressed to OBU. The major drawback of this approach is that it is designed to work in a highway environment where the next RSU selection is trivial.

Note that in an urban scenario, the AP selection process may not be as trivial as the highway scenario. An extended version of this approach is intended to work in an urban environment. The authors propose forwarding data packets to all the candidate RSUs.

When an RSU detects that the OBU has entered its coverage range, it is selected as the next RSU and sends a Move–Notify message to the remaining RSUs. However, such an approach implies a significant packet overhead. In order to allow the MS to anticipate the short-term evolution of the network, it is critical to provide information about the vehicle's mobility. Based on the fact that people usually drive on previously known routes, a scheme is proposed that replaced the scanning with an AP selection using historical information. While driving, the MS learns and caches information about nearby APs (ESSID, BSSID, and channel) by frequently sensing during inactive periods. This information is, then, used to script the handover location in advance such that the MS always connects to the best candidate AP. Another approach is proposed that suggests including the trajectory of the vehicle and neighbor information in order to select APs along the vehicle's path and predict an optimal handover location.

This approach was investigated in which an augmented version of the Mobile IPv6 (MIP6) architecture with a new component is updated with the location of the MS. Based on the evolution of the MS location and prior knowledge of AP locations, channels, BSSIDs and IPv6 prefixes, the GPS server triggers handover to the closest AP when the MS is about to leave the coverage range of the current AP by sending a handover indication packet to the MS. The author uses large datasets gathering mobility history of cellular network users and the large indoor 802.11 network. A scheme is proposed based on a cloud-based mobility prediction system that consists in detecting periodicity in the mobility pattern using the Fullback–Libeler divergence (KLD) as the metric and evaluates social interplay in order to identify some pairs of calls that will be colocated. In the literature, a model is presented in which the mobility behavior of users are in an 802.11 network as Markov Renewal Processed (MRP). This model is intended to predict handovers and the sojourn duration of a user based on the current location and the prior location of the user immediately before the transition into the current location. In the same way, an efficient prediction-based bandwidth allocation scheme using the Mobile Reservation Protocol (MRSVP) is proposed and described an analysis of users' mobility to ensure quality-of-service (QoS). These approaches propose long-term predictions that allow the MS to ensure service continuity in case the selected AP is unavailable (switch off or not able to provide enough bandwidth). In our previous contribution (road), the AP selection process uses prior knowledge of the route of the vehicle and the location of the APs along the road. The RSSs of the APs are modeled offline using the CORNER signal propagation model. Based on this information, road can predict the best handover location. This allows the MS to trigger the handover using its location as the single input.

9.4.1 COOPERS

In order to mitigate the limitations of the standard 802.11 handovers in a vehicular scenario, a roaming decision technique that intends to provide always best connected wireless access by avoiding the MS scanning process is proposed. The choice of the AP providing the best connectivity has traditionally been done by selecting the AP with the highest RSS discovered through the scanning process. In this work, the AP selection process on prior knowledge of the road topology, the locations of the APs and a model of their RSSs is proposed. Using this information, the MS is able to determine its location on the road network and use the modeled RSSs of nearby APs to choose the one potentially providing the best signal in the new vehicle location. As illustrated in Fig. 9.4, COOPERS is composed of three main modules intended to provide seamless transitions between the best candidate APs regardless of

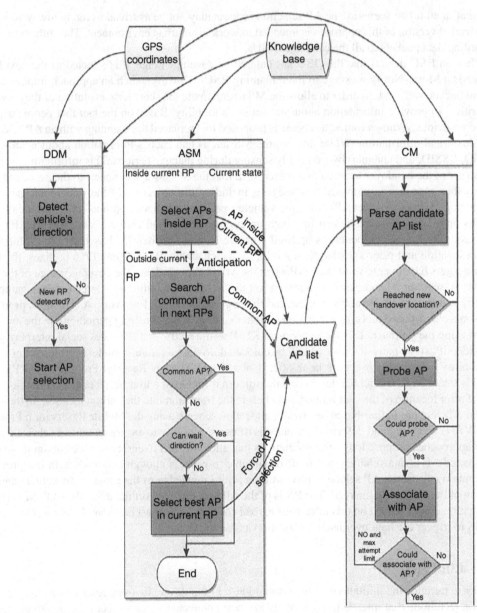

FIGURE 9.4 COOPERS Module

the vehicle's route. To this end, the Direction Detection Module (DDM) anticipates the direction of the vehicle using a fuzzy logic–based analysis trajectory that considers the road characteristics stored in a precomputed CDB. For this direction prediction, the AP Selection Module (ASM) makes use of the simulated AP RSS stored in the CDB in order to look for the best APs and the best locations to trigger handovers. Finally, the Connection Module (CM) detects when the vehicle is entering a handover area and attempts a connection by probing the selected AP and associating with it. The following sections describe the construction of the CDB and the COOPERS modules.

9.5 REAL-TIME PATH PLANNING BASED ON HYBRID-VANET-ENHANCED TRANSPORTATION SYSTEM

Traffic congestion, as an important societal problem, has received considerable attention. The 2007 Urban Mobility Report stated that traffic congestion causes nearly 4.2 billion hours of extra travel every year in the United States; the extra travel almost accounts for 2.9 billion extra gallons of gasoline. Although many existing advanced personal navigation devices have functionalities of providing an optimal end-to-end path, traffic congestion problems in ITSs have not been fully resolved; on the contrary, conventional approaches still face a number of technical challenges. For example, Google Maps involve existing networks (e.g., Global Position System, Wi-Fi, cellular networks, etc.) for individual paths, planning to avoid the traffic congestion. However, the provided services are very costly, and more importantly, they cannot make a quick response to an emergency caused by an accident/incident. The essential reason for this imperfection lies in the lack of real-time traffic information. Thus, to enhance the adaptability of path planning, it is indispensable to study how to efficiently collect and further exploit the real-time traffic information for path planning and traffic congestion avoidance.

First, to collect the real-time traffic information, the emerging VANETs can provide an ITS system with enhanced communication capabilities for cost effective and real-time traffic information delivery. Both V2V and V2R communications are supported in VANETs to efficiently collect/report traffic updates from/to vehicles as well as roadside units (RSUs). As a result, the collected real-time traffic information can be utilized for freeway-traffic-flow management, individualized vehicle path planning, and vehicle localization. However, most of the related work assumes that the incorporated VANETs have a sufficiently small delivery delay for real-time information collection. As VANETs rely on short-range multihop communications, the end-to-end transmission delay cannot be neglected in some scenarios. Therefore, evaluations should be conducted to study how the end-to-end transmission performance of vehicular communications affects the performance of path planning in different scenarios and how to design the transmission mechanisms to reduce the delay when delay cannot be neglected. Second, to exploit the obtained real-time traffic information, many algorithms are designed to discover optimal paths for individual vehicles. However, individual path planning may lead to a new congestion if performed uncoordinatedly. To smooth the overall network flow, many works plan optimal paths from a global perspective for a group of vehicles simultaneously.

However, most existing globally optimal path-planning algorithms focus on the network-side performance improvement and neglect the drivers' preferences (e.g., shorter travel length or time). Since the replanning decisions are made to avoid congestion and balance the traffic rather than discover optimal paths for individuals, some vehicles may pay additional costs (e.g., a longer traveling length). Therefore, algorithms should be designed to jointly consider the balance of the network traffic and the reduction of average vehicle travel cost. To this end, a real-time global path-planning algorithm that exploits VANETs communication capabilities to avoid vehicles from congestion in an urban environment is proposed. Both the network spatial utilization and vehicle travel cost are considered to optimally balance the overall network smoothness and the drivers' preferences. Specifically, the contributions of this work are as follows.

First, to facilitate the application of real-time path planning, a hybrid-VANET-enhanced ITS framework is proposed that exploits both the VANETs and the public transportation system. Based on the proposed hybrid ITS framework, a multihop message forwarding mechanism is designed to collect the real-time traffic information or the emergent warning messages, which usually have strict delay bounds. A theoretical analysis on the end-to-end transmission delay performance of the mechanism is presented as well. Second, a real-time global path-planning algorithm to not only improve network spatial utilization but also reduce average vehicle travel cost per trip is designed. A low complexity algorithm is developed based on Lyapunov optimization to make real-time path-planning decisions. With the proposed path-planning algorithm, the trade-off between the overall network, spatial utilization, and drivers' preferences can be well balanced. Finally, the transmission performance of the hybrid VANETs is first evaluated under different vehicle densities via VISSIM, and then, extensive simulations validate the effectiveness and efficiency of the proposed path-planning algorithm. The results confirm that our proposed path planning algorithm is able to find alternative paths for vehicles to bypass congestion areas while reducing the average travel cost in an efficient, timely, and coordinated way.

9.5.1 SYSTEM MODEL

Aiming at providing real-time planned paths for vehicles from a global perspective, we first described the following network architecture. The traffic flow model followed by the vehicle categorization and mobility model. A summary of the important mathematical notations used in this work is given in a Hybrid-VANET-Enhanced Transportation System. The architecture of the considered hybrid-VANET-enhanced transportation system consists of vehicles, RSUs, cellular base stations (BSs), and a vehicle-traffic server. Vehicles are equipped with the onboard units that enable multihop V2V communication used in delivering the periodic vehicle information (e.g., vehicle velocity, density, and location). When vehicles sense accident-related congestion, the warning message can be generated to alert the emergency accident information and then be shared not only among vehicles but with the nearest RSU via V2R communications as well. Moreover, pure VANETs, cellular communications, for example, a GSM system that is set up for the functions such as mobile telemonitoring and management systems for intercity public transportation, are also involved.

Hence, the taxis or buses can directly upload the received warning message to the nearest cellular BS, and the BS will deliver the message to the vehicle traffic server as shown in Fig. 9.5. RSUs deployed along the roads are assumed able to obtain vehicle-traffic statistical information (e.g., the vehicle arrival/departure rate on each road). They consider that taxis and buses are perfectly connected to the cellular system, and RSUs are well connected with each other through wire line. If RSUs are deployed at intersections, the traffic information can be detected by the equipped cameras or traffic flow meters connected to RSUs directly. Otherwise, the traffic flow can be predicted by the nearest RSUs based on the obtained vehicle information (e.g., periodically obtained vehicle density and velocity) from the VANETs. An RSU can share its own collected information with other RSUs and the vehicle-traffic server. When an accident happens, based on all the collected information, the vehicle-traffic server is

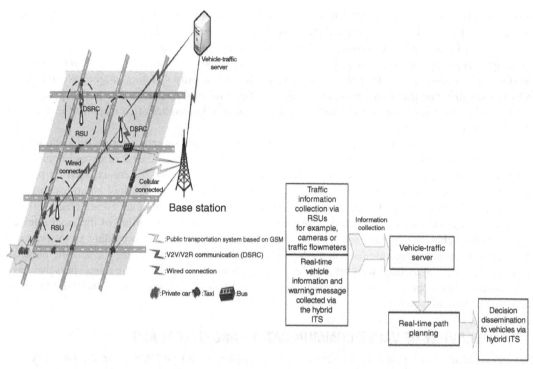

FIGURE 9.5 System Model for Hybrid-VANET-Enhanced Transportation System

capable of performing real-time path planning to provide globally optimized travel paths for vehicles of interest. In order to further define a road network, four main components (i.e., intersections, roads, vehicles, and RSUs) are designated as $\zeta = (I, \Gamma, V, R)$. The set of all intersections is denoted as I. Let Γ be the set of all the roads in the network. Each road between two adjacent intersections is assumed bidirectional, possibly with multiple lanes in one direction. Each of those lanes with the same direction in a road is a road segment; that is, one normal bidirectional road between two adjacent intersections i and j has two different road segments with opposite directions, that is, road segment (i, j) and road segment (j, i). The set of vehicles and that of RSUs are defined as V and R, respectively.

9.6 RECENT ADVANCES IN CRYPTOGRAPHIC SOLUTIONS FOR VEHICULAR NETWORKS

During the past years, vehicles have become increasingly reliable and comfortable. The need for reliability and comfort is accompanied by several security requirements related to driving and the knowledge of the internal and external environmental parameters. Numerous services are currently deployed in modern vehicles, including localization, path selection, and collision avoidance. To provide such services, advanced communication systems have been introduced. They mainly ensure V2V, V2I, and vehicle-to-home (V2H) communication services. These systems are used to implement a number of promising applications, such as early hazard prevention, adaptive route planning, and coordination of traffic flows. Even truly cooperative and therefore extremely challenging applications like crosstraffic collision avoidance are being considered. Unfortunately, the proliferation of VANET applications is severely affected by the potential attacks that may alter the services provided across vehicular networks. Such threats, ranging from denial-of-service (DoS) to identity spoofing, might have disastrous effects since they can lead to the partial or total loss of control of the vehicle. Due to the specific features of vehicular communication channels, existing security solutions are often inapplicable to thwart the aforementioned threats.

A security solution for VANETs has to account for the contention-based opportunistic communication medium, the ad hoc group formation strategies between vehicles, the ease of eavesdropping and capturing the data exchange, the high mobility of the network nodes, and the crucial need for privacy and anonymity. Cryptographic protocols have often been presented as potential solutions to cover the vulnerabilities of VANETs and improve their robustness to the malicious events characterizing the hazardous environment in which they operate. In this section, a description of the most relevant cryptographic schemes that have been proposed for VANETs. We begin by providing an overview of the communication architecture used in the VANET context. Then, we underline the specific network security challenges associated with vehicular communication. An overview of the researchers that have been published to propose cryptographic solutions for VANETs is also given with some insights on the future development issues.

9.6.1 OVERVIEW OF VANET COMMUNICATION ARCHITECTURES

Several approaches are proposed for the networked services based on VANET. In the literature, the authors divided the network applications of VANETs environment can be into three main categories: road safety, traffic monitoring categories are discussed in the following.

- Road safety: Safety applications are always paramount to significantly reduce the number of accidents, the main focus of which is to avoid accidents from happening in the first place. The main purpose of these applications is informing drivers through vehicular communications of the traffic conditions in their close proximity and further down the road. Vehicle platooning is also another technique to improve safety. For example, this can be achieved by eliminating the amount of lane changing and/or speed adjustment, and platooning helps vehicles to travel both more closely and more safely. Fuel economy cars benefit also from the aerodynamic drag reduction as the vehicle headway is more tightened. Used with adaptive cruise control system assisted by V2V communications, the vehicle crash problem due to human error can be mitigated.
- Traffic monitoring and management: Traffic monitoring and management are essential to avoid traffic congestion and increase road capacity. In the city streets, crossing intersections can be dangerous and tricky at times. Thus, scheduling traffic lights can help drivers to cross intersections. Allowing regular smooth traffic can greatly reduce travel time and promotes vehicle throughput. On the other hand, drivers can optimize their driving routes. Thus, the problem of highway traffic congestion can be highly reduced with knowledge of real-time traffic conditions. Real-time location system (RTLS) is one of the several technologies that allow the current geolocation detection of a target, which may be anything such as a vehicle, or person, or also an item in a manufacturing plant. RTLS-capable products are used more and more in an ever-increasing number of sectors such as retail, recreation, military, and courier and postal services. RTLS are

typically embedded in a product, like navigational system or mobile phones. The majority of the systems consist of wireless nodes— typically tags or badges—that emit signals and readers that receive those signals. Current real-time location systems are basically based on wireless technologies, such as Bluetooth, Wi-Fi, ultrawide-band, GPS, and RFID.

• Infotainment delivery: The goal of infotainment applications is to provide convenience and comfort to both drivers and passengers. For example, the capacity to yield peer-to-peer transferring files tools and games on the road. A real-time parking navigation system is also proposed to inform drivers of any available parking space. Digital display panels for VANETs devices and users are proposed for advertisement and warning. V2I communications can easily provide Internet access.

Therefore, in a VANET environment, business activities can be performed as usual, bringing out the notion of a mobile office. On-the-road media streaming between vehicles also can be available, making long travel more pleasant. The communication schemes used in a VANET will be classified into two categories. The first category concerns V2V communication while the second category covers communications between mobile vehicles and the roadside infrastructure (V2I). The main advantage of V2V communication is that it overcomes the need for expensive infrastructure; the major drawback is the comparatively complex networking protocols, and the need for significant penetration before applications can become effective. 802.11p enables communication between devices, moving at the vehicular speed of up to 200 km/h. It is part of the WAVE framework. Besides the PHY, 802.11p defines the lower part of the MAC layer, while the IEEE 1609 family of standards address the upper part of the MAC (1609.4), networking (1609.3), security (1609.2), resource management (1609.1), communication management (1609.5), and overall architecture (1609.0). With a maximum communication range of 1 km, the time for data exchange between two moving devices is limited to a few seconds before connectivity is lost.

If the connectivity time is short, devices neither associate nor authenticate before data exchange. V2I communications systems assume that all communications take place between roadside infrastructure (including RSUs and OBUs). Depending on the application, the author distinguished two different types of infrastructure, that is, the sparse RVC (SRVC) and the ubiquitous RVC (URVC) systems. SRVC systems are able to provide communication services at hot spots. Among applications that require SRVC system, applications like parking space identification in airport, a busy intersection scheduling its traffic light, and a gas station advertising its existence and its prices are predominant. An SRVC system can be gradually deployed, thus not requiring additional investments before any possible available benefits. A URVC system can be considered as the holy grail of VANET communication: providing all roads with high-speed communication would enable applications unavailable with any of the other existing systems. Unfortunately, a URVC system may require important investments for providing significant coverage of available roadways, especially in wide countries like the United States or China. The network layer may provide either fixed or geographical addressing. In the case of an unsuitability, it also needs to grant a mapping service between them. In an IVC system, if fixed addresses are used, a query may be flooded in the target area. Any vehicles in the action area will reply with their fixed addresses. Then the message can be sent in unicast to each vehicle (or better yet, in multicast). On the other hand, if geographical addresses are used, an additional identification field may be added to the geographical address such that the message is delivered to only one vehicle. 4G emerging wireless technologies such as LTE and IMAX have been proposed to implement V2I. 4G involves technologies that provide faster downlink speeds and packet-switched delivery for VoIP. 4G systems support a wide variety of services, which include interactive multimedia, video streaming, wireless broadband Internet, and video streaming. This type of Internet connection is superfast, high capacity, and costs less per bit. A few of the distinct advantages include global mobility and the capability to access the Internet anywhere in the world. The 4G wireless Internet also allows for greater service portability and mobile networks that are more versatile. Although 3G wireless Internet was created to provide faster speeds for multimedia and Internet connectivity, most of the 3G connections provide WAN coverage as well as restricted coverage for Mbps. For this reason, 4G wireless Internet can handle broadband access, allowing mobile users access to high-speed Internet both at home and on the road.

9.6.2 SECURITY REQUIREMENTS AND CHALLENGES FOR VANET

To protect the VANET services against the attacks identified in the foregoing section, a set of security primitives should be considered. These requirements are specific to the vehicle context and, therefore, they slightly differ from the traditional security needs. In the following, the authors identify the security needs at different locations of the architecture based on the characteristics of the transmitted information.

- Authentication: The authentication process has to verify the driver's identity or the identity of the person authorized to drive the vehicle. Similarly, beacons frames should be authenticated in order to avoid spoofing attacks.
- Integrity: Data and information issued from various sources of information should not be either amended or altered by an attacker. Relevant information from the OBU, RSU, sensors and SU systems, and V2I and V2V communications should be protected against unauthorized falsifications.
- Nonrepudiation: It is important to ensure that any of the parties engaged in a VANET communication (V2I and V2V) cannot deny a communication/transaction that took place.
- Confidentiality: The confidentiality of exchanging information must be ensured in all vehicle systems (RSU, OBU, GPS, sensors). It is extremely important that only authorized persons can access information, especially for V2V and V2I communications.
- Access control: The vehicle systems are a transport means that belongs to individuals or to legal entities. Access to systems must be strictly controlled by more and more secure means.
- Privacy: Vehicular systems are private devices. Their operations are governed by practices and regulations. The privacy of the driver and passengers is of extremely high importance as one of the major security aspects.
- Accessibility: The vehicular systems have a long lifetime. The proper functioning of sensitive subsystems must be ensured throughout the lifecycle of the vehicle.
- Responsibility enforcement: Vehicle drivers are fully responsible for their actions in driving the process. Vehicles should provide information to identify or assist in the responsibility attribution. Generally, in the case of accidents (insurance experts, police officers), authorities are entitled to the identification of responsibilities.
- Evidence and proof management: During the vehicle motion on highways and roads, and to identify the vehicle in case of illegal travel speed or accidents, some services require evidence or proof. The proof may include photography of the EPL (Electronic License Plates) of the vehicle supported by a timestamp of a legal certification authority.

- Vehicle tracking: The precise location of the vehicle has become vital information for vehicle safety, in particular against theft and vehicle tracking. Addressing the balance between authentication and nonrepudiation versus privacy is an important challenge that a secure scheme of communication for VANETs faces. The trade-off between authentication and anonymity is also a critical concern. The real-time constraint is an added challenge because it prohibits the use of security protocols that have high delay overhead or rely on multiple stages of full-duplex sessions between nodes.

Moreover, mobility constitutes a barrier to the implementation of traditional security schemes in VANETs. Vehicles move at a fast rate, moving in and out of the reception area of other vehicles participating in the network. We can expect that a pair of vehicles can communicate for a limited period of time. It is also expected that communication between nodes that have never interacted before and will never interact again will be the norm. Thus, VANETs are different from existing mobile ad hoc networks where communication between pairs of nodes can be of relatively long duration. This prevents the use of security protocols where a cluster head should be elected to operate security tasks since the lifetime of the connectivity graph is too short.

9.6.3 ATTACKS AGAINST VEHICULAR NETWORKS

Attacks against VANETs could be roughly classified from three different levels of views. One category includes the attacks against the communication infrastructure (e.g., routing protocols), the second relates to attacks against the major function of the VANET (e.g., location monitoring), and the third class consists of attacks against the security requirements (e.g., authentication protocols, integrity checking algorithms). For the sake of brevity, the authors only consider the attacks on authentication, availability, and confidentiality.

9.6.3.1 Attacks on Availability

Multiple techniques can be used by malicious users/drivers to make the VANET experience service interruptions. These techniques encompass the following:

- Black hole: In VANETs the nodes collaborate to forward packets from one node to another. This attack occurs when a malicious node refuses to participate in the packet forwarding process or even drops the data packet. This has a substantial effect by increasing the packet rejection rate and the packet transmission delay. In order to preserve their resources, the selfish nodes have the possibility of advertising less optimal routes or nonexisting routes among its neighbors. This behavior has the consequence of disrupting the network and the traffic. The only reason for using the network is when they need it.
- Sinkhole: In this attack, the intruder attracts the neighbor nodes with forged routing information, and then performs selective forwarding or alters the data passing through it. The attacking node claims to offer a very attractive link. Therefore, a lot of traffic bypasses this node. Besides simple traffic analysis, other attacks like selective forwarding or denial of service can be combined with the sinkhole attack.
- Selfish/greedy behavior: Selfish drivers may aim at using the network resources only for themselves. This can be done by causing an illusion of traffic congestion in the attacker's neighborhood. A greedy driver may convince the neighboring vehicles that there is considerable

congestion ahead, so that they will go through secondary routes and allow the selfish driver a clear path to his/her destination. To detect these possible attacks, Dahl et al. have proposed FLSASC.

- Broadcast tampering: The nodes that are elected to act as network relays can affect the communication to/from the other nodes by corrupting the messages that go through them, thereby meaningfully modifying these messages. As a result, the reception of valuable or even critical traffic notifications or safety messages can be manipulated. The consequence of these attacks might be very heavy when the target service is related to driver safety.
- Denial-of-service: The objective of this attack is to cause service interruptions. This can be achieved, for example, when the attacker gets access to VANET and sets up paths between all nodes. Once the paths are correctly established, the attacker injects an immense amount of unwanted data packets into the network, which is directed to all the other nodes in the network. These immense useless data packets greatly degrade network services. Any vehicle that serves as a destination node will be busy and will not forward properly the received data. The impact of these attacks is generally measured by proportion to the time needed to recover the VANET system to its normal operation status.

9.6.3.2 Attacks on Authentication

The vulnerabilities due to the open-access to the radio medium are often exploited by attacks to perform various types of identity spoofing techniques. Some of these techniques are detailed in the following.

- Message replay: The attacker injects forged messages or suppresses transmitted messages. The motives of an attacker might be manifold. An attacker might want to introduce flawed information to convince other vehicle drivers to take an alternative route, giving them a clear path. Replaying previous message is particularly useful when the attacker's objective is to be granted access to a protected system. In this case, he captures the authentication messages of other authorized vehicles and tries to inject them into the system in order to bypass the protection infrastructure.
- Sybil: Large-scale peer-to-peer systems face security threats from faulty or hostile remote computing elements. To resist these threats, many such systems employ redundancy. However, if a single faulty entity can present multiple identities, it can control a substantial fraction of the system, thereby undermining this redundancy. The Sybil attack is especially aimed at distributed system environments. The attacker tries to act as several different identities/nodes rather than one. This allows him to forge the result of a voting used for threshold security methods.
- Masquerading: The attacker actively pretends (impersonates) to be another vehicle by using false identities and can be motivated by malicious or rational objectives. Message fabrication, alteration, and replay can also be used toward masquerading. A masquerader can be a threat: consider, for example, an attacker masquerading as an emergency vehicle to mislead other vehicles to slow down and yield.
- Location service spoofing: Location information is extremely important in the vehicular communication context. VANETs have special requirements in terms of position-dependent applications and vehicle's mobility. These requirements are generally satisfied by geographic based routing protocols.

These protocols are mainly based on the same principles, that is, every vehicle determines its current position using a positioning system such as GPS. The obtained position is broadcasted periodically in beacon packets so that every vehicle is able (within the wireless transmission range) to build up a neighboring vehicle table of including their positions. If a vehicle has to forward a packet, it selects the possible next hop from the neighbor table using a prechosen rule (e.g., it selects the closest vehicle to the destination). When a vehicle disseminates wrong position data, routing messages in VANETs are affected. Wrong position information is due to a malfunction in the positioning hardware or forged intentionally by attackers to reroute data. Malfunctioning nodes may degrade the performance of a system to some extent while rerouting of data through malicious nodes violates basic security goals such as confidentiality, integrity, authenticity, and accountability.

9.6.3.3 Attacks on Confidentiality

Due to the high mobility of the nodes involved in VANETs, the establishment of secure encrypted tunnels is nearly impossible.

This increases the ability of the attacker to gain access to the messages exchanged through the infrastructure. The need for confidentiality is particularly crucial when the driver accesses to services requiring the submission of sensitive information. For instance, when being authenticated by a payment platform, the driver submits a confidential code that can easily be sniffed by malicious users. Therefore, for data, it is not unusual to be eavesdropped on by the vehicles where it is ultimately routed to the RSU for example. Often, for an adversary to effectively render the useless network, the attacker can, for example, simply disable the RSU (in such cases). To make matters worse, an approach is given in the literature where two attacks can identify the base station in a network (with high probability) without even understanding the contents of the packets (if the packets are themselves encrypted). A rate monitoring attack relies on the fact that the nodes further from the base station tend to forward fewer packets than closer ones. An attacker needs to monitor only the nodes that are sending packets and follow the vehicles sending the most packets. In the time correlation attack, an adversary simply generates events and try to monitor packets receivers.

9.7 STANDARDS HARMONIZATION EFFORTS ON FUTURE ITS

Connected vehicular networking acts as one of the most critical enabling technologies, indispensable to implementing numerous applications related to vehicles, vehicle traffic, drivers, and pedestrians. These applications are more than novelties and far-fetched goals of a group of researchers and companies. ITS is one initiative in securing vehicular networks. The term ITS refers to added information and communications technology to transport infrastructure and vehicles, to improve safety, reduce transportation times, and reduce fuel consumption. ITS aims to modernize the operation of vehicles, manage vehicle traffic, and assist drivers with security and other information. ITS has provision convenience applications since passengers are no longer confined to laboratories and test facilities of companies.

ITS embrace a proper kind of communications-related applications meant to minimize environmental impact, improve traffic management, and maximize the advantages of transportation to both business users and the general public. Some of the prominent examples of the intelligent transportation are Tollgate Management Systems and systems for driver assistance. These systems are being supported by the organized efforts of governments and various organizations. The government organization, which frames the Governing Principles, primarily considers the real-time scenarios for vehicles and the users inside the vehicles. To accomplish effective ITS, vehicular standards act as a barrier because of differences in various standardization groups. Furthermore, along with that, there is an enormous regional variation among different countries. To eliminate the difference and to harmonize the standards and communication technologies, a Standards Harmonization research program initiative is carried out.

The purpose of the Standards harmonization research program is to collaborate with the international standards community to harmonize standards and architecture to extend ITS. Harmonization facilitates ability between products and systems, which may profit transportation management agencies, vehicle manufacturer, and so forth. Efforts underneath this research program embrace collaboration with standards development organizations (SDOs), original equipment manufacturers (OEMs), and different stakeholders to seek agreement and supply applicable incentives. As a worldwide business, it's crucial to scale back the barriers to standardization and come to a broad agreement on harmonization that will profit both the general public and also the automobile manufacturers. Henceforth, the organization has established a Joint Declaration of resolve on Research Cooperation in Cooperative Systems in the European Union (EU). The intention of the arrangement is to provide advance cooperation on research in communication technologies, in relation to transportation. The European Commission on Transportation and the US DOT will determine the research areas that might get pleasure from a harmonious approach and that should be self-addressed by an organization or joint research. Precisely, the parties will build efforts to preclude the event and adoption of redundant standards and to support and accelerate the preparation and win the approval of Cooperative Systems.

The European Union and the United States signed an agreement to develop a research initiative focusing the cooperative vehicular systems. Fig. 9.6 portrays two functional groups associated with the EU-US joint ITS venture. HWG facilitates the coordination and harmonization of one of the six working groups for harmonization action plans. HTG is a flexible organizational construct that allows joint alignment activity in vehicular networks. The typical venture focuses on roadmaps and policy requirements; it also deals with the identification of gaps and identification of areas that are appropriate for harmonization.

Furthermore, companies like Volkswagen, Daimler, and Renault along with automotive supplier industry representatives like NEC, Continental, Hitachi, and Renesas participate actively in the harmonization of cooperative ITS. In addition to that, manufacturers and network operators such as Cohda Wireless, Auto talks, T-Mobile, Telecom Italia, and Orange, and research centers like Eurecom, Fraunhofer, and INRIA are effectively evolved to attain C-ITS. In order to stimulate the deployment and implementation of cooperative ITS, iMobility initiatives play a nominal role. In the European region the European

FIGURE 9.6 Standards Harmonization Working Group Organization

Commission Mandate (M/453) in the field of ICT (Information Communication Technologies) supports C-ITS. In order to emphasize the importance of C-ITS, ETSI collaborates closely with international standardization bodies like ISO, CEN, IEEE, SAE, ARIB, TTA, IETF and ITU, and so forth, which is essential to achieve worldwide harmonization. In this article, the authors discuss the various standardization workgroup and its progress in the vehicular network. Furthermore, they also consider the possibilities of different communication technologies that can apply to intelligent vehicular communication.

9.8 A NOVEL VEHICULAR MOBILITY MODELING TECHNIQUE FOR DEVELOPING ITS APPLICATIONS

Improving the road traffic safety and comfort through ITS is getting much more attention in recent days. The standardization bodies have also taken a huge interest in developing technologies and protocols to implement the promising applications of vehicular communication. The domain of VANET has huge potential for both vehicle-to-vehicle (V2V) and vehicle-to-infrastructure (V2I) communications. In order to ensure road safety and comfortable journey, extensive research activities have been going on to disseminate several types of safety messages for VANET applications. Nevertheless, most of the recent protocols concentrate mostly on the V2V communications aspect. Hence, V2I communication technologies need to be explored extensively to be integrated with V2V communication. ITS applications like reducing traffic congestion, traveling time, and emission rate of the roads can be implemented through V2I communication. As the logistic difficulties are high and economic resources are very limited, it is practically impossible to test such kind of system under a test bed environment.

Therefore, simulation study plays an important role in terms of understanding the feasibility of the networking protocols with vehicular mobility, which requires a modeling of the vehicular mobility in a realistic manner. Due to the difficulties associated with collecting real vehicular traces, traffic simulators are widely used for mobility modeling and for generating realistic vehicular traces. The simulator must have the capabilities to offer realistic mobility scenarios where the vehicles will be reacting according to the various types of road conditions. In addition, strong bidirectional interactions are needed between the network and the vehicular mobility simulator. Thus, choosing the proper traffic simulator is a big challenge in order to obtain and validate the results. In general, vehicular traffic simulators fall into two categories, namely microscopic and macroscopic simulators. For macroscopic perspective, traffic density (number of vehicles per km per lane) or traffic flow (number of vehicles per hour crossing some point, usually intersection) is required to compute road capacity and the distribution of the traffic in the road network. Vehicular traffic can be viewed as a fluid compressible medium that can be modeled as a unique derivation of the Navies–Stokes equations. However, in the microscopic approach, the movement of each vehicle should be determined by the simulators that can provide simulated values for a wide range of parameters.

9.8.1 MOBILITY MODELS AND SIMULATION TOOLS

It has been identified that the following attributes are important while considering any simulator for vehicular mobility modeling as shown in Fig. 9.7.

- Accurate and realistic topological maps (intersections, lane and categories of streets with speed limits, etc.)
- Attraction/repulsion points (specifying source and destination points)

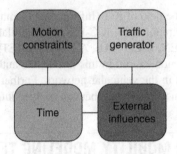

FIGURE 9.7 Mobility Model

- Vehicle characteristics (heavy duty, light duty, emergency vehicles, etc.)
- Smooth deceleration and acceleration
- Human driving patterns (overtaking, traffic jam, preferred paths, etc.)
- Intersection Management (Traffic lights, stop signs, obstacles, etc.): Based on control over the road traffic behavior and on the simulation performance, two types of modeling techniques are used: the Agent Centric and Flow Centric approaches. An Agent Centric approach is able to fully control individual vehicles with increased computational cost. However, the bidirectional interaction between the road traffic simulator and the network simulator with a very low latency and with high accuracy is essential for developing applications such as traffic management or the Intelligent Road Traffic Signaling System (IRTSS). Modeling sophisticated applications and safety message dissemination protocols require full control on the road traffic mobility patterns. Thus vehicular commutations researchesrs prefer to adopt an agent-centric modeling approach for mobility modeling.

9.9 CONCLUSIONS

In this chapter, we described the NGVNs, which deal with the augmented car data through a smartphones-based crowd sensing technique. Moreover, we present a detailed description about various architectures related to smartphones vehicular platform and their functionality. These architectures gives us the details about how to collect data, how to preprocess the data, and finally, how to visualize the data. In addition, we also give the details about the vehicular mobility based on the IEEE 802.11 through predictive handovers. In this system a communication is achieved between various technologies, such as V2I. Then, a real-time path planning system is described that is based on the enhanced transportation system. In this system, V2V and V2R communication is achieved in VANETS that collects or report traffic updates from/to vehicles. In this system, focus is given to achieve end-to-end transmission performance. Also, some of the security features are given in the said technology, which helps in providing security to vehicle communication. Last but not the least, mobility techniques are presented in developing ITS applications for V2V, V2I, and also describes various simulation tools for mobility model.

References

[1] US Department of Transportation. Technical Report, 2009 Executive summary of the ITS strategic research plan; 2010–2014.

[2] World Health Organization. Global status report on road safety: time for action. Geneva: World Health Organization; 2009.

[3] Dorle SS, Deshpande DM, Keskar AG, Chakole M. Vehicle classification and communication using ZigBee protocol IEEE Conference Publication on Emerging Trends in Engineering and Technology (ICETET); 2010

[4] He L, Ma S, Wu Y-C, Ng T-S. Data detection for cooperative vehicular communication systems with unknown channels. IEEE ICECS; 2010.

[5] Sepulcre M, Mittag J, Santi P, Hartenstein H, Gozalvez J. Congestion and awareness control in cooperative vehicular systems. Proc IEEE 2011;14(4):1708–17.

[6] Alam N, Dempster AG. Cooperative positioning for vehicular networks: facts and future. IEEE Trans Intell Transp Syst 2013.

[7] Jorge H, Elli K, Valenzuela JL, Alonso L, Laya A, Martínez R, Aguilar A. Experimental study of Bluetooth, ZigBee, and IEEE 802.15.4 technologies on board high-speed trains. IEEE Vehicular Technology Conference (VTC Spring); 2012.

[8] Chang K-L, Chang JS, Gwee B-H, Chong KS. Synchronous-logic and asynchronous-logic 8051 microcontroller cores for realizing the Internet of Things: a comparative study on dynamic voltage scaling and variation effects. IEEE Trans Emerg Sel Topics Circuits Syst 2013;3(1):23–34.

[9] Yin J. et al. Performance evaluation of safety applications over DSRC vehicular ad hoc networks. Proceedings of the first ACM international workshop on Vehicular Ad Hoc Networks 2004, Philadelphia, PA, USA; Oct. 1, 2004, p. 1–9.

[10] Hartenstein H, Laberteaux K. VANET: vehicular applications and inter-networking technologies. Wiley Online Library; 2010.

[11] Daniels RC, Heath RW. Link adaptation with position/motion information in vehicle-to-vehicle networks. IEEE T Wirel Commun 2012;11(2):505–9.

[12] Rawat DB, Treeumnuk D, Popescu D, Abuelela M, Olariu S. Challenges and perspectives in the implementation of notice architecture for vehicular communications. In: 5th IEEE international conference on Mobile Ad Hoc and Sensor Systems, 2008 (MASS 2008); 2008. p. 707–11.

[13] Abuelela M, Olariu S, Weigle MC. Notice: an architecture for the notification of traffic incidents. In: Vehicular Technology Conference, 2008. VTC Spring 2008. IEEE; 2008. p. 3001–5.

[14] Rawat DB, Bista BB, Yan G, Olariu S. Vehicle-to-vehicle connectivity and communication framework for vehicular ad-hoc networks. 2014 eighth international conference on complex, intelligent and software intensive systems; 2014.

[15] Brickley O, Pesch D. Communication management for cooperative vehicular systems. 2013 IEEE 24th international symposium on personal, indoor and mobile radio communications: services, applications and business track.

[16] Bhoi SK, Khilar PM. Vehicular communication: a survey. IET Netw J 2014;3(3):204–17.

[17] Singh KD, Rawat P, Bonnin J-M. Cognitive radio for vehicular ad hoc networks (CR-VANETs): approaches and challenges. EURASIP J Wirel Commun 2014;2014:1–22. 49.

[18] Ghandour AJ, Fawaz K, Artail H. Data delivery guarantees in congested vehicular ad hoc networks using cognitive networks. In: International IEEE Wireless Communications and Mobile Computing Conference (IWCMC); 2011.

[19] Akyildiz IF, Lo BF, Balakrishnan R. Cooperative spectrum sensing in cognitive radio networks: a survey. J Phys Commun 2011;4(1):40–62.

[20] Min AW, Shin KG. Impact of mobility on spectrum sensing in cognitive radio networks. In: Proceedings of the 2009 ACM workshop on cognitive radio networks. Beijing, China; 2009.

[21] Di Felice M, Chowdhury KR, Bononi L. Cooperative spectrum management in cognitive vehicular ad hoc networks. In: 2011 IEEE Vehicular Networking Conference (VNC); 2011.

[22] Li H, Drick DK. Collaborative spectrum sensing in cognitive radio vehicular ad hoc networks: belief propagation on highway. In: 2010 IEEE 71st Vehicular Technology Conference; 2010.

[23] Di Felice M, Doost-Mohammady R, Chowdhury KR, Bononi L. Smart radios for smart vehicles: cognitive vehicular networks. IEEE Veh Tech Mag 2012;7(2):26–33.

[24] Kim W, Gerla M, Oh SY, Lee K, Kassler A. CoRoute: a new cognitive any path vehicular routing protocol. Wirel Commun Mob Comput 2011;11(12):1588–602.

[25] Murroni M, Popescu V. Cognitive radio communications for vehicular technology—wavelet applications. In: Almeida M, editor. Vehicular technologies: increasing connectivity. In Tech; 2011.

[26] Ghasemi FA, Sousa Elvino S. Spectrum sensing in cognitive radio networks: requirements, challenges and design trade-offs. IEEE Commun Mag 2008;46(4):32–9.

[27] Di Felice M, Chowdhury KR, Bononi L. Analyzing the potential of cooperative cognitive radio technology on inter-vehicle communication. Wireless Days (WD); 2010 IFIP.

[28] Piran MJ, Cho Y, Yun J, Ali A, Suh DY. Cognitive radio-based vehicular ad hoc and sensor networks. Hindawi Int J Distrib Sens N 2014;2014:11. 154193.

[29] Rasheed H, Rajatheva N. Spectrum sensing for cognitive vehicular networks over composite fading. Hindawi Int J Veh Tech 2011;2011(2011):9. 630467.

[30] Danda B, Rawat, YZ, Gongjun Y, Song M. CRAVE: cognitive radio enabled vehicular communications in heterogeneous networks. IEEE Radio and Wireless Symposium (RWS); 2013.

[31] Nima N, Mehdi M, Ahmad B. Centralized and decentralized cooperative spectrum sensing in cognitive radio networks: a novel approach. IEEE Signal Processing Advances in Wireless Communications (SPAWC); 2010.

[32] Unnikrishnan J, Veeravalli VV. Cooperative sensing for primary detection in cognitive radio. IEEE J Signal Proc 2008;2(1):18–27.

[33] Jiang C, Yan Chen KJ, Liu R, Ren Y. Renewal-theoretical dynamic spectrum access in cognitive radio network with unknown primary behavior. IEEE J Sel Area Commun 2013;31(3):406–16.

[34] Ejaz W, Hasan N, Kim HS. Distributed cooperative spectrum sensing in cognitive radio for ad hoc networks. J Comput Commun 2013.

[35] Wang B, Liu KR. Advances in cognitive radio networks: a survey. IEEE J Sel Top Signa 2011;36(12):1341–9.

[36] Fawaz K, Ghandour A, Olleik M, Artail H. Improving reliability of safety applications in vehicle ad hoc networks through the implementation of a cognitive network. In: IEEE 17th international conference on telecommunications (ICT); 2010.

[37] Pan M, Li P, Fang Y. Cooperative communication aware link scheduling for cognitive vehicular networks. IEEE J Sel Area Commun 2012;30(4):760–8.

[38] Wong C-M, Hsu W-P. Short paper: a study on the cognitive radio in IEEE 802.15.4 wireless sensor networks. In: Proceedings of the IEEE World Forum on Internet of Things (WF-IoT'14); 2014.

[39] Letaief KB, Zhang W. Cooperative communications for cognitive radio networks. Proc IEEE 2009;97(5):878–93.

[40] Sadek AK, Liu KJR, Ephremides A. Cognitive multiple access via cooperation: protocol design and stability analysis. IEEE Trans Inform Theory 2007;53(10):3677–96.

[41] El-Sherif AA, Liu KJR. Joint design of spectrum sensing and channel access in cognitive radio networks. IEEE T Wirel Commun 2011;10(6):1743–53.

[42] Jianfeng W, Monisha G, Kiran C. Emerging cognitive radio applications: a survey. IEEE Commun Mag 2011;49(3):74–80.

[43] Daniel A, Paul A, Ahmad A. Embedded surveillance system for vehicular networks. IEEE international conference on Electronic and Communication Systems (ICECS); 2014.

[44] Stiller C, Farber G, Kammel S. Cooperative cognitive automobile. Proceedings of IEEE Symposium on Intelligent Vehicles, 2007, Istanbul, Turkey, June 13–15; 2007.

[45] Wang R, Tao M. Blind spectrum sensing by information theoretic criteria for cognitive radios. IEEE T Veh Technol 2010;59:8.

[46] Liu C, Qi A, Zhang P, Bu L, Long K. Wideband spectrum detection based on compressed sensing in cooperative cognitive radio networks. Eighth international ICST conference on communications and networking in China (CHINACOM); 2013.

[47] Big data: the next frontier for innovation, competition, and productivity. McKinsey Global Institute [Online]. Available from: http://www.mckinsey.com/insights/business_technology/big_data_the_next_frontier_for_innovation; 2011.

[48] Barlow M. Real-time big data analytics, emerging architecture. [Online]. Available from: http://www.pentaho.com/assets/pdf/CqPxTROXtCpfoLrUi4Bj.pdf; 2013

[49] Lu H, Sun Z, Qu W. Big data-driven based real-time traffic flow state identification and prediction. Hindawi J Discrete Dyn Nat Soc 2014;2015(2015):11. 284906.

[50] Hu H, Wen Y, Chua T-S, Li X. Toward scalable systems for big data analytics: a technology tutorial. IEEE Access 2014;2:652–87.

[51] Twardowski B, Ryzko D. Multi-agent architecture for real-time big data processing. IEEE/WIC/ACM international joint conferences on Web Intelligence (WI) and Intelligent Agent Technologies (IAT); 2014.

[52] Mishra N, Lin C-C, Chang H-T. A cognitive adopted framework for IoT big-data management and knowledge discovery prospective. Hindawi J Distrib Sens N 2014;2015(2015):12. 718390.

[53] Reza SM, Rahman Md M, Al Mamun S. A new approach for road networks—a vehicle XML device collaboration with big data. IEEE Conference on Electrical Engineering and Information & Communication Technology (ICEEICT); 2014.

[54] Bhattacharya D, Mitra M. Analytics on big fast data using real-time stream data processing architecture. EMC Proven Professional Knowledge Sharing; 2013.

[55] Khan N, Yaqoob I, Abaker I, Hashem T, Inayat Z, Kamaleldin W, Ali M, Alam M, Muhammad Shiraz, Gani A. Big data: survey, technologies, opportunities, and challenges. Hindawi Sci World J; 2014.

[56] Bedi P, Jindal V. Use of big data technology in vehicular ad-hoc networks. IEEE ICACCI; 2014.

[57] Liu X, Iftikhar N, Xie X. Survey of real-time processing systems for big data. ACM IDEAS'14 July 07–09; 2014.

[58] Di Felice M, Doost-Mohammady R, Chowdhury KR, Bononi L. Smart radios for smart vehicles: cognitive vehicular networks. IEEE Veh Tech Mag 2012;7(2).

[59] Marfia G, Roccetti M, Amoroso A, Gerla M, Pau G, Lim J-H. Cognitive cars: constructing a cognitive playground for VANET research testbeds. In: Proceedings of the fourth international conference on cognitive radio and advanced spectrum management; 2011.

[60] Stephenson S, et al. Network RTK for intelligent vehicles: accurate, reliable, available, continuous positioning for cooperative driving. GPS World 2013;24(2):61–7.

[61] Alam N, Balaei AT, Dempster AG. Relative positioning enhancement in VANETs, a tight integration approach. IEEE Trans Intell Transp Syst 2013;14(1):47–55.

[62] Sharifi F, Chamseddine A, Mahboubi H, Zhang Y, Aghdam AG. A distributed deployment strategy for a network of cooperative autonomous vehicles. IEEE T Control Syst T 2015;23(2):737–45.

[63] Tan R, Xing G, Wang J, Liu B. Performance analysis of real-time detection in fusion-based sensor networks. IEEE T Parall Distr 2011;22(9):1564–77.

[64] Akselrod D, Sinha A, Kirubarajan T. Information flow control for collaborative distributed data fusion and multisensor multitarget tracking. IEEE T Syst Man Cy C 2012;42(4):501–17.

[65] El Faouzi N-E, Leung H, Kurian A. Data fusion in intelligent transportation systems: progress and challenges—a survey. J Inf Fusion 2011;12(1):4–10.

[66] Daniel A, Paul A, Ahmad A. Near real-time big data analysis on vehicular networks. IEEE international conference on Soft Computing and Network Security (ICSNS); 2015.

[67] Mujica F. Scalable electronics driving autonomous vehicle technologies. Texas Instruments; 2014.

[68] Baydere BA, Erondu K, Espinel D, Jain S, Madden CR. Car-sharing service using autonomous automobiles; 2014.

[69] Daily Camera. Self-driving cars could be a decade away. Available from: http://www.dailycamera.com/the-bottom-line/ci_24021170/self-driving-cars-could-be-decade-away; 2013.

[70] The travel and environmental implications of shared autonomous vehicles, using agent-based model scenarios. Transport Res Part C 2014;40:1–13.

[71] MIT Technology Review. Data shows Google's robot cars are smoother, safer drivers than you or I. Available from: http://www.technologyreview.com/news/520746/data-showsgoogles-robot-cars-are-smoother-safer-drivers-than-you-or-i/; 2013.

[72] Bai F, Krishnan H. Reliability analysis of DSRC wireless communication for vehicle safety applications. In: Intelligent Transportation Systems Conference, 2006 (ITSC'06). IEEE, Toronto, Ontario; 2006.

[73] ISO 24102-3:2013. Intelligent transport systems—communications access for land mobiles (CALM)—ITS station management—Part 3, Service access points, ISO STD; 2013.

[74] US Department of Transportation. IEEE 1609—family of standards for wireless access in vehicular environments (WAVE), intelligent transportation systems standards fact sheet; 2013.

[75] Kokkoniemi J, Ylitalo J, Luoto P, Scott S, Leinonen J, Latva-aho M. Performance evaluation of vehicular LTE mobile relay nodes. IEEE 24th international symposium on personal, indoor and mobile radio communications; 2013.

[76] Saifan R, Kamal AE, Guan Y. Efficient spectrum searching and monitoring in cognitive radio network. IEEE international conference on Mobile AdHoc and Sensor Networks; 2011.

[77] CVIS (Cooperative Vehicular Infrastructure Systems). [Online]. Available from: http://www.cvisproject.org/; 2015.

[78] ITS JPO. Vehicle safety applications. US DOT IntelliDrive(sm) Project—ITS Joint Program Office, Technical Report; 2008.

[79] US DOT, RITA. ITS Standards Fact Sheets. [Online]. Available from: http://www.standards.its.dot.gov/Factsheets/Factsheet/71; 2013.

[80] European Commission, US Department of Transportation. International deployment of cooperative intelligent transportation systems—bilateral efforts of the European Commission and United States. Department of Transportation; 2012.

[81] Bento, LC. Inter vehicle sensor fusion for accurate vehicle localization supported by V2V and V2I communications. Fifteenth international IEEE conference on Intelligent Transportation Systems (ITSC); 2012.

[82] Singh P. Comparative study between unicast and multicast routing protocols in different data rates using VANET. In: 2014 international conference on Issues and Challenges in Intelligent Computing Techniques (ICICT), Ghaziabad; 2014.

[83] Sharma HL, Agrawal P, Kshirsagar RV. Acute direction route node selection multipath routing for VANET: design approach. In: 2014 international conference on Signal Processing and Integrated Networks (SPIN), Noida; 2014.

[84] Levinson, D. The evolution of transport networks. In: Hensher D, editor. Handbook 6 transport strategy, policy and institutions. Oxford: Elsevier; 2005. p. 175–88 [chapter 11].

[85] Zeadally S, Hunt R, Chen Y-S, Irwin A, Hassan A. Vehicular ad hoc networks (VANETs): status, results, and challenges. J Telecommun Syst 2010;50(4):217–41.

[86] Daniel A, Paul A, Ahmad A, Rho S. Cooperative intelligence of vehicles for intelligent transportation systems (ITS). Springer Wireless personal communication; 2015.

[87] Daniel A. Vehicle to vehicle communication using ZigBee protocol. ACM Proceedings of the 29th annual Symposium on Applied Computing (SAC); 2014.

[88] Daniel A, Paul A, Ahmad A. Queuing model for cognitive radio (CR) vehicular network. IEEE international conference on Platform Technology and Services (PLATCON); 2015.

[89] Rho R, Nam Y, Paul A, Daniel A, Ahmed A. Cooperative cognitive intelligence for Internet of vehicles (10-2015-0046184); patent submitted (Korean patent); 2015.

[90] Aalamifar F, Vijay G, Abedi P, Ibnkahla M. Cognitive wireless sensor networks for highway safety. First NSERC DIVA network workshop, Ottawa; 2011.

[91] Naft NS, Khan JY. A novel vehicular mobility modelling technique for developing ITS applications. IET international conference on wireless communications and applications; 2012.

[92] Mejri MN, Hamdi M. Recent advances in cryptographic solutions for vehicular networks. International symposium on Networks, Computers and Communications (ISNCC); 2015.

[93] Wang M, Shan H, Lu R, Zhang R, Shen X, Bai F. Real-time path planning based on hybrid-VANET-enhanced transportation system. IEEE T Veh Technol 2015;64(5):1664–78.

[94] Mouton M, Castignani G, Frank R, Engel T. Enabling vehicular mobility in city-wide IEEE 802.11 networks through predictive handovers. In: Elsevier Vehicular Commun; 2015 [special issue on advances on networking and information systems technologies for ITS].

[95] Briante O, Campolo C, Iera A, Molinaro A, Paratore SY, Ruggeri G. Supporting augmented floating car data through smartphone-based crowd-sensing. Vehicular Commun 2014;1(4):181–96.

[96] Kuklinski S, Matei A, Wolny G. A framework for next generation vehicular networks. IEEE international conference on communications (COMM); 2010.

[97] Qiu RG, Wang K, Li S, Dong J, Xie X. Big data technologies in support of real time capturing and understanding of electric vehicle customers dynamics. Fifth IEEE international conference on software engineering and service science; 2014. p. 263–7.

[98] Yan Z, Zeadally S, Park YJ. A novel vehicular information network architecture based on named data networking (NDN). IEEE Internet Things J 2014;1(6):525–32.

[99] Griggs WM, Shorten RN. Embedding real vehicles in SUMO for large-scale ITS scenario emulation. Connected Vehicles and Expo (ICCVE); 2013. p. 962–3.

[100] Mylonas Y, Lestas M, Pitsillides A. Speed adaptive probabilistic flooding for vehicular ad-hoc networks. IEEE Personal Indoor and Mobile Radio Communications (PIMRC); 2011. p. 719–23.

[101] Lu N, Cheng N, Zhang N, Shen X, Mark J. Connected vehicles: solutions and challenges. IEEE Internet Things J 2014;1(4):289–99.

[102] Hussain R, Son J, Eun H, Kim S, Oh H. Rethinking vehicular communications: merging VANET with cloud computing. Proceedings of IEEE fourth international conference on Cloud Computing Technology and Science (CloudCom); 2012. p. 606–9.

[103] Amadeo M, Campolo C, Molinaro A. Enhancing IEEE 802.11p/WAVE to provide infotainment applications in VANETs. Ad Hoc Netw 2012;10(2):253–69.

[104] Rostamzadeh K, Nicanfar H, Torabi N, Gopalakrishnan S, Victor CM, Leung VCM. A context-aware trust-based information dissemination framework for vehicular networks. IEEE Internet Things J 2015;2(2).

[105] Dimitrakopoulos G, Bravos G, Nikolaidou M, Anagnostopoulos D. Proactive, knowledge-based intelligent transportation system based on vehicular sensor networks. IET Intell Transp Sy 2013;7(4):454–63.

[106] Ding J-W, Wang C-F, Meng F-H, Wu T-Y. Real-time vehicle route guidance using vehicle-to-vehicle communication. IET Commun 2010;4(7):870–83.

[107] Elkosantini S, Darmoul S. Intelligent public transportation systems: a review of architectures and enabling technologies. Proceedings of 2013 international conference on Advanced Logistics and Transport (ICALT), p. 233–8.

[108] Ye P, Chen C, Zhu F. Dynamic route guidance using maximum flow theory and its MapReduce implementation. Proceedings of 2011 14th international IEEE conference on Intelligent Transportation Systems (ITSC), p. 180–5.

[109] Barba CT, Aguirre KO, Igartua MA. Performance evaluation of a hybrid sensor and vehicular network to improve road safety. Proceedings of the seventh ACM workshop on performance evaluation of wireless ad hoc, sensor, and ubiquitous networks, October 17–18, 2010, Bodrum, Turkey.

[110] Tuohy S, Glavin M, Hughes C, Jones E, Trivedi M, Kilmartin L. Intra-vehicle networks: a review. IEEE Trans Intell Transp Syst 2015;16(2):534–45.

[111] Sivaraman S, Trivedi M. Looking at vehicles on the road: a survey of vision-based vehicle detection, tracking, and behavior analysis. IEEE Trans Intell Transp Syst 2013;14:1773–95.

[112] Tian B, Morris BT, Tang M, Liu Y, Yao Y, Gou C, Shen D, Tang S. Hierarchical and networked vehicle surveillance in ITS: a survey. IEEE Trans Intell Transp Syst 2015;16(2).

[113] Siraj M, Abbasi ZA. An efficient video on demand system over cognitive radio wireless mesh networks. 2013 international symposium on Computational and Business Intelligence (ISCBI); 2013.

[114] Chouhan L, Trivedi A. Priority based MAC scheme for cognitive radio network: a queuing theory modelling. 2012 ninth international conference on Wireless and Optical Communications Networks (WOCN); 2012.

[115] Li L, Wen D, Yao D. A survey of traffic control with vehicular communications. IEEE Trans Intell Transp Syst 2014;15(1):425–32.

[116] Gerla M, Lee E-K, Pau G, Lee U. Internet of vehicles: from intelligent grid to autonomous cars and vehicular clouds. 2014 IEEE World Forum on Internet of Things; 2014. p. 241–6.

[117] Chaqfeh M, Lakas A, Jawhar I. A survey on data dissemination in vehicular ad hoc networks. Vehicular Commun 2014;1(4):214–25.

[118] Xiaonan W, Huanyan Q. Mobility management solution for IPv6-based vehicular networks. Comput Stand Interf 2013;36(1):66–75.

[119] Meneguette RI, Bittencourt LF, Madeira ERM. A seamless flow mobility management architecture for vehicular communication networks. J Commun Netw 2013;15(2):207–16.

[120] Cespedes S, Shen X, Lazo C. IP mobility management for vehicular communication networks: challenges and solutions. IEEE Commun Mag 2011;49(5):187–94.

[121] Zhu K, Niyato D, Wang P, Hossain E, Kim DI. Mobility support and handoff management in vehicular networks: a survey. Wirel Commun Mob Comput 2012;11(4):459–76.

[122] Paulo R, Pereira R, Rodrigues JJPC, Triay J. From delay-tolerant networks to vehicular delay-tolerant networks. IEEE Commun Surv Tutor 2012;14(4):1166–82.

[123] Bouhoute A, Berrada I, El Kamili M. A formal model of human driving behavior in vehicular networks. IEEE international Wireless Communications and Mobile Computing Conference (IWCMC); 2014. p. 231–6.

[124] Bali RS, Kumar N, Rodrigues JJPC. Clustering in vehicular ad hoc networks: taxonomy, challenges and solutions. Vehicular Commun 2014(1):134–52. Available from: http://dx.doi.org/10.1016/j.vehcom.2014.05.004

[125] Al-Sultan S, Moath M, Al-Doori H, Al-Bayatti AH, Zedan H. A comprehensive survey on vehicular ad hoc network. J Netw Comput Appl 2014;37(1):380–92.

[126] Amoozadeh M, Deng H, Chuah C-N, Zhang HM, Ghosal D. Platoon management with cooperative adaptive cruise control enabled by VANET. Vehicular Commun 18(1):217–241. Available from: http://dx.doi.org/10.1016/j.vehcom.2015.03.004

[127] Jia D, Lu K, Wang J, Zhang X, Shen X(S). A survey on platoon-based vehicular cyber-physical systems. IEEE Commun Surv Tutor; 2014;18(1):217–41.

[128] Dafflon B, Gechter F, Gruer P, Koukam A. Vehicle platoon and obstacle avoidance: a reactive agent approach. IET Intell Transp Sy 2013;18(1):263–84.

[129] Yu R, Zhang Y, Gjessing S, Xia W, Yang K. Toward cloud-based vehicular networks with efficient resource management. IEEE Netw J 2013;27(5):48–55.

[130] Barba CT, Aguirre KO, Aguilar M. Igartua. Performance evaluation of a hybrid sensor and vehicular network to improve road safety PE-WASUN'10. Proceedings of the seventh ACM workshop on performance evaluation of Wireless Ad Hoc, Sensor, and Ubiquitous Networks; 2010.

[131] Huang J, Lu J. A RESTful information service method in hybrid sensor and vehicular networks. ZTE Technol J. 2012;18(2):27–31.

[132] Bayram S, Papapanagiotou I. A survey on communication technologies and requirements for internet of electric vehicles. EURASIP J Wirel Commun 2014;2014:223. Available from: http://jwcn.eurasipjournals. com/content/2014/1/223.

[133] Alam KM, Saini M, El Saddiky A. Towards social Internet of vehicles: concept, architecture and applications. IEEE Access 2015;3:27–31.

[134] Gerla M, Lee E-K, Pauz, G, Leey U. Internet of vehicles: from intelligent grid to autonomous cars and vehicular clouds IEEE World Forum on Internet of Things (WF-IoT); 2014.

[135] Wang T, Song L, Han Z. Coalitional graph games for popular content distribution in cognitive radio VANETs. IEEE T Veh Technol 2013;62(8):4010–9.

[136] Li M, Yang Z, Wenjing L. CodeOn: cooperative popular content distribution for vehicular networks using symbol level network coding. IEEE J Sel Areas Commun 2011;29(1):223–35.

[137] Zhou L, Chao HC. Multimedia traffic security architecture for the Internet of Things. IEEE Netw 2011;25(3):35–40.

[138] Misra S. A fault-tolerant routing protocol for dynamic autonomous unmanned vehicular networks. Proceedings of IEEE international conference on communication (ICC 2013); 2013. p. 3525–9.

[139] Daniel A, Paul A, Ahmad A. Cooperative Cognitive Intelligence for Internet of Vehicles. IEEE Syst J 2015;99(99):1–10.

[140] Rathore MM, Ahmad A, Paul A, Daniel A. Hadoop-based real-time big data architecture for remote sensing earth observatory system. Sixth IEEE ICCCNT, July 13–15, 2015, Dallas, Texas, USA; 2015.

[141] Wang S-S, Lin Y-S. PassCAR: A Passive Clustering aided routing protocol for Vehicular ad hoc networks. J Comput Commun 2013;36(2):170–9.

Index

Printed in the United States
By Bookmasters